MW01278217

SECOND EDITION

# MEDICAL
# MALPRACTICE
# CLAIMS
# INVESTIGATION

## A Step-by-Step Approach

Nancy Acerbo-Kozuchowski, RN, MS, CPHRM
Risk Management Consultant & Education Director
FOJP Service Corporation, New York, NY


Kathleen Ashton, RN, BSN
Education Coordinator
FOJP Service Corporation, New York, NY

JONES AND BARTLETT PUBLISHERS
*Sudbury, Massachusetts*
BOSTON    TORONTO    LONDON    SINGAPORE

*World Headquarters*

| Jones and Bartlett Publishers | Jones and Bartlett Publishers | Jones and Bartlett Publishers |
|---|---|---|
| 40 Tall Pine Drive | Canada | International |
| Sudbury, MA 01776 | 6339 Ormindale Way | Barb House, Barb Mews |
| 978-443-5000 | Mississauga, Ontario | London W6 7PA |
| info@jbpub.com | L5V 1J2 | UK |
| www.jbpub.com | CANADA | |

Jones and Bartlett's books and products are available through most bookstores and online booksellers. To contact Jones and Bartlett Publishers directly, call 800-832-0034, fax 978-443-8000, or visit our website www.jbpub.com.

Substantial discounts on bulk quantities of Jones and Bartlett's publications are available to corporations, professional associations, and other qualified organizations. For details and specific discount information, contact the special sales department at Jones and Bartlett via the above contact information or send an email to specialsales@jbpub.com.

This publication is designed to provide accurate and authoritative information in regard to the Subject Matter covered. It is sold with the understanding that the publisher is not engaged in rendering legal, accounting, or other professional service. If legal advice or other expert assistance is required, the service of a competent professional person should be sought.

6048

**Library of Congress Cataloging-in-Publication Data**

Medical malpractice claims investigation : a step-by-step approach / [edited by] Nancy Acerbo-Kozuchowski, Kathleen Ashton. — 2e.
    p. cm.
  ISBN-13: 978-0-7637-4042-9 (alk. paper)
  ISBN-10: 0-7637-4042-X (alk. paper)
  1. Insurance, Physicians' liability—United States—Handbooks, manuals, etc. 2. Liability insurance claims—United States—Handbooks, manuals, etc.  I. Acerbo-Kozuchowski, Nancy. II. Ashton, Kathleen.
  HG8054.A27 2007
  368.5'6420140973—dc22

                              2006013017

**Production Credits**
Executive Editor: David Cella
Production Director: Amy Rose
Associate Production Editor: Rachel Rossi
Editorial Assistant: Lisa Gordon
Associate Marketing Manager: Laura Kavigian
Manufacturing Buyer: Amy Bacus
Composition: Paw Print Media
Cover Design: Timothy Dziewit
Printing and Binding: Malloy, Inc.
Cover Printing: Malloy, Inc.

Printed in the United States of America
10 09 08 07 06        10 9 8 7 6 5 4 3 2 1

# Contents

## Chapter 8—Developing Interview Questions on Occurrence in Long-Term Facilities . . . . . . . . . . . . . . . . . . . . 95

*Jose Guzman, RN, MS*

## Chapter 9—Developing Interview Questions on Obstetrical Claims . . . . 109

*Nancy Acerbo-Kozuchowski, RN, MS, CPHRM and Irene Kassel, BSN, RN*
with *Peter Bernstein, MD, MPH*

## Chapter 10—Investigating Equipment-Related Occurrences . . . . . . . . . 129

*Patricia Kischak, RN, CPHRM* with *Allison M. Barth, Esq.*

## Chapter 11—Reviewing and Maintaining the Claim File . . . . . . . . . . . . 143

*Ruth H. Axelrod, RN, JD*

## Chapter 12—Writing the Investigation Report . . . . . . . . . . . . . . . . . . . 155

*Kathleen Ashton, BSN, RN*

*Lori Breslow, PhD*

# Foreword

Welcome to the second edition of *Medical Malpractice Claims Investigation: A Step-by-Step Approach.* This book is the result of many years of hard work by its two authors, Nancy Acerbo-Kozuchowski and Kathleen Ashton, and by other risk management experts at FOJP Service Corporation and elsewhere.

This edition incorporates key developments in the handling of malpractice claims since publication of the first edition in 1997. New chapters offer guidelines on electronic medical records and patient confidentiality after passage of the Health Insurance Portability and Accountability Act (HIPAA). Also new is a chapter covering risk management in long-term care, with specific suggestions for developing interview questions. Expanded chapters on preparing for interviews include substantially enhanced questions for providers in the disciplines of surgery, anesthesia, obstetrics, pathology, and psychiatry. Revised chapters give detailed instructions for writing obstetrical claim reports and conducting root cause analyses. Throughout the text, helpful forms illustrate how to organize the investigation process, and these forms may be downloaded from the CD-ROM included in the back of this book.

FOJP has been involved in the education of malpractice claim investigators for nearly 30 years. We believe that thorough and careful investigation of adverse occurrences is the first step in the defense of claims. Our orientation program, which every new FOJP investigator attends, covers all aspects of medical malpractice claim investigation, including the fundamentals of risk management, claim management, and various aspects of law and insurance.

The authors have adapted this work from the manual used for the education and training of our own staff. It is our opportunity to share the expertise we have developed in training malpractice claim investigators and creating comprehensive investigation reports.

*Medical Malpractice Claims Investigation: A Step-by-Step Approach* represents the thinking of some of the leading people in the field of risk management and risk management education. I hope you find it a valuable professional tool.

*Lisa Kramer*
President and CEO
FOJP Service Corporation

# Introduction

This text is designed as a primer for medical malpractice claims investigation. It can be used by claim investigators, healthcare risk managers, paralegals, healthcare organization (HCO) counsel, and others whose duties include the investigation of actual and potential medical malpractice lawsuits. It can be used as a desktop reference, a self-study guide or—as is the practice at FOJP—as part of a formal orientation program. FOJP established a formal in-house claim investigation orientation program over 20 years ago. This manual was developed as a teaching tool and self-study guide for new investigators.

Although more complex technology and procedures have improved the ability of health care providers to treat diseases, the risk of injury and adverse outcome has also increased. At the same time, the public has come to expect more from medical institutions and will not accept poor results arising from mismanaged care. With the growing frequency of claims and severity of malpractice awards, claim investigation has become a vital part of an HCO's risk management activities.

Part I of this text is a quick-start study guide for medical malpractice claim investigators.[1] It provides an overview of risk management principles, medical/legal concepts, investigation techniques, and the various activities involved in the investigation and claim process. These subjects are covered in enough depth to prepare the reader to begin to function as a claim investigator. All forms presented in this section can be downloaded from the companion CD-ROM for the reader's use.

A practical, step-by-step approach to the investigation of a claim, Part I enables the investigator to:

- extract and organize relevant information from medical records
- understand the relevance of the electronic medical record
- identify the issues of a case

- interview the individuals involved in a given occurrence
- prepare a comprehensive investigation report focused on the pertinent issues

Part II supplements Part I. It gives further information on risk management and the related fields of law and insurance. Guidelines for clear and concise writing are also included, because preparation of a written investigation report is the concluding activity of the initial investigation.

Figure I-1 illustrates the investigation process as set forth in Part I, as well as the topics in Part II that can be used to strengthen the investigator's knowledge and skills.

An investigation report prepared by a well-trained investigator is an asset to the HCO, defense counsel, and the insurance carrier. The investigation report can:

- be a valuable tool for defense counsel engaged in defending a case
- help defense counsel determine whether to settle a claim or take the case to trial
- enable insurers to establish prudent reserves

Perhaps most important, the investigation can spark initiatives by the health care facility's risk management and quality improvement programs for the management of adverse patient care outcomes. Information uncovered by the investigation can be helpful in studying the process that gave rise to the adverse outcome.

A good investigator needs perseverance and initiative to do the job well. These basic attributes, together with the information in this manual, can help him or her function effectively as a medical malpractice claim investigator.

Before getting started with the investigation of a claim, we briefly address the interplay between risk management and claim management in the health care setting.

## WHAT IS RISK MANAGEMENT?

It is important for the medical malpractice claim investigator to understand the risk management process as a means to identify and reduce the risks facing an HCO and promote safe patient care. The risk management

*Part I contains information about...*

| Reviewing Notices of Potential Claims | Reviewing Medical Records | Analyzing the Medical/ Legal Issues | Identifying, Locating, and Interviewing Parties Involved | Reviewing the Claim File | Writing the Investigation Report |

*Part II supplements Part I by covering information on...*

| Insurance | Claim Management | Confidentiality of Medical Records | The Life of a Medical Malpractice Claim | Responding to Potential Lawsuits | Informed Consent | Writing Clearly and Concisely |

**Figure I-1** The Investigation Process

process protects the organization's financial assets, reduces liability from adverse patient occurrence and lawsuits, and fosters quality improvement and patient safety initiatives.

Because the claim investigator works closely with the risk manager, it is important to know what the risk manager does and the impact of the claim investigation on the risk management process.

Depending on the organization's structure, the risk management professional is generally a member of an HCO's administrative team. The risk manager identifies and evaluates problems that may result in injury to patients or have already caused a patient injury. He or she reviews and analyzes adverse patient occurrences, as well as lawsuits that have been thoroughly investigated. A comprehensive investigation thus allows for a more insightful analysis of an adverse event and provides critical information that will be needed to understand the root cause of an event and prevent its recurrence.

The risk manager's responsibilities may include quality management, workers' compensation, safety, and insurance and contractual review. For the purposes of this text, however, we concentrate specifically on claim investigation, which may be done by the risk manager or by a claim investigator.

### The Risk Management Process

The medical malpractice investigator needs to understand how the particular clinical risk management program operates within a specific HCO. The program's effectiveness depends on the cooperation of the entire medical and healthcare staff. The exchange of information between the risk management department and the various clinical departments, as well as implementation of risk control recommendations, is essential. Most HCO risk management programs include the components of risk identification, risk analysis, risk treatment, and risk financing.

#### Risk Identification

Risk identification is a process of gathering information—from sources both within and outside of the HCO—that pertain to actual or potential patient injury and consequent loss exposure for the HCO. Such sources include incident reports, verbal and written occurrence reports, generic screens, medical malpractice lawsuit experience, minutes from morbidity and mortality meetings, safety committee minutes, and quality management reviews. External sources include surveys of the Joint Commission on Accreditation of Healthcare Organizations (JCAHO), investigations by state health departments, and assessments performed by outside consultants.

Risk managers use risk assessment as a tool to uncover situations that may cause injury or unsafe practices. Using a checklist of accepted standards, risk managers identify deviations or problem areas and also review systems, procedures, and policies. Another method of risk identification is a process known as Failure Modes and Effects Analysis (FMEA). Using FMEA methodology, one can examine the design of procedures and processes to identify points of potential risk to patient safety (failures) and what their consequences (effects) would be—before any error actually happens. Weaknesses identified in the system or process can then be redesigned or avoided.

## Risk Analysis

Risk analysis is a determination of which of the identified risks pose significant exposure to the HCO and of the probability that a loss will occur or recur. Risk managers have generally given priority to clinical areas that have the greatest risk of financial loss: obstetrics, surgery, and anesthesia. Reviewing the losses associated with closed medical malpractice cases is one way to assess the risks associated with various clinical activities. Analyzing the contents of an investigation report can also help the risk manager focus on an area of exposure.

## Risk Treatment

Risk treatment[2] is the establishment of a plan of action to avoid recurrence of certain incidents or to minimize their impact on the hospital's risk management program. There are two approaches to risk treatment: risk control and risk financing.

### Risk Control

Risk control encompasses loss prevention, loss reduction, and risk avoidance. *Loss prevention* is the approach commonly used in the health care setting to minimize the number of adverse occurrences. Traditional methods include staff in-service education programs, employee orientation, and preventative maintenance for biomedical equipment. Loss prevention also calls for the development of procedures and policies designed to reduce the frequency of certain loss-producing events. One example is the implementation of a protocol to prevent wrong-site surgery. Such a protocol requires a series of checks by various members of the health care team during the preoperative and intraoperative period, aimed at verifying the correct surgical site.

To affect changes that will reduce the risks associated with a particular situation, the risk manager must synthesize the information from a thoroughly investigated occurrence or carefully analyzed loss data and present it to a quality management or risk management committee. Such a committee is usually composed of individuals who have the policy-making authority necessary to avoid a recurrence of a particular adverse event or to reduce the risk or system vulnerability identified in an assessment.

The risk manager may be responsible for preparing a root cause analysis (RCA) as required by the JCAHO. The RCA is designed to study serious adverse patient occurrences, determine the underlying causes, and develop corrective actions. Such corrective actions are actions or policy changes that must be instituted in response to the adverse event and are generally determined by the department involved. Their intent is to ensure that the event does not recur. HCOs are encouraged to report sentinel events to the JCAHO. The information gained from the investigation process may be critical for the preparation of an RCA.

*Loss reduction* involves implementing risk control techniques that limit the potential consequences or severity of an identified risk or loss. One important means of loss reduction is the early investigation of adverse occurrences. Accurate and comprehensive investigation of an actual or potential claim puts the HCO in a more advantageous position to defend the claim and therefore minimize loss. If investigations are done quickly and thoroughly, records, X-rays, specimens, and equipment can be easily located, reviewed, and stored for safekeeping, and witnesses can be interviewed while the details are still fresh. Prompt investigations also allow the risk manager to troubleshoot a potentially litigious event. An informed risk manager can encourage the initiation of frank discussions with the patient and his or her family regarding the adverse event. Some of the information obtained in the claim investigation may be used by the health care team to understand what happened and to establish a unified and informed approach to communicating with the patient.

*Risk avoidance* is a risk treatment strategy that recognizes that certain activities expose the facility to serious levels of risk. When it is believed that losses associated with these activities cannot be prevented, reduced, or transferred, an HCO may decide to avoid the activities altogether. For example, an HCO might close an emergency department in a community where clinical specialists are not available to provide on-call emergency care. However, such a business decision may cause the HCO to lose revenue as well as to diminish its reputation.

### Risk Financing

An HCO may also employ risk financing to cover financial losses. This risk treatment strategy includes the choices of risk retention (acceptance of risk) and risk transfer (transferring the risk to another party in order to protect the institution's assets).

*Risk retention* occurs when the HCO assumes all or part of the financial burden of certain risks. Some of the techniques used include:

- setting up a self-insurance trust
- maintaining a significant deductible in a commercial insurance policy
- setting aside funds to pay for small losses, such as the reimbursement of patients for lost dentures or eyeglasses

A more formal method of self-insurance is the establishment of a multi- or single-owner captive insurance company. This is an insurance company controlled by its owners and whose principal beneficiaries are its insured.

*Risk transfer* involves the purchase of a commercial insurance policy or the transfer of liability to another entity by contractual agreement. For example, a contractual transfer of risk could be in the form of an agreement with an outside nursing service agency that provides the HCO with nurses and accepts liability for their actions. Either way, unavoidable risk can then be managed in order to protect the institution from catastrophic loss.

In most cases, identified risks are managed through a combination of risk transfer and risk retention techniques. This dual approach to risk financing is discussed in greater detail in Chapter 15, "What the Investigator Needs to Know about Insurance."

**Claim Management**

Despite the efforts and strategies to prevent, reduce, and avoid risk, malpractice claims continue to be brought against HCOs and their employees. It is imperative that a comprehensive plan be in place to investigate, evaluate, and manage all claims so that individualized risk reduction techniques can be implemented. The risk manager monitors the HCO's claims. Depending on the insurance program, the insurer's claim examiner may share or assume this responsibility, working with the risk manager and defense counsel to monitor the development of individual cases. The risk manager should follow closely all the institution's claims. Internal monitoring ensures that important developments are evaluated from the hospital's standpoint and prevents an unnecessary lapse in defense activities.

The risk manager fulfills his or her role in safeguarding the institution's assets through a loss prevention and claim management program. This role requires the risk manager to take an active interest in all aspects of claim management. The HCO is then able to evaluate fully its position on all claims and make sure defense counsel supports that position. See Chapter 19 for more information on claim management.

**The Investigator's Role in the Risk Treatment Process**

Depending on the HCO's professional liability program, the medical malpractice claim investigator's role in the investigation of potential and actual medical malpractice claims may include the following activities:

- Analyzing medical records and other institutional documents, including doctor's office records, laboratory data, and department-specific data such as logbooks, policy and procedure manuals, rules and regulations, and mortality and morbidity minutes and worksheets
- Consulting, as needed, with in-house experts for guidance on intricate clinical issues
- Undertaking research on medical and biomedical issues, as needed, on topics relevant to the claim
- Preparing a comprehensive investigation report on the case that includes reviewing all relevant clinical data, conducting and documenting witness interviews and descriptions, and analyzing the med-

ical/legal issues of the case (Exactly how an investigation is conducted is discussed in detail in Chapters 1 through 13.)

• Channeling information and reports to the HCO risk manager and defense attorneys, as well as bringing relevant information to the attention of insurance claim examiners

• Corresponding with defense attorneys regarding the need for additional information to support the defense process and to meet discovery demands. This process may include, for example, retrieving hospital by-laws, policies, regulations, and copies of potential evidence pathology slides and/or X-rays; locating the parties involved in the claim; and identifying signatures in the medical record.

• Informing interviewed parties about such risk management techniques as documentation and protection of the integrity of medical records

The claim investigator must understand and respect the confidential nature of the information gathered during the course of a claim investigation and should consult legal counsel regarding any legal restrictions on the investigation process. Medical records may contain information about a patient's or a family member's private life. Refer Chapter 14, "Confidentiality of Medical Records and Other Documents" for more information on this topic. The facts uncovered in an investigation should be divulged only to the appropriate parties for the specific purpose of developing a defense or settlement strategy. A business associate agreement, under HIPAA, may be required of the investigator before patient health information is made available.

A claim investigator employed by an outside entity needs to become aware of the "personality" of the HCO and also the personalities of key individuals with whom he or she will come into contact. There is generally a "procedural protocol" that must be learned. For example, how does the investigator set up an interview with a nurse, resident, or salaried attending physician? The investigator who is not an employee of the HCO needs to be sensitive to the feelings of the staff who may perceive the investigator as a threat.

Suffice it to say, the role of the claim investigator is an integral part of the HCO's risk management program. Ultimately, the investigator's services will prove an invaluable part of an HCO's efforts to reduce future patient injuries and minimize the impact on the HCO of actual adverse events.

## NOTES

1. This text assumes that the investigator has some knowledge of the principles of medicine. Individuals without this knowledge base should supplement this text with medical reference texts to obtain an understanding of basic anatomy and the general principles of medicine and surgery. Please see the list of resources at the end of this text for references.
2. American Society for Healthcare Risk Management, *Risk Management Program Development Tool Kit* (Chicago, Ill: American Society for Healthcare Risk Management, 2000).

# Part I

---

# The Investigation

Investigating a claim is much like solving a mystery. The who, what, when, where, and how of each case must be addressed. Part I of this text details the steps necessary to prepare for and conduct a medical malpractice investigation.

Special attention is given to the review of the medical record (both paper and electronic), which contains a great deal of information crucial to the investigation. Other chapters in Part I address how to identify areas of potential liability and appropriate parties to interview. Tips for organizing the medical records to facilitate the investigation process are also included. All of these steps are done to accomplish one of the investigator's main goals: to assist defense counsel in developing a strong defense strategy.

The text provides a section on interviewing techniques that describes the communication process essential for a successful interview. Practical suggestions for preparing and conducting an interview are included along with guidelines for handling a "difficult interview." Several chapters are devoted to sample interview questions designed to help the novice interviewer formulate appropriate, tactful, and succinct questions for different types of claims. Interview questions on occurrences in such areas as surgery, anesthesia, psychiatry, and laboratory are covered in one chapter.

Another chapter is devoted to the investigation of obstetrical events, including clinical information needed to understand the maternal medical record and develop interview questions. Chapters on long-term care and equipment-related occurrences address the special considerations necessary for those types of investigations. These chapters will help the investigator become aware of the extent of questioning needed to explore an occurrence thoroughly.

Finally, the process of analyzing the fact pattern of a case (i.e., a description of all salient factors in a case and their interrelationships) is discussed. This "sorting out" of facts enables the investigator to define clearly the relevant issues and to address the who, what, when, where, and how questions posed at the onset of the investigation. It is the final step before the investigator begins writing the comprehensive investigation report.

# Chapter 1

# Reviewing the Medical Record

---

- When to Review Medical Records
- Reviewing Notices for Potential Claims
- Reviewing a Medical Record for Investigation
- Tips for Managing Documents

---

Medical records are the foundation of every claim investigation. The goal of this chapter is twofold: to instruct the investigator on how to determine when medical records require a review and to explain how to extract the information needed to evaluate a case for potential liability. Reviewing a medical record for claim investigation requires the development of a medical/legal sense. That is, the investigator must apply clinical experience, as well as concepts in law and risk management, as he or she reviews records in health care organizations (HCOs) and physicians' offices. Also required is the ability to differentiate between medical records that require only a cursory screening and those for which an in-depth review is necessary.

## WHEN TO REVIEW MEDICAL RECORDS

Several factors can alert an investigator to the need to review the records of an HCO or an insured physician. Each of the following notices requires different degrees of review, based on the potential liability or financial risk. First, we define the various terms used to describe these alerting mechanisms. Specific guidelines follow for reviewing the records on the various types of cases.

3

## Alerting Mechanisms

### *Attorney Request Letters (ARLs)*

Physicians' private offices and HCO health information departments receive many requests from attorneys for copies of patients' medical records. Such requests are referred to as attorney request letters (ARLs). These requests should be reviewed promptly for issues of liability so the HCO can be alerted to a potential lawsuit.

### *Notices of Motion/Order to Show Cause*

The court notifies the HCO or HCO-insured physician when the court has ordered a copy of the medical record or when an attorney has petitioned the court for a copy. In most cases, the health information management department (HIM) notifies the risk manager it has received such a request. Depending on the HCO's policy, insured physicians may then forward a copy of the requested patient's office record to the risk management department for review by an investigator, or the investigator may review the record in the physician's private office.

### *Reported Adverse Patient Occurrences*

Verbal or written communications to the HCO risk manager about an adverse occurrence to a patient are also called alerts. Such notices usually come from a health care worker, nurse, physician, quality management coordinator, or other HCO personnel and generally include a description of an untoward event involving actual or potential patient injury. Written communication might take the form of a formal occurrence report or a handwritten, typed, or e-mailed note to the risk manager.

Risk managers can use a form such as the **Alert Transmittal Form (Exhibit 1-1)** to track reported events and/or to transmit them to the investigator for screening and review for potential liability. Most HCOs investigate serious alerts immediately, while the recollections of all involved parties are still fresh. Prompt response enables the risk manager to secure the documents and make an early assessment of liability and financial risk. After reviewing the medical record, the investigator can complete the **Alert Screening Form** shown in **Exhibit 1-2**. This form helps the risk manager decide whether a more in-depth review is necessary or whether sufficient reason exists to open a claim file and begin an investigation.

**Exhibit 1-1**   Sample Alert Transmittal Form

---

This report is confidential and is prepared solely in anticipation of or in connection with litigation.

Date Reported_____   Time Reported _____

Patient Name_____   Age _____

Unit Number_____   Room Number _____

Date of Occurrence_____   Time of Occurrence _____

Location _____

Attending M.D. _____

Admitting Diagnosis_____
_____

### DESCRIPTION OF OCCURRENCE
_____
_____
_____

### CONDITION OF PATIENT PRIOR TO OCCURRENCE
_____
_____

### SUBSEQUENT CONDITION OF PATIENT
_____
_____

### DOCUMENTATION ON CHART RELATIVE TO THE OCCURRENCE AND BY WHOM
_____
_____

### FOLLOW-UP ACTION AND/OR PLAN (e.g., TESTS PERFORMED OR PENDING)
_____
_____

| Persons Involved | Status | Extension |
|---|---|---|
| 1. | | |
| 2. | | |
| 3. | | |
| 4. | | |

REPORTED BY_____   Date_____   Ext._____

Courtesy of Jane Whitney, Director of Risk Management, Regulatory and Insurance Affairs, Mount Sinai Hospital, New York, New York.

**Exhibit 1-2**    Sample Alert Screening Form

This report is confidential and is prepared solely in anticipation of or in connection with litigation.

PATIENT LAST NAME        FIRST NAME                        M.I.        AGE

_____

UNIT NUMBER_____ DEPARTMENT _____

LOCATION OF OCCURRENCE _____

ATTENDING/ADMITTING M.D. _____

ADMITTING DIAGNOSIS _____

_____

DATE OF ADMISSION _____

OCCURRENCE DATE _____

DATE OF OCCURRENCE _____

DESCRIPTION (see summary for details)

_____

_____

_____

_____

PARTIES INVOLVED

1. _____

2. _____

3. _____

4. _____

ACTIVITY

| | | |
|---|---|---|
| AWAITING MEDICAL RECORD | Y / N | _____ |
| PRIORITY REVIEW | Y / N | _____ |
| REVIEW MEDICAL RECORD | Y / N | _____ |
| INVESTIGATE | Y / N | _____ |
| CLAIM FILE | Y / N | _____ |
| NO ACTION | Y / N | _____ |

REPORTED BY_____ Date_____ Ext._____

*continues*

**Exhibit 1-2**    continued

PATIENT LAST NAME        FIRST NAME

_____

UNIT NUMBER_____

SUMMARY:_____

_____

_____

_____

_____

_____

_____

_____

_____

_____

_____

Courtesy of Jane Whitney, Director of Risk Management, Regulatory and Insurance Affairs, Mount Sinai Hospital, New York, New York.

## *Legal Action*

A summons or subpoena is a legal document that signals the start of a lawsuit and is usually delivered to the risk management department or another designated office. At this point, all medical records must be secured.

## *Letters of Complaint*

Letters of complaint are generally addressed to the hospital president, administrator, or risk manager. The patient or the patient's family describes an event that allegedly resulted in an injury to the patient. The HCO patient representative may become involved in investigating and responding to the complaint.

## Letters of Claim

A letter of claim comes from an attorney, a patient, or a patient's family member. This type of correspondence, which is generally sent to the HCO risk manager or to HCO counsel, alleges an injury to the patient and sometimes demands compensation. Depending on HCO policy, such letters are sent immediately to the HCO's insurance carrier or claim examiner and/or to a designated person within the HCO.

## Patient Requests for Access to Medical Record

Under the Health Insurance Portability and Accountability Act (HIPAA), patients or their legally authorized representatives are entitled to review medical records pertaining to their own medical treatment. Such requests may or may not indicate an intention to sue the HCO.

## Notification of State Review of Complaint

When a state regulatory agency begins investigation or review in response to a complaint received from a patient, a family member, or another individual, the agency notifies the named HCO. A preliminary review of the medical record can put this complaint in context and may signal the need for further investigation.

## Billing Disputes

Patient complaints about billing may be an indication of dissatisfaction with the quality of the care received. The investigator may be notified by the risk manager of such a situation, in which case a review of the medical record may be appropriate.

## Preliminary Reviews of the Medical Record

Before the HCO responds to any of these alerting communications, the investigator should evaluate the medical record for possible liability, identifying the adverse patient occurrence and evaluating the outcome. The risk manager may make a recommendation regarding the depth of the initial investigation to be undertaken.

ARLs, billing disputes, and patients' requests for copies of their medical records usually require only a quick review for documented evidence of apparent liability. Cases involving severe adverse occurrences, letters of claim, and lawsuits require an in-depth record review plus the preparation of an investigation report that includes an evaluation of any departures from standard medical practice. Patient complaint letters and follow-ups to incident reports tend to fall somewhere in between; they need attention, but they may not require a detailed report. **Table 1-1** illustrates the different types of notices and the suggested levels of review.

A review of the patient's condition upon admission and discharge, as well as the records of procedures or surgery performed, generally gives the investigator an idea of whether there was an adverse occurrence. Reviewing the following items in the medical record may help to expedite the preparation of a summary of the patient's hospitalization:

- discharge summary (compare the discharge diagnoses to the admitting diagnoses and physical examination)
- operative report or brief handwritten operative note
- patient's condition on discharge
- progress notes relevant to any occurrence identified during the review or to any date of occurrence included in the ARL
- relevant X-rays and laboratory reports

**Table 1-1**   Types of Notices of Potential Litigation and Suggested Medical Record Review

| Brief Review* | In-Depth Review |
| --- | --- |
| Attorney requests for copy of medical records | All medical malpractice lawsuits |
| Notices of motion /orders to show cause | All serious "alerts" or reported |
| "Alerts" or reported occurrences | occurrences |
| Patient/family letters of complaint | All letters of claim |
| Patient/family requests for copy of medical record | |
| State notices of intent to investigate a complaint | |
| Billing disputes | |

**\*When any brief review reveals a serious iatrogenic patient injury, an in-depth review is the next step.**

The **Case Summary Form (Exhibit 1-3)** can be used to summarize most medical records in order to identify the existence of potential liability exposure as well as any need for a more in-depth review. This form can be used to highlight the occurrence and injury, if any, and other pertinent information. Caution: Even the most skilled investigator can miss information regarding a potential lawsuit during this quick review, and a summons might later be served upon the hospital. Be aware that this can happen, and do not panic!

**Exhibit 1-3**    Sample Case Summary Form

TO:_____        REVIEW DATE:_____

FROM:_____        INVESTIGATOR:_____

PATIENT:_____

UNIT NO:_____        DATE OF OCCURRENCE:_____

DATES OF TREATMENT:_____

TYPE OF NOTIFICATION:        ☐ Alert        ☐ Complaint        ☐ Other

_____

_____

SUMMARY:_____

_____

_____

_____

_____

_____

_____

_____

_____

_____

### Securing and Requesting Copies of the Medical Record

If the investigator completes a preliminary record review and concludes there is a potential for litigation (or if actual litigation has begun—as in the case of the commencement of legal action), it is necessary to secure the patient's medical records. As noted in Chapter 2, "Locating Other HCO Documents," associated documents (e.g., X-rays) pertaining to the case also must be secured. Once the record is secured, no alterations should be made. If a claim file has not already been opened (e.g., in response to an ARL or a serious adverse patient occurrence), one should be opened immediately.

The **Request Form** (**Exhibit 1-4**) can be used by the investigator or the risk manager to both secure and request copies of hospital documents that are, or may become, part of the litigation process. If a hard copy of this form is used, one copy should remain on file with the risk manager. The form contains spaces for the patient's name, date of birth, Social Security number or hospital medical record number, and admission and discharge dates. Instructions for both securing and copying the documents can be given next to the item being requested. The name of the individual or entity requiring a copy can be entered next to the item. Beneath this name, the full address(es) can be included. This form allows the department to invoice the appropriate party for the cost of duplication.

It is important to keep this information confidential, and this form should not become a part of the patient's medical record.

## REVIEWING NOTICES FOR POTENTIAL CLAIMS

### Responding To Attorney Request Letters (ARLs)

An attorney's request for medical records does not necessarily mean the HCO will be sued. Nevertheless, it is recommended each request be screened for medical liability issues. This screening may be done by staff in the HIM department. The obvious disadvantage of responding at this point is it may not be clear why the record is being requested, and there may not be any apparent injury or adverse patient occurrence. A request for a medical record—especially an emergency department (ED) record—could merely involve motor vehicle liability or a worker's compensation claim. In such cases, it is often apparent there is no liability to the hospital.

**Exhibit 1-4**    Sample Attorney Request Form

TO:    Supervisor
         Medical Information
         Department of Medical Records

FROM _____

REVIEW DATE _____                ☐ Hard Copy      ☐ Microfilm

PATIENT _____                   INSURANCE_____

DATES OF                                                             UNIT NO. _____
TREATMENT_____
            _____               DATE OF
            _____               OCCURRENCE_____

☐  The medical record may be released without further action.

☐  The medical record may not be released. It is missing the following authorizations:
_____

☐  The chart is missing the following items:_____
_____

☐  A copy of the chart may be released when the original has been secured and a copy sent
    to the Risk Management Department. We will advise you of our file number.

MEDICAL RECORDS COPY
. . . . . . . . . . . . . . . . . . . . . . . . . . . . . . . . . . . . . . . . . . . . . . . . . . . . . .

SUMMARY _____
_____
_____
_____
_____
_____
_____
_____

ATTORNEY _____

INVESTIGATOR'S COPY

On the other hand, the requesting attorney's letter may indicate the reason the records are being requested. For example, a date of occurrence, an injury, or a fall during the hospital stay may be mentioned, or the patient may be referred to as "the deceased." A preliminary review may indicate this is not a routine ARL.

## Reviewing Requests for the Release of Medical Records

In addition to reviewing the medical record for liability, a designated HCO employee needs to ensure the specific aspects of any request for medical records meet with legal compliance. The reviewer should be aware these requirements differ depending on the state statutes.

The request to release the medical record should:

- be written on attorney's letterhead stationery, in the case of an ARL, or contain the complete name and address of the patient if the request comes directly from the patient
- include the patient's signature (If the patient is deceased, incompetent, or a minor, a legally appropriate individual, such as the parent, estate administrator, or legal guardian, should sign.)
- have a current notary or commissioner of deeds' stamp validating the party's authorization signature, in the case of an ARL
- include a special release form (complying with any state and federal requirements) for patients being treated for a psychiatric illness, alcohol or drug abuse, or for *any* patient whose medical record documents any HIV- or AIDS-related information

If the request fails to meet any of these requirements, the HIM employee must obtain the missing information by mailing to the requesting party an explanation for the HCO's inability to release the requested documents.

## Reviewing Alerts of Serious Adverse Patient Occurrences

In the case of alerts—unlike with ARLs—the person referring the information usually provides some clue to the nature of the occurrence and injury. Sometimes, however, the investigator may discover the information in an alert differs from facts uncovered while investigating the case.

A benefit to the early review of records of a serious occurrence, *while the patient is still in the hospital,* is that the staff involved can make any necessary and factual addenda to the progress notes so the documentation more accurately reflects the events. This should be done only under the guidance of the risk manager! Such additions can be helpful or harmful to the defense of a claim, and the risk manager may want to seek the advice of legal counsel before advising an employee or insured physician to make an addendum to the medical record entry. The resulting addendum should include the date and time of the entry. The note should not be self-serving and must be written very soon after the occurrence. If the case involves a potential lawsuit, it is advisable to open a claim file. Serious reported occurrences may require extensive investigation in anticipation of litigation. Additionally, all records and associated documents should be secured after the patient's discharge. Once the record is secured, no alterations should be made.

## Reviewing Summonses

Extensive investigation is necessary for all cases involving litigation— summonses and letters of claim from an attorney. A detailed investigation report with a summary of the medical record and interviews conducted is recommended for all cases in suit. These summaries help the defense counsel prepare for depositions, identify witnesses, and develop a vigorous strategy to defend the claim.

To facilitate a focused investigation, allegations are generally noted from the complaint or other legal documents. For example, if it is alleged there was a failure to safeguard a patient who fell, the record should be checked for evidence of documentation regarding the patient's mental status, use of side rails, and patient activity orders.

The lawsuit usually names specific people and entities as defendants. The investigator then interviews these individuals if they are covered by the HCO's insurance policy, as well as others (where legally permissible) who may be helpful in preparing the defense of the case.

If the occurrence and injury are unknown or unclear, the investigator may wait to receive additional legal documents before completely investigating the claim. However, it is a good idea to do a quick review of the entire medical record before deciding to delay the investigation. An unanticipated occurrence may provide a clue as to the issues involved in the case. To the extent legally permissible, the investigator should check for other related admission information (clinic or outpatient department and ED records) to help shed light on the case. The investigator may also want to interview one person who was involved in the greater part of the patient's care for background information. This early analysis may be beneficial to the claim management process.

## REVIEWING A MEDICAL RECORD FOR INVESTIGATION

The following guidelines are general steps for reviewing HCO or doctor's office records in response to notice (other than an ARL) of a possible patient injury, potential claim, or lawsuit. (See **Figure 1-1**.)

### Step 1: Reviewing the Letter or Document

This review of the alerting documents helps to focus the investigation on specific complaints or allegations regarding the occurrence or injury.

### Step 2: Obtaining the Record from the Health Information Department or Physician's Office

Most states have regulations regarding the maintenance of medical records and other HCO documents. For example, health department regulations may require HCOs to keep these documents for six years after the completion of treatment. For easier storage, most HCOs transfer medical records to microfilm, microfiche, or digital format after a few years. See the next two chapters, "Locating Other HCO Documents" and "The Electronic Health Record" for a more detailed discussion of how to assemble a complete medical record.

### Step 3: Making Sure the Medical Record Is Complete and the Copy Is Clear

Once the medical record has been obtained, it must be reviewed for completeness. In addition, the investigator should pay particular attention to the presence or absence of certain items that may be relevant to the case, such

STEP 1

> Review the documents, letters, legal papers,
> etc., that gave rise to the need for a review.

STEP 2

> Obtain the original medical record and copy.

STEP 3

> Check to ensure the record is complete:
>
> • history and physical
> • progress notes
> • physician's orders
> • TPR
> • consults, etc.

STEP 4

> Read through the record for an overview.
> Look for adverse patient occurrences and
> patient injury.

STEP 5

> Reread original record and scrutinize:
>
> • Take copy apart to correlate activities.
> • Highlight areas of concern.
> • Conduct research if necessary.
> • Note persons to interview.
> • List questions for parties involved.

Note: TPR, temperature, pulse, and respiration

**Figure 1-1**    Steps for an In-Depth Review of a Medical Record

as a typed operative report or pertinent laboratory reports. If anything essential is missing, the HIM department should be contacted. It is possible some items have been misplaced or have not yet been filed. In such cases, the investigator should determine whether individual departments have maintained a log of tests performed and their results.

*The typical medical record might have the following components (not an all-inclusive list):*

- history and physical
- physician's progress notes
- physician's order sheets
- nurse's notes (general and special care unit)
- graphic and flow sheets (temperature, pulse, and respiration [TPR]; intake and output [I&O]; activities of daily living [ADL])
- medication record
- nursing care plan
- laboratory transfusion and X-ray reports
- surgery documents
- consultations
- emergency department record
- records of special health care disciplines (e.g., rehabilitation therapy)
- consent forms
- discharge summaries
- autopsy report

**Step 4: Reading through the Medical Record**

This initial review provides an overview. It is important to try not to focus on every word, to be objective, to not start theorizing about what happened, to not assume that something happened if it is not documented, and to validate the occurrence and injury, if any. When possible, the outcome (extent and permanence) of the alleged injury should be determined. Any outpatient department records may need to be reviewed, if this is legally permissible, to assess the subsequent treatment the patient needed for the injury.

**Step 5: Scrutinizing the Medical Record**

This read-through is a thorough clinical review. The investigator should read the entire medical record. At some point during this review, it may be necessary to research an unfamiliar subject or contact an appropriate clinical specialist. All aspects of care given must be examined and the following assessed:

- Were all appropriate tests ordered in response to the patient's signs and symptoms? (Researching the type of testing done at the time of the patient's hospitalization may be necessary.)
- Was the information from the test results properly acted upon? (This one factor can have a crucial bearing on the outcome of the patient's treatment.)
- Were the physician's orders in response to abnormal test results carried out?
- Are the dates of tests and reported test results accurate?
- Is the record chronological, or are there incorrect or inconsistent dates or times?

This more extensive review covers progress notes and nurses' notes and also should include:

- ADL sheets
- TPR sheets
- addressograph information
- laboratory reports
- consultation notes

During this review, the investigator should look at the record with a plaintiff attorney's eye by:

- identifying the people involved in the occurrence and making lists of questions to ask each person who might be interviewed
- scrutinizing every word that describes or details the occurrence; looking for inflammatory or angry notes, discrepancies in notes, untimed

or unsigned notes, writing in the margins, and any other potential "red flags"

- whenever possible, looking at the original document and examining any alterations or questionable entries; looking for the use of different colored inks in critical notes, missing pages, scratching out, writing over, and the use of correction fluid
- making sure the original medical record matches the copy sent to the plaintiff's attorney (The original medical record will be the one used at the time of deposition.)
- looking at subsequent and prior treatment records, if appropriate, and consulting with legal counsel to determine if patient authorization is required for such review

This critical evaluation helps the defense attorney assess liability and develop a defense. The in-depth read-through is time well spent at the outset of each investigation.


## TIPS FOR MANAGING DOCUMENTS

Each investigator eventually develops his or her own organizational system and review style that produces a smooth investigation process. The following methods may help investigators organize and facilitate a review:

- photocopying the record so notes can be written on the copy
  - using paper clips to divide the record
  - using self-stick notes to make notes on individual pages
- numbering the progress-note pages on the copy if this has not already been done; reorganizing the record after the interviews, if necessary
- taking the photocopied chart apart and putting it into organized sections so the different sections can be easily cross-referenced (e.g., "Doctors' Orders" and "Laboratory Reports")
- clipping or marking pages with important names, dates, and any other information that will be referred to during the interviews
- creating timelines and research notes for the investigator's own use

If the case covers a long course of treatment involving an injury or adverse occurrence, it is important to try to isolate the times when a particular medical or nursing action, judgment, or decision led to a negative consequence. For example, suppose it is alleged that a cancer patient undergoing a course of radiation therapy received too high a dose, resulting in unnecessary tissue damage. The investigator should review medical record entries regarding the radiation treatment, looking for documented signs and symptoms of toxicity and the rationale for continued treatments.

If the patient had numerous hospitalizations or an extremely long hospital stay—and the charts are voluminous—the investigator should not try to give a day-by-day review in the investigation report. A summary of the hospitalization and/or office visits with special attention to the occurrence and injury is sufficient (see Chapter 12, "Writing the Investigation Report"). Summaries in the medical record by specialists and consultants, as well as residents' "off-service" notes, should be identified to guide in preparing the summary. However, the information in these summaries should be compared with the progress notes to validate their accuracy and completeness.

If the case involves a serious injury, brain damage, permanent coma, paralysis, or death, the record review requires even greater care. These cases generally carry a high monetary exposure and the potential for adverse publicity. Therefore, a great deal of effort should be put into investigating these cases, as the results of the investigation guide the defense strategy.

Chapter 2

# Locating Other HCO Documents

- Clinical Documents
- Electronic Information
- Miscellaneous Documents

As described, after obtaining the medical record, the investigator reviews the record for completeness. The investigator pays particular attention to the presence or absence of certain items, such as a typed operative report or pertinent laboratory reports that may be relevant to the case. If anything essential is missing, the investigator should contact medical records personnel to see if they are holding reports that have not yet been filed. Individual departments generally maintain duplicates of these items as well. Each department may also keep a log of tests performed and the results. This log can be reviewed when hard copies of the reports have been misplaced.

Many documents are stored in electronic format. The investigator should know what records are maintained electronically by the facility. He or she may need a password to access electronic records or may need to contact another authorized person for access. For further discussion, see the following chapter, "The Electronic Health Record: Getting It All Together."

The next step is to obtain documents that augment the medical record but may not actually be a part of it. Whenever possible, these documents should be secured. Such documents may provide important information that can be used to support or refute allegations and to further the defense of a claim. The following examples are listed alphabetically.

## CLINICAL DOCUMENTS

### Cardiac Catheter Laboratory Technician Records

The cardiac catheter laboratory flow sheet contains information about a catheterization procedure that may prove helpful to a case. The patient's and physician's names are recorded, along with information pertaining to the timing of specific aspects of the catheterization. For example, the technician records the length of time the catheters remained in the right heart and/or left heart (called the *arterial* and *venous times*, respectively). The types of catheter and dye used are also recorded, as are the approach used and the patient's vital signs during the procedure. Because there are standards relative to arterial and venous times, knowing the actual time may help the investigator focus on possible risk issues. The patient's blood pressure and the interpretation of cardiac monitoring are also maintained in the medical record during the procedure.

### Cardiothoracic Surgery (Bypass) Pump Records

These records may be part of the medical record, or they may be kept by the perfusionist in the cardiothoracic department. They relate to the patient's hemodynamic and metabolic status during procedures that require cardiopulmonary bypass and contain information that can help the investigator understand what occurred during cardiothoracic surgery.

### Dialysis Flow Sheets

Dialysis flow sheets, which may include the nursing assignment sheets for the dialysis unit, could prove helpful in renal cases by further identifying personnel, equipment, or treatment administered to patients during individual dialysis sessions. For example, the sheets may describe the dialysis station (bed or chair) assigned to the patient. In general, patients assigned to a chair cannot undergo femoral dialysis. The records may also note the type of dialysis (hematological versus peritoneal) and the patient access used (a femoral stick versus an upper extremity fistula or shunt).

## Epidemiology Logs

The departments of microbiology and epidemiology generally maintain some form of database that tracks the results of all body fluid cultures. Tracking positive cultures helps to monitor the frequency of institutionally acquired infections, along with the need for and problems with infection control on various patient care units. This information may be helpful when investigating a case that involves a nosocomial infection.

## Fetal Monitoring Strips

These strips record the progress of labor, indicating the duration and frequency of maternal contractions and the corresponding fetal heart rate and variability. The strips may also contain notations regarding the treatments and medications administered at a specific point during labor. The strips may be stored separately, in either hard copy or electronic form, or kept in the maternal medical record. Fetal monitoring strips are essential to the defense of most obstetrical claims. The strips can support the care given and the decisions made during the mother's labor. Many cases have been lost because of missing fetal monitoring strips.

## Hospital Bylaws

These rules are adopted by a health care organization (HCO) for the government of all hospital personnel.

## Implantable Devices

HCOs are required to maintain records of all implanted devices for a number of reasons, including federal regulations (e.g., the Safe Medical Devices Act), device recalls, third-party reimbursements, and legal liability. The documentation of implantable devices should include the name of the device, the manufacturer, and the serial or model number. The patient's name and address are also necessary for device tracking under federal regulations.

**Incident/Occurrence Report Forms**

The investigator should always check for the presence or absence of an incident/occurrence report. These reports contain details regarding the "who, what, when, and where" of an occurrence and are a valuable source of information.

**Needle and Sponge Count**

This information may be part of a circulating slip or may be noted on a separate form. The documentation should specify the number of needles, sponges, and instruments used during an operation, as well as the opening and closing counts of sponges, needles, and instruments. These counts are performed by the scrub and circulating nurses. It is important to review the count when a case involves a retained foreign body.

**Nursing Administration's Report**

At most institutions, the department of nursing maintains a formal report sheet that is submitted daily by nursing administrators. This report contains information on patients who are very sick or who have special problems. Information from the nursing administration's report sheet may supplement occurrence reports or the information contained in the patient's medical record.

**Nursing Assignment Records**

The department of nursing generally maintains a record of the nursing assignment for a given unit on various dates. This information is useful in supplementing the nurse's notes or progress notes to identify the nurses caring for a patient on a particular day.

**On-Call Schedules**

All of the clinical specialty departments generally maintain an on-call schedule or a rotation schedule that indicates the names of the attending and/or resident physicians scheduled to work on a certain day. These schedules are usually made up on a monthly basis and can be obtained from the individual departments. The on-call schedules can help identify which physicians to interview regarding an occurrence.

## Operating Room Circulating Slips

These forms generally contain the names of all individuals present during a surgical procedure, including the attending surgeons, house staff assistants, operating room nurses, and anesthesia staff, as well as any non-healthcare personnel such as medical equipment sales representatives. The slips may note the use of special equipment, such as prostheses, graft material, and special surgical instruments, and may also include information about a patient's blood loss and fluid replacement. The slips can be found in the operating room or in the patient's medical record.

## Other Departments' Records

Most departments maintain copies of records of activities related to patient care. The investigator should seek out individuals in the various departments who can help clarify the types of documents maintained, where the documents are stored, and how to access the information. These other departments might include social services, occupational therapy, physical therapy, pharmacy, and anesthesia.

## Patient Data Logs

Listed below are some departments that maintain logs or computerized databases that include the names of all individuals they have treated:

- operating room
- delivery room
- emergency department
- outpatient clinics
- radiology department

- cardiac catheterization department
- laboratory
- blood bank
- donor bank

Logs have many uses for the investigator. During the discovery phase of a lawsuit, both defense and plaintiff attorneys often request copies of these logs to determine the whereabouts of a particular person at any given time. For example, they would check to see whether a particular obstetrician or anesthesiologist was listed as operating in more than one area at once or whether he or she was noted to be in a different area than the one involving the patient or case. The logs can also be used to indicate how many patients were being treated on a particular day and to identify further potential witnesses to an occurrence.

**Private-Duty Nursing Logs**

These logs are maintained by the nursing department. Private-duty nursing logs may record the nurse's name and license number, the date, the time, the patient, the room number, and the agency sending the nurse. These logs can help identify a private-duty nurse for an interview, if permissible. The investigator may also be able to determine whether the HCO administration or the patient requested a private-duty nurse.

**Psychiatry Flow Sheets**

Most psychiatric units use some form of flow sheets to monitor patient activity throughout the day. Patients who are at risk for suicide or for going "absent without leave" (AWOL) are monitored frequently by the staff to verify their presence on the unit. The staff generally performs these types of patient checks anywhere from every 15 minutes to once an hour. Proving that patients were monitored and observed at certain times during the day can aid the defense of certain types of psychiatric cases. Because these flow sheets may not be kept for a long period of time, it is important they be sequestered immediately.

## MISCELLANEOUS DOCUMENTS

The following documents may not relate directly to the clinical management of the patient but may nevertheless help one understand the fact pattern of a case and thus better defend the case.

### Biomedical Engineering Records

This department maintains records of preventative maintenance and equipment repairs throughout the HCO, as well as work order request logs. These records may be helpful when investigating patient injuries that involve equipment-related occurrences.

### Blueprints or Floor Plans

Blueprints of former buildings, current floor plans, and any documents that can serve as evidence to illustrate a location that has been reconstructed or demolished may be helpful when investigating injuries in which the patient's physical surroundings are related to the occurrence (especially when these surroundings have been renovated or demolished).

### Contracts and Agreements

HCOs maintain many different contracts and written agreements with outside parties, including physicians, vendors, and such groups or entities as physician groups, health maintenance organizations, and other HCOs. These documents specify the terms and conditions under which the parties to each respective agreement conduct themselves and do business with the HCO. The so-called "hold harmless" clause is a very important part of the contract. This clause describes the assumption of one party's liability by the other party; obviously, it is desirable for the HCO to transfer liability in this manner if contract negotiations so allow.

### Crisis Management Records/Reports

If they exist, these documents detail extraordinary events, such as employee strikes, fires, blackouts, and other natural disasters. Crisis management records also include copies of medical personnel coverage during the occurrence. This information is helpful when one is investigating an event that occurred during an HCO crisis and may explain why routine procedures were not carried out.

### Department of Admissions and Census Sheets

The admissions department should maintain a record of the patient census for a given date. Individual patient room assignments and information on roommates may also be available. Information regarding the patient census within the HCO and/or on specific units can help the investigator support or question a decision to divert or transfer patients from the emergency department to another HCO. These records can also be used to determine the availability of beds in critical care or specialty units.

### Medical Staff Bylaws

These bylaws are the terms and conditions all members of the HCO's medical staff must follow to admit and treat patients. The bylaws generally specify the duties and responsibilities of the medical staff and the requirements for maintaining and renewing medical staff privileges.

### Patient Bills

Billing is an integral part of a claim investigation. Defense counsel needs copies of the bills for the course of treatment under review. Defense counsel must verify and respond to claims made for damages relevant to medical expenses incurred. A form addressed to the HCO's billing/finance department would make this a routine part of the investigation of every claim that is in suit. Be aware patient bills can sometimes contain inaccurate information stemming from the International Classification of Diseases, 9th Revision, but this is not always the case.[1]

## Physician Credentialing Files

The medical staff office generally maintains these confidential files. The files contain information on a physician's educational background, work history, and claim history. They also contain a list of current privileges and any disciplinary actions or reprimands against the physician.

## Policies and Procedures

The department of nursing keeps manuals listing all policies and procedures related to the nursing function. Each policy is reviewed periodically and updated. Outdated policies may also be available for the investigation of older claims.

Each clinical department maintains similar manuals detailing protocols for department operations. Information on medical devices is generally kept in the department where the device is used. The HCO administrator for each department can usually help the investigator obtain this information.

## Root Cause Analyses

The Joint Commission on Accreditation of Healthcare Organizations (JCAHO) requires all accredited HCOs to establish policies and procedures to identify, report, and respond to serious adverse patient occurrences (JCAHO refers to these as "sentinel events"). All HCOs must complete a root cause analysis of such an event, implement improvements to reduce the risks associated with the event, and monitor the effectiveness of the implemented changes. The root cause analysis may be a good source of information for the investigator. Check with the HCO's legal counsel to see if it is permissible for you to review these documents. For more information on this subject, see Chapter 18, "Responding to Adverse Occurrences and Potential Lawsuits."

## Security Logs

Security officers generally maintain logs of patient incidents and their response. The security department may also keep separate security reports for patient and visitor occurrences. These reports generally identify patients, physicians, and nurses and may indicate whether any care was rendered, along with the dates and times of that care. The security department also files reports when called to provide manpower or assistance in restraining patients or visitors.

## Training/Assessment Files

These files are generally kept in the nursing department but may also exist for other clinical specialties. The files detail the educational programs an individual has completed successfully and which procedures he or she is credentialed to perform. These documents can be used to refute allegations that an individual was not qualified to perform a certain procedure.

## NOTES

1. American Medical Association, *ICD-9-CM 2006: The International Classification of Diseases, Ninth Revision, Clinical Modification*, (Chicago, Ill.: American Medical Association, 2005). ICD-9-CM is based on the World Health Organization's Ninth Revision, International Classification of Diseases (ICD-9). ICD-9-CM is the official system of assigning codes to diagnoses and procedures associated with hospital utilization in the United States.

Chapter 3

# The Electronic Health Record: Getting It All Together

---

- Assembling the Electronic Health Record
- Working Paperless
- Where To Begin

---

The components of a traditional medical record can be widely distributed within a health care organization (HCO). The "chart" is generally kept in the medical records or health information management (HIM) department; X-rays are kept in the radiology department; diagnostic studies, such as angiography, may be kept in the department performing the study; clinic records may be kept in a satellite treatment location; and so on. The results of testing are sent to the individual patient record, but the specific study is kept within the department. The collection, maintenance, and use of health care information is very much organization- and system-specific. Knowledge of the organizational structure and how it functions is key to sorting out the record of care.

## ASSEMBLING THE ELECTRONIC HEALTH RECORD

The electronic health record (EHR) offers the promise of pulling everything together into a single patient database. This can contain information required for patient treatment decisions as well as information that is collected for other purposes such as billing. Identification and review of every component is not necessary for every investigation but anticipating what you will need in a particular case is important.

## The Electronic Treatment Record

The electronic treatment record is the record used by the provider to manage patient care and, depending upon the electronic system an organization uses, it can include many different types of patient information in a variety of formats:

- graphic images, such as digitized X-ray images from the picture archiving and communication system (PACS) or fetal heart rate monitor tracings from the obstetrics department
- audio recordings, such as a child's abnormal heart sounds or a speech defect
- diagnostic videos in occupational/physical therapy, neurology, and psychiatry
- scans of paper documents
- direct links to clinic, emergency department, and prenatal care records

Portions of the patient database become the official or legal medical record.[1] Other portions of that database, such as clinical audit trails, provider alerts or prompts, decision support suggestions, security audits, billing and insurance records, and performance improvement activity, may not be so easily categorized. The challenge for the investigator is to identify what information is located in the official record used for patient treatment and what information is stored but is not part of this official record.

The investigation process remains unchanged regardless of the form of the treatment record. As with any patient record, all portions of the EHR must be collected and systematically reviewed. The form of the record may be all electronic, a mixture of electronic and paper (a hybrid record), or all paper. Be aware that a paper copy of an electronic or hybrid record may look different from a traditional record or be arranged in a different order. Scanned pages will look like their paper counterparts. However, they might be placed in a single location—for example, at the end of the record—because the scanning is a batch process, and the pages are images of documents that are then incorporated into the record at one time. Also, keep in mind that data fields in the electronic portion of the record may resemble a series of forms consisting of check boxes, phrases, and short sentences. The use of forms can improve the consistency of documentation but it may present a new appearance so the investigator must learn where to look for the desired information.

## Nontreatment Patient Information

Much patient information is not directly related to treatment or the management of health care and would not normally be considered part of the patient's official or legal record.[2] Administrative data, although not part of the health record, do contain patient-identifiable information. The investigator may need to locate such information in an attempt to answer an attorney's request. Examples include billing and insurance information, event history and audit trails (which are especially important in electronic records systems), incident/occurrence report forms, and treatment logs such as those in the emergency department, operating room, and labor and delivery room. There may also be nonspecific information, such as standard abbreviation lists and protocols, guidelines, and policies and procedures—all of which may be available online for easy reference. You will need to know whether such reference documents that were existent at the time of the occurrence would still be available, in an archive, years later.

## Patient-Supplied Information and the Personal Health Record

Patient-supplied information, such as X-rays, test results, pathology specimens, and prior treatment records may be incorporated into the record. Determine, if applicable, how they are incorporated and where original documents are kept. A personal health record (PHR) may also be submitted for inclusion in a record. The PHR is an electronic health record assembled and submitted by the patient or a third party acting on behalf of the patient. It is not a physician's record of medical care.[3] If a PHR was provided, it may be revealing for what the patient chose to exclude from the history or for what the physician failed to appreciate. Either way, the investigator should review it carefully.

**Records Here, Records There**

Although the practice is not advised, duplicate records of treatment (shadow records) are sometimes kept by satellite areas such as clinics. Such duplication ensures that information is always available, even in treatment areas where the electronic system is not yet in place. However, there should only be a single medical record in existence; otherwise it becomes difficult to find the one true record as notations are made on different copies. If shadow records are encountered in an investigation, the risk manager should be notified, because this is a practice that requires immediate review. The entire collection of original plus shadow records then constitutes the patient's legal record.

In the event of a lawsuit, a litigation hold notice should be issued by counsel. This notifies the HCO to secure and copy all documents, including electronic documents and e-mail relevant to the claim. The content, format, and distribution of these hold notices should be determined, with counsel, in advance.

It is a good idea to know what is secured, where it is located, and in what form it is held.

**WORKING PAPERLESS**

**Navigating the System**

In some cases, the investigator may have to work with an e-record on a computer screen, particularly if the case is not in litigation. Confidentiality is better protected if printing of records is prohibited except under specially defined circumstances. Prohibiting copies also insures that only a single copy of a medical record exists. The investigator should become familiar with the arrangement of pages in the record and the navigation process used to proceed from page to page and section to section. He or she must also know how to quickly move to specific sections of the record, such as the progress notes, laboratory and diagnostic testing results, operative reports, consents, and nurses' notes.

Reviewing records on the screen can take longer than reviewing a hard copy. Details can be missed if the technical skill for navigation has not been mastered. This skill is particularly important if a record must be reviewed on the computer with a physician during an interview. It is also important to determine how familiar the practitioner is with the electronic record and how he or she feels about using it. What are the problems encountered when using it? How easy is it to check a patient's status or test results before writing an order or a narrative note?

The investigator must also consider what the practitioner would have seen during the patient encounter. What screens would have been readily available for viewing, and which ones would have taken longer to access? Many systems are designed for ease of information entry but become more cumbersome to use if a physician wants to review past information before making a decision. Requiring even a few extra seconds or minutes on the part of the provider, multiplied by many patients, can make a system discouraging to use. What is the custom and practice of this physician when documenting a patient visit? Does he or she document several encounters at one time or document each during or after seeing the patient?

**Correcting Mistakes**

It is important to know how mistaken entries are corrected in the record. Examples might include someone documenting in the wrong patient's record or documenting the wrong information in the correct patient's record. Generally, it is not possible to delete information once it is entered, so the investigator needs to ask how the erroneous information is marked and how the corrected information is displayed. Are corrections seen in date/time order at the same location as the error, or is it necessary to go to a corrections page to see the new information? It is important to review the pages that contain these corrections, as they may give the appearance of indecision on the part of the practitioner.

**Timing Is Everything**

Access to and entry of information is dated and timed in the EHR at the precise time it occurs. A note summarizing an acute event, such as a cardiac arrest resuscitation effort or a surgical mishap, that is written hours or days later can therefore appear self-serving. Delays in notation are inevitable, but the investigator must determine the reason for this type of delay, as well as the HCO's policy on delayed documentation. When are delays acceptable and for what period? Access to information may also be dated and timed. It might be possible to determine when a provider accessed laboratory or diagnostic study results. These electronic "footprints" left by a physician could make it difficult to plead ignorance of a critical result.

**Computerized Physician Order Entry**

Another important issue is whether computerized physician order entry (CPOE) is part of the EHR structure. CPOE can be fully integrated into the EHR, or it may be an independent system with few or no direct links to the patient's treatment record. Although it is in place to reduce error,[4] CPOE may fall short on this promise, depending on its design. Awareness of potential problems related to sources of error is important.[5] The investigator must find out what the provider saw when entering an order and whether any provider alerts, prompts, decision support suggestions, or questions would have automatically been displayed as a result of an order. For example, if a physician tried to order the adult dose of a medication for a pediatric patient, what would have happened? Some CPOE systems are very smart; others are less so.[6] These alerts must be consistent with accepted standards of practice and conform to the organization's guidelines, policies, and procedures. It is also important to understand how changes in orders appear in the record. An order log or order audit trail will contain all orders, including those written and then canceled before given, either because the physician rethought the order or because it was merely a mistake that was caught. Because everything is dated and timed, these logs can give the impression that the physician was unable to make a decision or lacked knowledge. It is helpful for the defense team to know about this ahead of time.

An appreciation of electronic system delays is also important. If an order for an antibiotic were being changed from one drug to another drug, how long would it take to accomplish that change and would another physician viewing the record be able to see the ordered change immediately? These kinds of situations can lead to errors and, certainly, to lawsuits. Many of these systems are new; the investigator should ask providers during the interviews about their comfort with the system and determine their usual practice in responding to alerts and prompts.

Some of these treatment alerts may be transmitted to the physician directly by e-mail, so asking about the provider's management of e-mail as it relates to the case is also important. Most HCOs have strict policies regulating the use of e-mail for the exchange of patient information. You should determine what they are.

## Sources of Error When Working Electronically

Electronic records make some errors less likely, but they may be sources of new types of error.[7] The investigator needs to be aware of the possibility of error when reviewing electronic records and interviewing the users. Some errors are the result of screen design, such as drop-down boxes packed with too much information placed too close together that make a wrong choice (e.g., from a list of medications) possible. Hand-eye coordination is not everyone's strength. Error trapping-routines can prevent many errors, but some will always get through; knowing the system and the questions to ask is essential.

## The Crash

Computer downtime is an important factor to understand. The investigator needs to be aware of the HCO's procedures for handling medical records during such periods:

- What happens if the computer is shut down or unavailable for a period of time?
- What measures are taken to insure continuity of care and continuity of record keeping? For example, is there an expectation that paper should be used temporarily? Are necessary forms and paper available when needed?
- How easy is it to assemble all the interim records after e-service is restored? If paper is used, how is this information incorporated back into the electronic patient record.
- Will the record the provider uses subsequently contain all the information in a readily reviewable format?

The investigator must also know the length of any downtime period and whether it affected treatment records during any portion of the investigation's timeline.

## WHERE TO BEGIN

Electronic systems may be a diverse collection of a number of different patient databases, new and legacy, and their interfaces with users—providers, other health care professionals, administration representatives, insurers, and others. Each system needs to be assessed regarding its components, attributes, and capabilities.[8] The investigator needs to understand the risks and benefits of these systems for health care delivery and the exposure they present to the organization, the individuals who provide care, and the patient who receives care. All of this knowledge helps the investigator to formulate the questions necessary to conduct a competent investigation.

Keeping the investigation and all information organized and following a consistent process are important (see **Exhibit 3-1**), as is knowing the system well enough to ask informed questions. Here are some suggestions for an initial assessment:

- determining the components of the medical record, how information is entered and retrieved, and the relevant risk management concerns and questions
- determining the form of the record (i.e., electronic, paper, or hybrid) and the location of each component of the record
- determining the health care professional's experience using the electronic record system (Include a description of the interface and display characteristics.)
- determining the system's integrity (e.g., maintenance and security profile and procedures)

**Exhibit 3-1**    The Electronic Health Record: A Checklist

**Record Components**
- Patient treatment record
  - Demographic information
  - Problem list
  - Medication list
  - Treatment dates
  - History and physical
  - Allergy list
  - Immunization records
  - Progress notes
  - Nurses' notes, care plans, and assessments
  - Medication administration records
  - Consults
  - Procedures
  - Implanted devices
  - Diagnostic testing
  - Laboratory testing and results
  - Blood transfusion records
  - Monitoring records
    - Vital signs
    - Skin integrity
    - Intake and output
    - Turning and positioning
    - Neurological checks
    - Dressing changes
  - Informed consent
  - Advance directives
  - Records from clinics and/or the emergency department
  - Any other components

- Provider electronic orders
  - Are all orders electronic or only some or none?
  - Who can order and from what locations?
  - How are stat orders handled and recorded?
  - How are orders needing cosignature handled and recorded?
  - How are telephone orders handled and recorded?
  - How are verbal orders handled and recorded?

*(continues)*

**Exhibit 3-1**    The Electronic Health Record: A Checklist *(continued)*

- ○ What is the process for canceling an order and what is the time delay between cancellation and execution?
- ○ How are erroneous orders corrected?
- Graphic files
  - ○ What graphic files are included in the record, and what graphic files are kept elsewhere? Is there a PACS system for radiology?
    - Radiology studies
    - Specialty diagnostic studies (gastrointestinal [GI] studies, cardiac catheterization, cardiac electrophysiology studies, magnetic resonance imaging [MRI] and computed tomography [CT] scans)
    - Electrocardiograms
    - Fetal heart rate monitoring
    - Ultrasound
    - Photographs (e.g., decubitus ulcers, dermatology, plastic surgery)
    - Other graphic files—specific institution should be checked
- Video files—specific institution should be checked
- Audio files
  - ○ Heart sounds
  - ○ Other audio files (institution- or department-specific)
- Coding and billing records
- Patient-submitted records, PHRs , records from other treatment organizations
- Discharge summary
- Discharge instructions
- Patient teaching materials
- Telephone messages
- E-mail exchanges. If used, are they appropriate and how are they documented? What is the policy of the HCO regarding use of e-mail for patient-care related communication?

**Exhibit 3-1**    The Electronic Health Record: A Checklist *(continued)*

**Form of Each Component**

- Is the record completely electronic or is it a hybrid record?

- What differences exist between the components of the electronic portion and those of the paper portion?

- Are paper documents such as narrative notes scanned into the electronic record?

- Does the HCO keep a list of record types stored for different time periods (e.g., paper and films used until a certain date, scanned records available for certain dates, hybrid records available for certain dates, all electronic records available for certain dates)? Does the policy reflect this?

- Is any patient information kept on personal devices or equipment such as PDAs, flash drives, iPods, and other storage items or on home computers?

**Provider/Health Care Professional Interface and Display Attributes**

- Determining whether interface or display characteristics promote inefficiency, time delay, or error

- Determining the provider/health care professional's ability to use the system at the time of the occurrence (i.e., evaluate the adequacy of training and the length of experience)

- Determining whether the system performed as intended at the time of the occurrence

- Determining if any system upgrades occurred and whether training was provided

**Systems Integrity**

- What procedure is to be used in the event of a system outage?

- Were there any system outages at the time of the occurrence?

- In the event of an outage, were the HCO's policies and procedures followed?

## NOTES

1. American Health Information Management Association e-HIM Work Group on the Legal Health Record, "Update: Guidelines for Defining the Legal Health Record for Disclosure Purposes." *Journal of AHIMA* 76, no.8 (September 2005): 64A-G.
2. Ibid.
3. American Health Information Management Association, e-HIM Personal Health Record in the HER, "The Role of the Personal Health Record in the EHR," *Journal of AHIMA* 76, no.7 (July–August 2005): 64A-D.
4. D. W Bates and A. A. Gawande, "Improving Safety with Information Technology," *New England Journal of Medicine* 348, no. 25 (2003): 2526–2534.
5. J. S. Ash, M. Berg, and E. Coiera, "Some Unintended Consequences of Information Technology in Health Care: The Nature of Patient Care Information System-Related Errors." *Journal of the American Medical Informatics Association* 11, no. 2 (2004): 104–112.
6. R. Koppel et al., "Role of Computerized Physician Order Entry Systems in Facilitating Medication Errors," *Journal of the American Medical Association* 293, no.10 (2005): 1197–1203; J. R. Nebeker et al., "High Rates of Adverse Drug Events in a Highly Computerized Hospital," *Archives of Internal Medicine* 165, no. 10 (May 2005): 1111–1116.
7. E. S. Patterson et al., "Identifying Barriers to the Effective Use of Clinical Reminders: Bootstrapping Multiple Methods," *Journal of Biomedical Informatics* 38, no. 3 (2005): 189–199; J.S. Ash, M. Berg, and E. Coiera, "Some Unintended Consequences of Information Technology in Health Care: The Nature of Patient Care Information System-Related Errors," *Journal of the American Medical Informatics Association*, II, no. 2 (2004); 104–112.
8. American Health Information Management Association, *Update*.

# Chapter 4

---

# Identifying the Medical/Legal Issues

---

- What Is a Medical/Legal Issue?
- Analyzing the Facts

---

Once all the pertinent facts have been gathered and reviewed, the investigator can begin to identify the medical/legal issues of the case. It is helpful to review the components of medical malpractice (duty owed, breach of duty, proximate cause, and damages), which are discussed in Chapter 16, "The Life of a Medical Malpractice Claim."

## WHAT IS A MEDICAL/LEGAL ISSUE?

An "issue" is anything problematic in the medical care rendered that relates to the occurrence or may adversely affect the defense of a case. *Here are some other ways to define this concept:*

- any deviation from the accepted standard of care at the time of the occurrence
- any fact in the case that suggests liability related to the occurrence
- any action or omission on the part of the health care provider that could be construed as negligent
- anything that may need to be addressed and clarified: for example, inconsistencies in documentation that may weaken the defense of the case

Reviewing any allegations specified by the plaintiff's attorney in the legal documents can help focus the investigation on possible issues. For example, a plaintiff's attorney may allege the defendant failed to place a Posey restraint on a patient who fell and sustained a fractured hip. The issue would be whether a Posey restraint was appropriate for this patient at the time of the occurrence.

Issues may also be alluded to in the broad allegations in a complaint. For example, if a complaint contains an allegation of a failure to diagnose a brain tumor, the specific issue may be whether the failure to perform a computed axial tomography scan or magnetic resonance imaging on a patient with long-standing complaints of headaches and visual disturbances was a breach of the applicable accepted standard of care at the time of the occurrence.

Issues might also be identified through the investigator's own independent knowledge of the standard of care. For example, investigators who are nurses are aware of the routine tests and procedures (i.e., temperature, complete blood count, and cultures of the infected area) performed for patients with an infectious process.

Once the responsible parties have been identified, the investigator must determine whether their acts or omissions could be considered a departure from acceptable standards of medical care. The individuals interviewed may have opinions on the issues. If the departure from the standard of care could have resulted in the occurrence that gave rise to the alleged injury, one of the medical/legal issues of the case may have been identified.

Of course, there may be other types of departures or issues, but whatever is contended must be supported with documented evidence (medical records) and/or oral statements made by the parties interviewed. Once again, when the issues have been clarified, the main objective is to identify any link between the alleged departure from accepted standards and the plaintiff's injuries. This link, known as *proximate cause*, is discussed in detail in Chapter 16.

There may be no relationship whatsoever between the care rendered and an adverse outcome. The occurrence may have been unavoidable or a known complication of a procedure or treatment. In that event, it is important to assess carefully all aspects of the medical course of treatment to fully support this defense position.

The potential medical/legal issues identified by the investigator are ultimately addressed by expert physicians and/or nurses who review the documented facts and the testimony of all parties involved and then make a determination about whether any standards of care have been breached.

A knowledgeable investigator's analysis at an early stage of litigation helps defense counsel focus its theories of liability and develop an appropriate defense strategy based on the existence—or absence—of medical malpractice. The written analysis of the issues identified in a case should be discussed thoroughly and placed in the "Comments" section of the investigation report.

**Table 4-1** presents examples of five occurrences, the possible allegations, and the medical/legal issues of the cases obtained from the investigation. Using such a table helps the investigator organize his or her thoughts and distinguish the issues from the occurrence and allegations.

## ANALYZING THE FACTS

Investigating a claim involves more than merely repeating the information gleaned from the medical record and the witness statements. It should also include a thorough analysis of all the contributing factors leading to an occurrence, as well as an examination of the occurrence itself and its aftermath. Therefore, it is essential all the information gathered from the legal documents, as well as from the medical records, interviews, and other investigation, be reviewed prior to the investigation report being written. All relevant information can then be pieced together to develop a fact pattern about the case.

The following suggestions can facilitate the process necessary to sort through all of this information and prepare a report that highlights the occurrence and clearly defines the issues of the case.

In developing a fact pattern that will be used to describe the events to the reader, the investigator should review the principal questions already asked. This helps develop an overview of the claim.

*It may also help to rethink some of the following questions:*

- What happened to the patient, and in what time frame?
- What were the causative factors?
- What systems problems might have been involved?
- Was a root cause analysis indicated?
- If a lawsuit has been filed, what are the allegations?

**Table 4-1**    Examples of Occurrences, Allegations, and Issues in Medical Malpractice

| Occurrence | Possible Allegations | Issues |
|---|---|---|
| A 16-year-old female was treated and released from the emergency department for a complaint of right lower quadrant pain, nausea and vomiting, and fever. She had a white blood cell count of 18. No rectal exam was done, and no abdominal X-rays were taken. A diagnosis of gastroenteritis was made. The patient returned to the emergency department the next day with a ruptured appendix. | • Failure to diagnose acute appendicitis <br> • Failure to perform appropriate diagnostic tests <br> • Lack of supervision of an inexperienced physician | • Inexperience of resident in the emergency department and lack of supervision by emergency department attending physicians <br> • Lack of a pediatric surgical consult <br> • Inadequate and incomplete physical examination of the patient to make a differential diagnosis, including no rectal exam and no abdominal X-rays |
| A 65-year-old female was admitted for bilateral lower extremity occlusion. The patient underwent a femoral bypass with the insertion of a Gore-Tex graft. Reversal anesthetics were administered. The patient was taken to the recovery room alert and with stable vital signs. The patient sustained a cardiopulmonary arrest 25 minutes after admission to the recovery room and remained comatose for six months before she expired. | • Failure to administer anesthesia properly <br> • Failure to monitor and observe the patient properly in the recovery room | • Premature extubation <br> • Inadequate reversal of general anesthesia by giving too small a dose of reversal anesthetic <br> • Lack of experience and supervision of anesthesia resident <br> • Poor recovery room monitoring by nursing staff; vital signs not taken or recorded every 15 minutes |

**Table 4-1**    Examples of Occurrences, Allegations, and Issues in Medical Malpractice *(continued)*

| Occurrence | Possible Allegations | Issues |
|---|---|---|
| A 59-year-old male was admitted for elective transurethral resection of the prostate (TURP) requiring prophylactic pacemaker insertion preoperatively for a history of bradycardia. Following the pacemaker insertion, the patient developed an 80% pneumothorax. The TURP was postponed indefinitely. | • Improper medical treatment rendered<br>• Improper technique used during insertion of pacemaker wire<br>• Lack of informed consent | • Lack of a skillful assistant for the physician during procedure<br>• Delay in recognizing that the patient had a pneumothorax<br>• Physician admitted to having never informed the patient of the risk of pneumothorax associated with the insertion of a pacemaker |
| A 44-year-old female was admitted for repair of umbilical hernia. Electrocautery was used during the surgery. A burning smell was noted by operating room staff during the procedure. The recovery room nurses noted a reddened area on the patient's right thigh. A diagnosis of third-degree burn was made that required plastic surgical repair. | • Failure to use equipment properly<br>• Failure to monitor the patient<br>• Failure to prepare the patient properly for use of electrocautery during surgery | • Manufacturer's instructions indicate the electrocautery ground pad should be placed *under* the patient's thigh; the pad was placed on the *side* of the thigh. The burning smell and the need for higher voltage should have alerted the operating room staff to a potential problem with the device or the grounding pad |

*(continues)*

**Table 4-1**   Examples of Occurrences, Allegations, and Issues in Medical Malpractice *(continued)*

| Occurrence | Possible Allegations | Issues |
|---|---|---|
| A 60-year-old female was admitted for chemotherapy treatment for cancer of the bowel. After receiving the first treatment, the patient complained of weakness and dizziness. During the night shift, the patient attempted to get out of bed to use the bathroom and was found on the floor by the nurse. The diagnosis of fractured hip was made. | • Failure to supervise the patient properly<br>• Failure to protect the patient properly | • Proper nursing intervention not instituted. Because of dizziness and weakness, the patient should have been assessed for the necessary intervention (e.g., an order for side rails)<br>• The patient should have been instructed to call the nurses when desiring to get out of bed<br>• Activity orders not updated. The patient's out-of-bed orders should have read "out of bed with assistance" instead of "out of bed" |

- How do the allegations compare to the statements made by the parties interviewed?
- Who was involved in or responsible for the occurrence?
- What were the underlying reasons for the actions taken (or not taken) for any care rendered?
- Were any standards of care breached?
- Is there evidence of contributory negligence?

In asking these questions, the investigator must dismiss his or her personal assumptions and objectively critique the documented clinical information and the witness statements.

Certain factors, including the following, may impede the data analysis and therefore must be addressed:

- Not all sources of information may agree with one another. For example, the medical record may appear to support one set of facts, whereas a witness may recall something quite different.
- Witnesses may provide conflicting descriptions of an occurrence.
- There may be no single specific occurrence, but rather a series of incidents, decisions, and actions that resulted in a particular outcome. Each event should be studied independently and then related to the entire situation to judge its impact on the ultimate outcome. This approach aids in determining the underlying causes of the occurrence.

The investigation report cannot be written until a review of all of the clinical factors and witness statements and an analysis of the entire situation for causation, responsibility, and contributory negligence (as well as the relationship of those factors to the patient's alleged injury) have been completed. The goal in writing the report is to present sufficient information to establish whether all of the components of medical malpractice exist and, most important, whether there has been a deviation from the accepted standard of care.

# Chapter 5

# Interviewing Techniques

- Identifying Individuals To Be Interviewed
- Setting Up the Interview
- Beginning the Interview
- Some General Guidelines for the Interview
- Closing the Interview
- The Difficult Interview

## IDENTIFYING INDIVIDUALS TO BE INTERVIEWED

When conducting a formal investigation, it is essential to personally interview all individuals involved in the occurrence(s). However, because there may be legal limitations on certain interviews, health care organization (HCO) counsel should be consulted for limitations applicable in specific jurisdictions. In the case of a lawsuit, all named codefendants insured by the institution's medical malpractice policy should be interviewed. A telephone interview may be necessary if a witness has left the area. The actual interviewing process is discussed in greater detail in the following four chapters.

### Parties Involved

The investigator begins by contacting only those parties directly involved in the occurrence and insured by the HCO's policy. These individuals may be identified during the medical record review.

*Questions to ask during the selection process include:*

- Which individual can provide the most information about the occurrence? This individual may be the most senior staff person, the physician or nurse who cared for the patient on a daily basis, the staff member who reported the alert, or supervising personnel.
- Who wrote the most pertinent notes regarding the occurrence (i.e., before, during, or after the incident)?
- Who might be able to provide background information or "fill in the gaps" in the progress notes?

If persons not directly involved in the occurrence, such as ancillary staff or professional staff from other departments (e.g., pharmacists), are selected for interviews, they should include interviewees who can provide background information or explain what would typically have taken place during a similar situation. The investigator may also need to interview supervising or management personnel for advice on policies and procedures.

**Early Clinical (In-House) Reviews**

In complicated cases, the investigator should contact the appropriate department chair or director, or other experts within the HCO, for an objective critique of the medical record. Once litigation is initiated, it is advisable to contact the risk manager or legal counsel to determine if such discussions should take place.

Expert input can be extremely helpful in explaining medical complexities and difficult technical issues. The investigator should ask these reviewers to identify the deviations from accepted practice in a case. An in-house expert (this is generally the chairperson of a department or designee) can also evaluate the validity of the plaintiff's allegations.

Expert reviews also serve to apprise individuals in authority positions of serious occurrences within their departments. If there are policy or procedure problems that need to be addressed, the risk manager will soon learn from the chair or director whether the matter can be resolved expeditiously or could prove to be politically explosive.

**Personal Information for Interview**

*The interviewer should obtain the following information from the HCO's human resources department or the individual being interviewed:*

- position
- job title at the time of the occurrence
- academic qualifications
- department affiliation at the time of the occurrence
- current home or business address and phone number
- employment status at the time of the occurrence

Each HCO has its own system for determining the employment status of witnesses. Therefore, inquiries must be made with the appropriate HCO office to verify employment status. The interviewer must also determine whether these individuals are not covered by the HCO's insurance program or cannot be interviewed for some other reason. It is essential to validate this information with the individual before beginning the interview.

The investigator should be aware of legal limitations on certain interviews. For example, in some states it may or may not be legally permissible to interview an insured physician who treated a plaintiff for a related or unrelated illness after an occurrence. For more information, refer to Chapter 14, "Confidentiality of Medical Records and Other Documents." It is important to consult legal counsel for advice regarding any limitations on interviewing witnesses in a particular jurisdiction.

**SETTING UP THE INTERVIEW**

An interview is a communication between two people with a specific purpose. In our experience, individual interviews are preferable to group sessions for several reasons. Each person can give his or her statement independent of pressure or influence from others, and therefore statements may flow more easily. In addition, any confidentiality protection that may apply to the interview may be jeopardized by group interviews.

Communication is a dynamic, ever-changing interaction with many variables. The following techniques are designed to teach novice interviewers the art of asking questions that elicit the maximum amount of information without alienating interviewees or putting them on the defensive.

For recent claims and occurrences, most individuals involved in the case are available for interviews, and a personal interview is advised. Individuals who have moved need to be interviewed by telephone. Depending on the institution's policies, there may be a protocol for contacting HCO employees and members of the medical staff. People who do not know the investigator may not respond to a request for an interview. In that case, they should be referred to the HCO administrator or risk manager who can verify the investigator's status.

## Locating Prospective Interviewees

When individuals have moved away or are no longer employed by the institution, the HCO's human resources department, the nursing department, or the medical house staff office can often provide the person's employment status and last known address.

If it is impossible to locate a physician or a nurse, the American Medical Association (AMA) or the state nursing society can be contacted. A physician's current address can be obtained from the AMA online at www.ama-assn.org. This Web site provides basic professional information on virtually every licensed physician in the United States. Clicking on "DoctorFinder" on the left side of the Home page, on "Patient and Consumer's Search for a Physician" at the bottom of the next page, and on "DoctorFinder" on the following page brings one to the DoctorFinder Usage Verification Page. As the directions are followed, the next screen asks the user to accept the Terms and Conditions. If these are accepted, a screen appears on which the user can type in the physician's last name (a "sound-like" feature is available when the exact spelling of the physician's name is not known).

## Telephone Interviews

Once the last known address of a physician or nurse is obtained, copies of the medical record or appropriate portions of it should be forwarded so he or she can review this information prior to a telephone interview. (Check with HCO counsel to make sure such "sharing" of the medical record is permissible under HCO rules and medical information confidentiality laws in your jurisdiction.)

*Here are some guidelines for contacting individuals for telephone interviews and for mailing medical records to these parties:*

- The investigator should verify the recipient's correct address by telephone or by letter before sending the medical record. Telephone contact is preferred. If the involved party cannot be located, the medical record should not be sent to the last known address without verification that it is correct. To verify the address, it may be necessary to send a brief letter to the involved party. Without discussing any facts in detail pertaining to the case, the investigator should identify himself or herself as an investigator, explain why the person is being contacted, and ask that he or she either call collect, write, or e-mail in reply. (See **Exhibit 5-1** for a sample letter of introduction for an interview.)

- After making contact with the involved party, the investigator may copy and mail the medical record, or pertinent parts referring to his or her role in the occurrence, and schedule a telephone interview.

- The investigator should send a cover letter with the medical record that states the date on which contact with the party was originally made, summarizes that conversation, and confirms the interview time and date. No questions about the claim should be posed in this letter. A request for the medical record to be returned after the interview should be included, along with a large, self-addressed, stamped envelope.

- It is important to keep a copy of all letters in the claim file to document efforts to investigate the claim and to review the file prior to the interview in order to be familiar with the facts of the case.

## Before the Interview

A successful interview depends on a well-prepared investigator. A polished, professional approach is most likely to elicit most of the information

**Exhibit 5-1**    Sample Letter of Introduction for Interview

---

                                           Date

Name
Address

       **RE:**     (Name of plaintiff and defendants)
                 File No:
                 Defense Firm File No: _____

Dear _____

    I am the claim investigator for (Name of company/institution).

    The case listed above is currently in litigation. As a result, we are trying to speak with those practitioners who rendered care to the patient in order to determine how best to defend the hospital and its employees.

    Briefly, this case involves . . . (include a two–three sentence summary).

    Because your name appears in the patient's medical record, it is important that I talk with you about this case. Please contact me at (phone number) as soon as possible.

    Please feel free to verify my status with (risk manager, title) at (phone number).

    Thank you for your time and cooperation.

                                   Sincerely,

                                   Claim Investigator

cc:

---

needed to prepare a thorough report. Therefore, it is very important for the investigator to allow enough time to study the medical record and claim file so he or she understands clearly the medical/legal issues. This evaluation helps to generate most of the questions that need to be asked.

The investigator also may need to do some research about the medical treatment rendered or the equipment used in order to formulate appropriate questions and to understand the answers. Conducting an "in-house" review can help in filling in the medical background. Research is also helpful when discussing complex cases with the clinical staff and enables the investigator to make intelligent comments on the investigation report. The HCO's medical library and the offices of supervisory personnel or department directors can be resources for any pertinent equipment manuals.

As mentioned earlier, the review of the medical record may already have generated an initial list of questions for various witnesses. Another approach is for the investigator to review the chart, decide who should be interviewed, and then draw up a list of questions. Developing a method to mark specific documentation for reference during each interview can also be helpful.

*Here are some additional guidelines to help prepare for an interview:*

- Writing out the issues and allegations for easy reference while developing questions for the interview
- Focusing on possible deviations in the standard of care
- Treating each interview separately and individually
- Organizing and writing questions in a logical, sequential manner. This helps in organizing information from the interview when writing up the investigation results. It sometimes helps to start with general, nonspecific questions and then proceed to more specific, complex questions.
- Incorporating investigation requests by the HCO defense counsel into the questions

The investigator should not assume that the information found in the medical record is absolute but should, instead, use the record as a foundation to build a case. The interviews add structure and cohesion to that foundation.

*Be prepared to ask questions to elicit:*

- Causation: What is/was the cause of the occurrence? What was the result or injury? This helps to elicit the interviewee's viewpoint regarding liability.
- All explanations and rationales about how and why the incident occurred, focusing on the details. It may help to begin by asking the interviewee to relate as much as he or she can remember about all aspects of the incident.
- The interviewee's exact role in the occurrence.

Whenever possible, the interviewee should be asked to support his or her statements with medical record documentation. The investigator should also be sure to ask the interviewee to support or refute the allegations in the complaint or the bill of particulars, if available.

## BEGINNING THE INTERVIEW

The first few minutes are crucial in setting the tone of an interview. If all goes well, the interviewee is encouraged to participate freely and communicate accurately.

*The two purposes of the interview opening are:*

- to establish rapport
- to orient the interviewee to the interview

These two processes often evolve simultaneously.

The interviewer begins by introducing himself or herself. If the interview is conducted in person, the investigator should shake hands. His or her role as an investigator should be explained if not already done when the interview was arranged. Emphasizing the need for cooperation in defending the case, the investigator should tell the person how long the interview is expected to take and how the resulting information will be used.

This is an appropriate time to make an initial assessment of the interviewee, paying particular attention to his or her physical appearance and emotional state (nervous? hostile? resentful? curious? upset? harried?).

## SOME GENERAL GUIDELINES FOR THE INTERVIEW

*During the interview, the following guidelines should be kept in mind:*

- The investigator should try elaborating on his or her impressions of the interviewee's role, if the person is hesitant to speak.
- The investigator should be nonjudgmental and not show any sign of criticism in facial expressions or tone of voice.

- Trying to be empathetic is important, as this is often a difficult discussion for the interviewee.
- The interviewee should not be allowed to talk about unrelated subjects. It is important to bring him or her back to the original question, even if this takes several attempts.
- If the interviewee wants to make an off-the-record comment, the investigator should explain that everything said must remain "on the record," impressing upon the interviewee the fact that all information helps the defense of the case.
- The investigator should not hesitate to ask the interviewee to clarify anything that remains unclear.
- If the interviewee asks, the investigator should tell him or her that the information will be disclosed only as necessary, only to the appropriate HCO administrators for risk management and quality management purposes, *and* as may be required by law.

## Evaluating the Environment

The environment (or context) in which the interview takes place often affects the outcome of the interview. Some interviews may have to be conducted in less-than-ideal surroundings. The investigator should note any variables that may adversely affect the situation and try to minimize their impact. *Examples include:*

- room temperature
- seating (sitting close enough to communicate a sense of "sharing" with the respondent, but being careful not to invade the person's private space)
- comfort level (particularly the seats)
- sound level
- privacy
- potential sources of noise

**Asking Questions**

Questions are the tools of the interviewer's trade. *There are four basic kinds of questions:*

- *Open questions* are broad and allow the respondent considerable freedom in determining the type of information he or she wants to provide. Open questions let the respondent do the talking while the interviewer listens and responds (e.g., "Tell me about your background." "Tell me how this procedure is usually done.").
- *Closed questions* are more restrictive and limit the possible answers. Closed questions give the interviewer more control (e.g., "Where did you go to medical school?" "On what date did you last see the patient?").
- *Primary questions* introduce topics or open up new areas for exploration (e.g., "I'd like to talk about the general routine. Please tell me . . .").
- *Secondary questions*, often called follow-up questions, ask for more information on the same topic (e.g., "Now that I understand when ibuprofen is indicated, will you identify any complications associated with its use in this patient?").

Interviews are not meant to become cross-examinations; the interviewee should not be pressured to answer in a specific way. The use of leading questions that allow the interviewer to suggest, either implicitly or explicitly, the answer that he or she expects or desires should also be avoided.

**Phrasing Questions**

A general rule is to start slowly by asking open-ended questions to get the person talking. Questioning should begin on the periphery (e.g., "When was your first encounter with this patient?"). The investigator should not bombard the interviewee with the most difficult, sensitive questions. Requests should be clear and simple, to elicit a reasonably delimited amount of information. Questions that are overly complex, require encyclopedic answers, or use language that the person may not understand or may find offensive should also be avoided. The investigator should allow the interviewee to express his or her feelings. The great potential for misunderstanding existing between two people who are trying to communicate should be minimized whenever possible.

Chapter 6 includes general questions that can be used for most situations. Chapters 7, 8, and 9 provide guidelines for developing interview questions for individual types of cases—specific types of occurrences (patient falls, failure to diagnose, medication errors), long-term care facilities, and obstetrical cases.

## Observing Nonverbal Communication

A great deal of information can be gleaned from observing the interviewee's nonverbal behavior. In fact, some communication researchers believe that as much as 75 percent of the information we get from others is transmitted nonverbally. Research also shows when two forms of communication conflict, people invariably trust the nonverbal body language over the spoken message.

*Nonverbal communication cues worth noting include:*

- facial expressions
- eye contact (or lack thereof)
- fidgeting
- rate of speech
- hand and arm movements
- head nods
- vocal inflections
- leg movements
- posture
- attire
- indications of stress

The investigator's own nonverbal behavior is also being communicated. He or she should be careful not to show feelings of boredom or frustration, as such communication may unintentionally influence the course of the interview.

**Note Taking**

Unless blessed with a photographic memory, the investigator should expect to take notes during the interview. He or she should not try to write down *everything* the person says. Instead, it is helpful to try to develop shorthand abbreviations that allow noting of the most important points as accurately and as quickly as possible. Yes, it *is* difficult to listen, take notes, and think of the next question at the same time, so it is common to feel a little overwhelmed during the first few interviews.

Because the interviewee may feel uncomfortable with note taking, it is best to mention the need to do so at the beginning of the interview. Saying something like, "We're going to be covering a lot of ground in the next half hour, and it would really help me if I could take some notes" or "It's very important that the information be accurate" can help ease the tension. If the interviewee is adamant about not wanting notes taken, the investigator should comply with this preference. If the interview comes to an impasse, using the gesture of putting down the pen signals that the meeting is now more "informal" and often helps a restrained interviewee to open up. The practice of taping interviews is controversial. FOJP does not tape interviews for several reasons. The interviewee may be less likely to give important and critical information, and such tapes may be discoverable. Legal counsel should be consulted regarding this issue.

**Listening**

It is very important to listen attentively. What the person is going to say should never be assumed. The investigator should stay alert so no valuable information is missed. It is also important to listen "actively," that is, providing instantaneous feedback to the interviewee by maintaining eye contact, nodding, and/or saying "uh-huh." The investigator should restate in his or her own words any responses by the interviewee that are confusing and have the respondent verify, clarify, or add to his or her statement.

**CLOSING THE INTERVIEW**

The interviewee should be thanked for his or her time and asked about any remaining questions. He or she should be told how to reach the investigator with any additional information. He or she should also be advised not to discuss the case with anyone except legal counsel or the HCO's risk management personnel. The investigator should take one-half hour as soon as possible after the interview to review his or her notes, making sure all the pertinent facts are included and filling in any details that were not written down.

## THE DIFFICULT INTERVIEW

*Here are some tips for handling interviewees who are not as cooperative as they should be:*

- Asking questions that require only "yes" or "no" answers should be avoided.
- The investigator should emphasize the need for the interviewee's cooperation and the importance of any information he or she can provide.
- An uncooperative interviewee can be asked if he or she would prefer to speak to the HCO's risk manager or an administrative liaison.
- If the interviewee is using abusive language and the situation cannot be defused, the interview should be terminated. The investigator might suggest, "Perhaps we should meet at another time."
- If an individual who is named coparty in a claim refuses to be interviewed, the investigator should seek legal counsel because this refusal may abrogate his or her right to insurance coverage and legal defense.

Chapter 6

# Preparing for Interviews

---

- Listing the Goals for Each Interview
- Doing Some Research
- Preparing a List of Questions

---

The following guidelines are presented to aid in the preparation of interview questions. Designed to elicit background information, they are applicable to almost any situation. The next three chapters offer further guidelines for developing questions to suit the needs of specific cases—such as cases about specific types of occurrences (e.g., patient falls, failures to diagnose, surgical mishaps and anesthesia incidents), cases involving patients in long-term care, and obstetrical cases. Although, in general, it is not necessary to ask each and every question, this sampling can help in customizing the interview. The investigator must remember that a great deal of advance thought and effort is required with each interview to formulate a series of questions that cover as much territory as possible.

## LISTING THE GOALS FOR EACH INTERVIEW

If not already done, the investigator should read the medical record (and the claim file, if applicable) to get a clear sense of the case. (See Chapter 1 for advice about thorough reviews of the medical record.) It is helpful to highlight areas where more information is needed and to note the names (if listed) of anyone who would be able to provide that information. Looking in particular for any discrepancies or inconsistencies (e.g., time conflicts), or any point in the record where the person involved should be offered a chance to comment is important. In addition to the involved parties named in the claim, other individuals involved in the care of the patient might be able to add explanations for certain aspects of the case (e.g., a nurse's aide or a technician who services the equipment in question). Only individuals insured through the HCO's medical malpractice policy may be interviewed. If possible, interviews should be conducted in person, with telephone or e-mail communication reserved solely for short follow-up queries.

Once a list of potential interviewees is established, the investigator should make notes about what to investigate during each interview. Clarifying the facts of the case is one of these goals. For instance, in a claim about informed consent, it would be important to determine the circumstances of the consent discussion (e.g., the location, duration, timing after receipt of diagnosis, identities of the individuals present, and the emotional state of the patient).

## DOING SOME RESEARCH

This is a process of investigating what actually occurred and comparing it with accepted standards of care. Thus, for every case, the investigator must know the HCO's policies and procedures aimed at preventing or at least minimizing the alleged injury. It may also be necessary to look up basic protocols and any unfamiliar terms noted in the medical record.

A good place to start is the HCO medical library, where reference texts and professional publications can be found. Consulting the textbooks listed in the Resources at the end of this book should also be considered. Many professional organizations offer clinical guidelines, practice standards, newsletters, and journal articles online. A key resource is www.Medscape.com. This website, sponsored by WebMD Corporation, is a searchable database of medical information. Other useful websites include:

* American Academy of Family Physicians           *www.aafp.org*
* American Academy of Pediatrics                       *www.aap.org*
* American Association of Neurological Surgeons   *www.aans.org*
* American College of Cardiology                        *www.acc.org*

- Association of periOperative Registered Nurses    *www.aorn.org*
- American College of Radiology    *www.acr.org*
- American College of Surgeons    *www.facs.org*
- American Nurses Association    *www.nursingworld.org*
- American College of Obstetricians
  and Gynecologists    *www.acog.org*
- American Dental Association    *www.ada.org*
- American Medical Association    *www.ama-assn.org*

Finally, the investigator might ask the interviewee for direction to any published professional standards that relate to the subject of the lawsuit.

## PREPARING A LIST OF QUESTIONS

This discussion of general guidelines, together with specific guidelines for different cases presented in the following three chapters, can help the investigator prepare for interviews of the parties involved in a claim. Although a set of prepared questions should be ready for each interview, the interviewer must remain flexible to follow up on points that he or she had not anticipated. There will be surprises!

The following questions are geared to physician interviews but can be adapted for use with other health care professionals as well.

### Focusing on the Interviewee's Background

*Getting the "housekeeping" information out of the way early:*

- What was the interviewee's role/status/degree of required supervision at the time of the occurrence? What was his or her area of specialty? Has he or she received board certification? What is his or her current address?
- If the interviewee is a medical resident, where does he or she plan to go after completing this residency?

**Focusing on the Patient**

*Starting to direct the questions toward the clinical details of the case:*

- How would the interviewee describe the patient's history, complaints, course of treatment, and overall condition throughout the hospitalization? What is the background information regarding the medical care that was rendered? Why did the patient seek treatment with this particular physician?
- When did the interviewee first and last treat or examine the patient? How was the patient referred to that individual?

**Focusing on the Occurrence and Injury**

*Asking the interviewee about the occurrence itself:*

- What were the circumstances leading up to the occurrence? What caused the injury? What was the reasoning behind the treatment prescribed? The investigator should clarify any inconsistent answers. If the individual does not remember the occurrence, what would he or she have done routinely (custom and practice) under such circumstances?
- What were the potential, immediate, and long-term (temporary versus permanent) consequences of the injury?
- Who were the parties involved in the occurrence? Can the interviewee help determine who was responsible and to what extent? Can the interviewee describe the involved parties' relationships to each other and help the investigator determine who was "in charge"?
- Does the interviewee consider that any of the patient's underlying conditions contributed to the occurrence and/or the ultimate outcome of the case? To what degree? Can the interviewee support his or her explanations with documentation in the medical record? In the interviewee's opinion, is there any reason to question patient culpability?
- In the interviewee's opinion, did the patient contribute to the untoward outcome?

- Does the interviewee think that the occurrence or injury was recognized and treated in a timely manner? What was the timeline?
- What were the normal policies and procedures relative to the occurrence (e.g., side rail policy, policy on fetal monitoring, use of heparin) and was there any departure from standard practice? Was the interviewee aware of these policies and procedures at the time of the occurrence?
- Can the interviewee develop or refute the existence of a causal connection between the occurrence and the injury? In cases in which the patient died, what does the individual believe to be the actual cause of death? Was the death a direct result of the occurrence? Does an autopsy report support this opinion?
- What were the patient and/or family told about the injury/prognosis and about the occurrence? How did they react?
- Can the interviewee identify signatures and, if necessary, decipher the handwriting?

## Focusing on Liability

*Asking the interviewee to help you determine the defensible aspects of the case and the severity of the patient's injury:*

- The investigator should ask the interviewee to carefully review any documentation pertaining to the occurrence. Does the documentation support the diagnosis and justify the treatment?
- Can the interviewee account for any gaps in time (e.g., a change in shift when there are no entries in the medical record, or the absence of progress-note entries for several days)?
- Are there now any options or treatments that might improve the patient's condition or diminish the extent of his or her injury? Were any of these remedies offered to the patient?
- What was the national/acknowledged standard of care for this procedure or treatment? Do any professional, federal, regulatory, or other standards apply? Do any published standard/clinical guidelines relate to the occurrence?

- Has the HCO completed a root cause analysis or any other internal study regarding the occurrence? Is it permissible for the investigator to review the results?
- What was the billing arrangement? (This fact is important in determining insurance coverage and collateral sources of payment.)

**Asking Essential Questions in All Cases**

- What could have been done differently to prevent the occurrence? In retrospect, would the interviewee do anything differently?
- Was an occurrence report filed regarding the incident?
- If the case involved surgery or invasive treatment, was the patient informed of the risks, alternatives, benefits, and possible outcomes of the procedure?

# Chapter 7

# Developing Interview Questions on Specific Occurrence Types

---

- Slips and Falls
- Intravenous Infiltrations
- Medication Errors
- Failures to Diagnose
- Surgical Mishaps/Technical Accidents at Surgery/Poor Surgical Outcomes
- Postoperative Infections
- Anesthesia Occurrences
- Suicide-Related Occurrences
- Clinical Laboratory Errors
  - Blood Bank Occurrences
  - Pathology Lab Occurrences
  - Radiation Therapy Occurrences
  - Informed Consent Issues
  - Gastroplasty

---

This chapter is designed to guide the development of interview questions by emphasizing potential areas of legal exposure. These areas can be studied prior to the interview during the in-depth medical record review and then confirmed and explored during the interview. Each section suggests issues and questions to use during interviews about a claim for a specific injury or adverse occurrence. The investigator should prepare for the interview(s) by following the guidelines in Chapter 6, beginning with the general questions and then modifying the questions suggested here to suit the needs of the specific case being investigated.

*The following guidelines for document review and question development are designed to elicit the information needed for the investigation report.*

## SLIPS AND FALLS

*This section is geared toward interviews of nursing personnel.*

- Is there any documentation of a prior history of falls, of the patient trying to climb out of bed, or of the patient being found wandering in the hall or in his or her room?
- Is there any evidence of an undiagnosed or untreated condition (e.g., uremia, anemia, hypoglycemia) that could have contributed to the fall? What do the laboratory results show?
- Was there a history of cancer or any other condition that might increase the potential for pathologic fractures?
- Was there a recent change in orders or the patient's condition that could have contributed to the fall? Based on a review of the medications for the twenty-four-hour period prior to the occurrence, what was the potential effect on the patient's mental status and gait?
- What is the interviewee's knowledge of the patient's condition prior to the fall?
  - What was the interviewee's knowledge of the patient's mental status?
  - What was the interviewee's knowledge of the patient's activity order prior to the fall? What are the indications of that order (e.g., what does "OOB w/assistance" mean)?
  - What was the patient wearing? Was there evidence of the use of inappropriate foot coverings (e.g., paper slippers) that could have contributed to the fall? Were appropriate foot coverings provided?

- ○ What was the patient's actual activity at the time of the occurrence? The activity flow sheet, if available, should be consulted.
- Was a private-duty nurse, private sitter, or companion present? If not, were there any indications for needing such a person or for needing more frequent observation prior to the fall?
- What was the proximity of the patient's room to the nurses' station?
- Did the patient ask to go to the bathroom?
- Was the patient noted to have called for assistance?
- From a review of the medical record, including flow sheets and medication sheets, the interviewee should determine exactly when the patient was last seen. When were the last rounds made on this patient prior to the fall? What was the health care organization's (HCO's) policy for checking patients?
- If mechanical restraints were used, what type was used? How often was the patient checked while restrained? Were restraints indicated? If so, were they ordered? If restraints were indicated but not ordered, why not? Were there any contraindications to restraints? What were the HCO's policy and procedures on the use of restraints?
- Were there any environmental problems? The interviewee should be asked to describe, in detail, the patient's environment, focusing on the details that relate to the occurrence.
  - ○ Was there any equipment in the room? If so, where was it located?
  - ○ What were the lighting conditions in the room?
  - ○ Was the floor wet or in need of repair? If so, were any warning signs in place?
  - ○ What was the position of the bed (e.g., high or low position)?
  - ○ What were the location, position, and type of side rails? What was the HCO's protocol regarding the use of side rails?
  - ○ What were the location, position, and condition of grab bars?
  - ○ Was the patient instructed to use the call bell for assistance? What was the location of the call light or call bell? How close was it to the patient? Was the patient able to use it?
  - ○ Could a visitor have changed any aspect of the environment (e.g., the level of the bed or side rails) without the knowledge of the nursing personnel?

- Were there any other witnesses (visitors, patients, or staff) to the fall?
- What is the HCO's protocol for responding to an occurrence? Was this protocol followed? For example, if the protocol required notifying the private attending physician, the hospitalist, and/or the resident and then documenting this notification, were these steps followed?
- What was the physician's response to the fall at the time? Did the physician respond promptly? Were appropriate consults called, in a timely fashion, to treat the patient's injuries?
- Does the interviewee consider that the patient's hospitalization was prolonged due to the fall? What treatment was necessitated by the fall?

## INTRAVENOUS INFILTRATIONS

*This section is geared toward interviews of nursing personnel.*

- What was the HCO's policy—and the interviewee's knowledge of those policies—at the time of the occurrence regarding the checking of intravenous (IV) infusion sites, assessment for infiltrations, and response to infiltrations?
- Does the nursing care flow sheet document how IV infusions were administered and monitored?
- What was the interviewee's knowledge of the signs and symptoms of an IV infiltration at the time of the occurrence?
- What was the interviewee's custom and practice regarding appropriate IV needle placement and flow rates?
- What was the extent of coverage during breaks? Was someone other than the interviewee checking the site?
- What were the conditions at the time of the infiltration?
  - Was the IV infusion site visible?
  - What was the appearance of the patient's arm or other IV infusion site?
- When was the IV removed?
- What was the immediate care given to the patient following discovery of the infiltration?

- What was the length of time that the IV site appeared to have been infiltrated? Does the extent of the infiltration reflect appropriate monitoring?
- What are the effects of the type of solution or medication being infused at the time of the infiltration? Was it routine to run the infusion that was in progress through a peripheral line?
- Was a plastic surgery consult indicated? Was there the possibility of permanent damage and scarring?

## MEDICATION ERRORS

*This section is geared toward interviews of nursing personnel and/ or physicians.*

- What details does the medical record document regarding the medication error?
  ○ What was the documentation for the medication orders? Were they questioned appropriately?
- What was standard medication administration procedure?
  ○ Were there any deviations from this procedure? Why?
  ○ Does the HCO use a computerized physician order entry system? If so, could the occurrence be attributed to a failure in the system?
- Did the pharmacy department provide proper medications in a timely fashion? Was there a unit dose system in effect?
- Did the injury that resulted from the medication error extend the patient's HCO stay?
- Was there any change in the patient's condition because of the medication error?
- Did any underlying medical problems affect the extent of the injury?
- What was the level of training required to administer the specific medications or intravenous fluids involved in this occurrence?
  ○ Were written guidelines outlining these necessary qualifications available?
  ○ At the time of the occurrence, what were the qualifications of the individual who administered the medication subsequently involved in error?

- Did the patient have any responsibility in contributing to the problem?
  - Did the patient understand the rationale for taking the medications?
  - Did the patient refuse medications?
  - Did the patient ignore restrictions regarding medications?
  - Did the patient take his or her own medications brought from home? Did the patient understand the risks associated with taking any medications brought from home?
- What was the nursing staff's responsibility for patient education?
- Was there any history of allergies that might have contributed to the patient's response to the medication?

## FAILURES TO DIAGNOSE

*This section is geared toward interviews of physicians.*

Review the usual symptomatology of the disease/condition missed on diagnosis.

- Questioning should focus on determining why the diagnosis was missed.
  - Were there any factors that could have obscured the real disease (e.g., did the patient ingest narcotics, barbiturates, or alcohol prior to being treated)?
  - Was there masking of symptoms by other disorders?
  - The differential diagnoses should be carefully reviewed. Was another diagnosis incorrectly attributed to the patient? What are the signs and symptoms of the incorrectly diagnosed condition? Did the patient exhibit these signs and symptoms?
  - Could any laboratory or radiologic tests have contributed to the missed diagnosis? Were any tests indicated but not performed *or* were any tests or radiologic studies misinterpreted?
- Were all formal laboratory and/or radiologic reports reviewed? Were any preliminary reports used to arrive at the diagnosis? Did any discrepancies exist between the two reports? If so, what action was taken to correct the situation?
- Is there any documentation that went unread regarding signs and symptoms of the disease?

- What was the impact of any delay or failure to diagnose? Did the delay or failure to diagnose adversely affect the patient's outcome? Did it alter the diagnosis? Did it hamper the physician's ability to treat the patient? Did it prolong the patient's HCO stay? Specifically, was the condition more severe as a result of the missed or delayed diagnosis?
- What would be the expected outcome if the diagnosis had been made earlier? Would the outcome have been different?
- Should consultations have been ordered? Was the patient's condition beyond the treating physician's realm of expertise? If the case involved a resident, was any attending physician involved? If so, does the documentation reflect his or her input?
- What was the interviewee's prior experience with this medical condition—including the diagnosis and treatment of such patients?
- Were there any prior or subsequent treating physicians who also may have missed the diagnosis?

## SURGICAL MISHAPS/TECHNICAL ACCIDENTS AT SURGERY/POOR SURGICAL OUTCOMES

*This section is geared toward interviews with physicians.*

- What were the indications for surgery? Was the patient a suitable candidate?
- Were the risks and benefits of the procedure explained to the patient? What were the risks? Was this discussion documented?
- What were the alternatives to surgery? Were the alternatives explained to the patient? Was this discussion documented?
- If the case involved wrong-site surgery, was the HCO's protocol for preventing wrong-site surgery adhered to? Was "time out" called during surgery?
- Was medical clearance indicated and, if so, obtained in accordance with HCO policy?
- Did the patient need to be stabilized prior to surgery, and if so, was the patient adequately stabilized? If recommended, was an intervention performed prior to surgery?

- Was there anything significant in the patient's past medical or surgical history relevant to the operation in question? Specifically, had the patient had any prior surgery, and if so, was it related to the procedure in question (either anatomically or by the nature of the disease)? For example, if the patient was undergoing a mastectomy, did she undergo prior biopsies on that or the other breast?
- Who performed the surgery or procedure? Was the surgeon adequately trained and privileged to perform the procedure? How many times had the surgeon performed this particular procedure?
- Ask the interviewee to describe the nature of the surgery and surgical procedure. Was the surgery performed properly (i.e., within the norms of standard practice)?
- Were other surgeons involved in the care of the patient before, during, and/or after surgery? If so, what were their roles?
- What was the role of each individual at the time of surgery? What surgical maneuvers did each perform that may have contributed to or caused the injury?
- What position(s) was assumed during surgery by the surgeon(s)?
- What type of equipment was used? Was the appropriate equipment available for the surgery? Was the equipment in good repair, sterile, and ready when requested?
- The surgeon should be asked to review the pertinent section of the operative note.
  - Does the operative report or note reflect the complications encountered?
  - Was there a procedural error?
  - Was each step performed in the proper sequence?
  - Is there any unusual language that requires an explanation (e.g., "we encountered a rent in the patient's bladder")?
- In cases involving intraoperative hemorrhage secondary to iatrogenic injury, the indications for blunt (forceps) versus sharp (scalpel) dissection during the procedure should be reviewed. The interviewee should be asked whether appropriate landmarks were identified. Did the patient have any unusual anatomical features or friable tissue that may have contributed to the occurrence?
- In a case involving nerve damage, was there a possibility of nerve damage during retraction, suturing, or from the development of a hematoma?

- In a case involving cautery burns, the nursing staff should be asked about the placement and appropriate use of Bovie pads.
  - Was the cautery unit checked prior to the procedure? Is there any documentation to support this?
  - What type of grounding was there for all the operating room (OR) electrical devices? Who checked the devices? Who repaired them? Who returned them?
  - What type of skin preparation was done? Were there any factors (e.g., hairy skin, skin lesions, cellulitis) that could have resulted in inadequate skin bonding?
- Does the anesthesia record reveal any unnoticed or untreated changes in vital signs? Does the operative note or scrub sheet include any comments on the occurrence?
- Are there any factors that may have contributed to the outcome? For example, was the anesthesia adequate during surgery? Did anesthesia contribute to the occurrence?
- Was the problem recognized immediately? Was appropriate equipment and blood available when needed? Were the appropriate consultations obtained intraoperatively, in a timely manner?
- What do the pathology reports reveal? Were the tissues submitted to pathology consistent with the tissue intended for removal and for the procedure performed?

## POSTOPERATIVE INFECTIONS

*This section is geared toward interviews with physicians.*

- Were infected wounds or a condition involving an infection documented preoperatively? What do any pertinent culture and sensitivity reports reveal?
- Was there a preoperative evaluation (medical clearance of the patient)? Did the private doctor or other consultant (e.g., endocrinologist for a diabetic patient) perform this evaluation or medical clearance?
- Was proper skin preparation performed preoperatively and intraoperatively? Were sterile instruments and proper techniques used? Was there a known break in sterile technique?

- What was the surgeon's usual practice regarding the use of preoperative and intraoperative prophylactic antibiotics at the time of the occurrence?
- In a case involving a wound infection, ask the surgeon, what type of suture or staple material was used? Was the stitching appropriate? Were retention sutures or silk sutures indicated?
- Were intraoperative drains indicated and, if so, for what reason? What type of drain was used?
- Were postoperative sterile dressing changes, drain maintenance, and wound observation performed? Were these procedures documented adequately?
- Was there early recognition, documentation, and treatment of fever, an indurated wound, or pronounced incisional pain?
- If indicated, were wound specimen cultures obtained? Were culture results reported in a timely fashion? If there was no improvement, was another culture performed?
- The record should be reviewed to determine sensitivity of the infecting organism(s) to the antibiotics ordered. Was the type and dosage of antibiotic used appropriate for this infection?
- Was an infectious diseases consultation obtained in a timely manner?
- If cross-contamination is suspected, consulting an in-house epidemiologist to establish whether similar infections were occurring in the HCO at the time of the occurrence should be considered.
- Did a fistula develop? Was the bowel or bladder inadvertently stitched or traumatized during surgery?

## ANESTHESIA OCCURRENCES

*This section is geared toward interviews with anesthesiologists and anesthetists.*

### Preoperative Care

- Review the informed consent process for anesthesia administration. Were all the actual risks, benefits, and alternatives discussed with the patient? What were the risks (e.g., brain damage, nausea, vomiting, and/or death, depending on the type of anesthesia administered)?

- Was an appropriate preoperative medical evaluation obtained?
- If the case involved a complication of endotracheal intubation, was a thorough preoperative anesthesia history taken?
  - Were physical and oral examinations performed?
  - Was a difficult intubation anticipated?
  - Did the patient have any predisposing anatomical anomaly (e.g., scoliosis; a short, fat neck; a small chin; or an overbite) that could have been a factor in a difficult intubation?
  - Was a nasal versus an oral intubation indicated?
  - What criteria were used to determine the placement of the endotracheal tube (e.g., patient size, type of procedure, use of anticoagulation)?
- Were all the preoperative laboratory and radiologic evaluations noted on the chart at the time of the preoperative evaluation? Did the anesthesiologist personally review these reports? If so, how was this review documented?
- What was the American Society of Anesthesiologists (ASA) classification given to this patient?[1] Did the patient have any risks (e.g., critical illness, history of smoking, asthma, anterior mediastinal mass) for complications of general anesthesia? Was an alternative to general anesthesia indicated?
- Was the patient in the best possible condition for anesthesia and surgery?
- Was the required preanesthesia apparatus check performed? Both the ASA and the Food and Drug Administration (FDA) have safety checks that include inspecting the gas-scavenging systems, flow control valves and meters, oxygen and nitrous oxide cylinder pressures, central pipeline and connect supply hoses, and oxygen monitor.
- If the case involved an equipment-related occurrence, was the problem due to human error (e.g., failure to do a machine check) or a system error (e.g., an equipment defect)?[2] If an equipment defect is believed to be the cause, what is the rationale for this determination?

- ○ Who serviced the equipment? How was the equipment maintained? How frequently was it serviced?
- ○ Was the problem noted during surgery? What was done to rectify the problem?
- ○ If contacted at the time of the incident, what did the manufacturer's representative tell the risk manager?
- ○ Who was called to service the equipment after the occurrence? What was done to repair the equipment?
- ○ A knowledgeable in-house individual (e.g., an administrator) should be asked to review the service contract.
- ○ Where is the equipment now? Has the equipment been sequestered and, if so, where?
- If it is suspected that the user was at fault, what was the individual's training with this equipment?
  - ○ How recently was he or she trained? Is the training documented? (For more information, see Chapter 10, "Investigating Equipment-Related Occurrences.")
  - ○ Were techniques used within the delineation of privileges for the anesthesiologist, nurse anesthetist, or resident performing them?
  - ○ Were there any restrictions for certain procedures? For example, was this individual prohibited from administering anesthesia to children?

**Intraoperative Care**

- What type(s) of anesthesia was used? What specific anesthetic agents were used?
- Were there any contraindications (e.g., renal or hepatic dysfunction) to the specific anesthetic agents used?
- What were the dosages and actual times for delivery of the anesthesia?
- Was there an anesthetic overdose?
- Who administered the anesthesia? Was the attending anesthesiologist in the room the entire time? What was the HCO's policy regarding his or her presence? Was there a change of anesthesiologists during the procedure? If so, what was the reason for the change? What does the

OR schedule document? Was appropriate supervision provided for the anesthesia resident, certified registered nurse anesthetist, anesthesia assistant, etc.?

- If the case involved a complication of endotracheal intubation, were appropriate checks done to ensure appropriate placement of the tube (e.g., capnography)? Was the intubation smooth or difficult? If the intubation was difficult, the interviewee should be asked to describe the problem.
- What type of intraoperative monitoring equipment was used?
  - If a mechanical vent was used, was an oxygen-analyzing alarm or disconnect alarm used?
  - Were equipment alarms turned on?
  - Were tubes positioned and taped?
  - Were there any unnoticed or unchallenged shifts in vital signs?
  - Were a pulse oximeter and an end-tidal $CO_2$ monitor used?
  - Are any monitoring strips available?
  - Are the input (blood, infusions) and output (urine, if patient was catheterized) sheets available?
- Was there any intraoperative discussion between the anesthesiologist and the surgeon about a problem? Who was the first person to notice a problem? What action was taken?
- What medications were used intraoperatively to treat any complications?
- If the case involved an intraoperative cardiac arrest, what was the availability of resuscitation equipment? What was the HCO's protocol for intraoperative arrest? Was this protocol followed? Were appropriate staff available to assist?
- If the case involved a cervical nerve or brachial plexus injury, the interviewee should be asked to describe the patient's positioning (e.g., popliteal nerve injury secondary to the use of stirrups).
- If the case involved a problem that occurred during the patient's transfer to the postanesthetic care unit (PACU), how was the patient delivered to the PACU?
  - Who transferred the patient to the PACU?
  - What was the patient's status en route to the PACU? How was the patient monitored en route to the PACU?

- ○ What kind of postoperative observation did the anesthesia department make?
- ○ What was the physical layout of the OR and the PACU suites? (This information is helpful in determining, for instance, the distance the patient traveled from the OR to the PACU.)

**Postoperative Care**

- If the case involved a complication of endotracheal intubation, who was present during extubation?
  - ○ What extubation criteria were utilized?
  - ○ Was the patient extubated prematurely?
  - ○ In the case of a difficult intubation, was there a backup plan on how to reintubate the patient?
- Was there adequate reversal of anesthesia? Were reversal agents used? Was a peripheral nerve stimulator used?
- Was pulse oximetry used in the PACU?
- Was a postoperative note written?

**SUICIDE-RELATED OCCURRENCES**

*This section is geared toward interviews with physicians and/or nurses.*

- What was the admitting diagnosis?
- Was there anything in the patient's previous history (e.g., depression) relevant to his or her hospitalization? The presence of any mood disorders, particularly those involving psychosis, should be noted.[3]
  - ○ In particular, was there a history of previous suicide attempts, suicidal ideation, or suicidal gestures?
  - ○ Was there a family history of suicide? (Suicide seems to have a genetic component.)
  - ○ Was a patient urine drug screen performed to indicate the presence of cocaine or other drugs that might have contributed to a rapid shift of mood, particularly dysphoria, and suicidal behavior?

- If the case involved a suicide, what do the documented behavior assessments reveal? For example, nursing notes may describe some odd behavior that could have been a signal of suicidal behavior. However, the notes may not have been reviewed, or the description may have been discounted by the medical attending physicians or other staff.
  - Was there a recent event that precipitated the suicide (e.g., a particularly emotional family therapy session, or a fight with another patient)?
  - Was the patient undergoing detoxification and in the period of peak withdrawal?
  - Was there an important anniversary date (e.g., loss of a loved one) that might have triggered suicidal behavior?
  - Was there a recent completed suicide or suicide attempt on the unit that might have initiated a copycat phenomenon?
  - Did the patient give away any personal articles to other patients or discuss the topic of death, or even suicide, with staff or other patients?
  - Is there documentation of suicidal ideation or discussions about suicide with the staff?
  - Did the staff ever observe any suicidal gestures? Were these observations documented?
  - Did the patient have a specific plan?
  - Did the patient leave a suicide note?
- What suicide precautions were used in this HCO?
  - What security measures (e.g., staffed exits, tamper-proof locks, window guards) were in effect?
  - What were the indications for 1:1 or constant observation; isolation; or 5-, 10-, or 15-minute checks?
  - Did the HCO's policy or practice allow a patient who was under constant or 1:1 observation to ever be by himself or herself (e.g., using the bathroom alone)?
  - Did the HCO have a policy for denying outpatient or activity passes following certain types of behavior?
  - What was the HCO's policy for handling devices that could be used in a suicide attempt, such as eating utensils, razors, and shower curtain rods?

- ○ What was the policy for checking patients and visitors of patients for contraband (drugs or other materials that may be used in future suicidal behaviors) when they go on and off the unit?
- ○ Was there a policy to check whether a patient swallowed medications or held them in his or her cheek or under the tongue in order to save the drugs for a possible overdose?
- Were any precautions breached in this case?
  - ○ All flow sheets should be carefully reviewed for information about patient checks. When was the patient last seen prior to his or her suicide or suicidal behavior?
  - ○ Who was responsible for initiating special observation? Was such observation carried out in accordance with orders?
  - ○ Were all staff's opinions reviewed regarding the suicidal behavior?
  - ○ Was the patient permitted to go into the bathroom alone?
  - ○ If an elopement occurred, were the doors and window guards secured? Was the patient wearing street clothes?
- Who was in charge of treatment decisions?
  - ○ What were the patient's symptoms? Were appropriate medications used, evaluated, and adjusted in accordance with the patient's symptoms and diagnosis?
  - ○ What judgment was made regarding the patient's suicide potential?
  - ○ If there were notations of self-mutilating behavior, was this identified as an "attention-getting mechanism" as opposed to actual evidence of intent to harm oneself?
  - ○ What treatment plan was developed to deal with this behavior? Was it adhered to?
  - ○ Was the patient adequately medicated?
- The therapist should be asked for a detailed evaluation of the patient's suicidal ideations or attempts.
- If the patient was not on a locked unit, was he or she on a medical unit or in the HCO's emergency department? Were there any contingency plans to transfer the patient to a more secure unit? Were safeguards instituted and in effect until and during the transfer?
- If the patient was discharged, what were the plans for follow-up and outpatient care? What was the patient's status on discharge? Was it

reasonable to discharge the patient on the basis of this status? Was there a mechanism to ensure that the patient would be safe and would take his or her medications?

## CLINICAL LABORATORY ERRORS

*This section is geared toward interviews with physicians and/or technicians.*

- If the case involved equipment failure, as opposed to human error, was the equipment properly maintained?
  - Was there a service contract?
  - Are recorded maintenance checks, logs, manuals, and schedules available for review?
  - Was preventive maintenance that should be performed by the manufacturer conducted as scheduled?
  - What was the standard operating procedure for the quality control (QC) testing of the equipment? Were QC procedures routinely done? Such procedures are especially important for antigen-antibody testing.
  - Were the (QC) data complete?
  - Is there documentation that the personnel who performed the testing of the equipment were trained and their competency was assessed?
  - Were there any out-of-range values (QC failures) during the period of time in which the event occurred? If so, is there documentation of corrective action(s)?
- If the occurrence happened on a weekend, a holiday, or at night, was there adequate coverage—including supervisory staff?
- What were the HCO's procedures for training and evaluating personnel who used the equipment?
- If the case involved a possible mix-up of specimens, what were the policies and procedures for accessioning specimens (putting them into the analyzing equipment) and, if applicable, for making aliquots (subdividing a specimen)? Do these policies assure specimen integrity and accurate labeling?

- If the case involved a delay in performing or reporting a test, what was the availability and timeliness of PRN and stat testing?
- If there was a procedure for reporting grossly abnormal or "panic" findings, to whom were they reported and by whom?
  - How were abnormal or alert findings ("flags") highlighted?
  - Do logs provide evidence of telephone transmittal of stat or abnormal lab findings?
  - For "panic" values, does the policy require "read back" by the clinical staff, and is this documented?
- What was the quality of the specimen?
  - Was the specimen usable (i.e., in a sufficient amount and not hemolyzed)?
  - According to the instrument logs, did the instrument identify a problem with its functions or a problem with the patient sample during this analysis?
- Was there a "look-back" procedure to check all specimens when new techniques are developed?
- If the case involved an error in a test result, what was the procedure for transmitting results from the analyzer to the laboratory information system (LIS)?
  - If the test results are read by a technician and manually entered into the LIS, were the results accurately transcribed from the worksheet to the LIS?
  - If the data were inaccurately entered manually into the LIS, what systems are in place to assure that this function is performed accurately?
  - If the data were not transmitted accurately to the LIS, what is the procedure for assuring the accuracy of the transmission of results from the instruments to the LIS and from the LIS to the clinical care system?
  - Was the result transmitted with appropriate flags to the clinical care system?
  - Is there documentation that the technologist reviewed these flags?
- What was the procedure for communicating stat test results, frozen sections, or other biopsy findings to the operating room, special care

units, or delivery room? Can the records establish the trail of communication, if necessary?

- Do the patient's medical history and any medications explain any false-positive or false-negative results?

## BLOOD BANK OCCURRENCES

*This section is geared toward interviews with physicians, nurses, and/or technicians.*

- Was proper consent for blood administration obtained prior to the transfusion?
- If the case involved the administration of the wrong unit of blood, what caused the error?
  - Was there an occurrence management system?
  - Was the blood mislabeled (i.e., wrong sticker on the right bag or right sticker on the wrong bag)?
  - What system was in place to identify mislabeled specimens?
  - Was the type and cross-match test misinterpreted?
  - What system was in place to prevent inappropriate release of blood products?
  - Was there a demographic or data entry error?
  - For systems that do not utilize bar code readers and/or are not directly interfaced with the information system, what checks were in place to assure specimen integrity and accuracy of result reporting?
- If the case involved the transmission of an infectious disease allegedly due to the blood administration, where was the blood obtained?
  - How many units were involved? (With 10 or fewer units, donors are usually placed on surveillance status.)
  - How was the blood screened?
  - Did the donor test positive for the infectious disease on the subsequent donation?

## PATHOLOGY LAB OCCURRENCES

*This section is geared toward interviews with physicians and/or technicians.*

- If the case involved a misinterpretation of a pathology specimen, what was the procedure for reviewing slides?
  - What were the resident's role and the attending pathologist's input in making the diagnosis?
  - Was the pathologist aware of the patient's history and other test results?
  - Is there any evidence that there was a secondary review of the case by another pathologist at the time of the microscopic examination?
- Can the pathologist review the slides again?
  - Are the original tissue samples available?
  - Is there enough tissue in the paraffin blocks to prepare recuts?
- What is the pathologist's opinion in retrospect (on re-review of the slides)?

## RADIATION THERAPY OCCURRENCES

*This section is geared toward interviews with physicians and/or technicians.*

- Was the patient informed of the risks, benefits, and alternatives regarding radiation therapy? (See the "Informed Consent Issues" section that follows.)
- What was the make and type of equipment used for administering the radiation?
- What was the treatment schedule?
- The interviewee should be asked to discuss the dose calculation and size and shape of protective devices used during treatments. These factors are of particular concern in cases in which the spinal cord and gonads must be protected.
- Were the symptoms of toxicity recognized early?
- Was treatment stopped?
- Were appropriate consultations requested?

## INFORMED CONSENT ISSUES

*This section is geared toward interviews with physicians.*

- If the case involved the allegation of a lack of informed consent, was consent legally required? Was informed consent required by HCO policy?
- Was consent implied by the patient's behavior? (See Chapter 17, "Informed Consent," for information regarding implied consent.)
- Did the patient ask for a waiver of the informed consent conversation?
- Did an emergency situation exist?
- When and where was consent obtained? When did the procedure take place? Was the interval between the two events legally valid and appropriate per HCO policy?
- What type of documentation was made regarding the consent (e.g., note in the medical record and/or completed and signed consent form)?
- Who obtained consent? Was there a language barrier? If so, was an appropriate interpreter available to translate?
- Did the patient have the mental capacity to consent? If not, how was the patient's incapacity determined and by whom? What type of documentation exists? Was the HCO policy followed? Was the incapacity temporary or permanent?
- What was the role of the witness in the consent process (e.g., did he or she witness the patient's signature or witness the conversation)?
- If the consent of a surrogate was involved, were there any problems or refusals? Were there any objections by other family members?
- If a minor was involved, were state laws regarding consent of minors observed? Was the minor considered emancipated or a mature minor?
- What types of information were given to the patient and/or the patient's family about the procedure? Was the procedure routine or extraordinary?
- What risks were disclosed to the patient and/or family? Were the most probable and/or the most serious risks disclosed?
- What alternatives were offered? What was the patient's response? What was documented?

- Were the risks, benefits, and alternatives discussed on the basis of what a reasonable physician would disclose or what a patient would need to know (i.e., which standard was used—physician-based or patient-based)?
- Were the risks commonly known to the general public or considered too remote to be mentioned?
- Did the physician consider it dangerous to give information to the patient, and did he or she therefore exercise therapeutic privilege? (See Chapter 17 for information on therapeutic privilege.)
- Were there any substitutions entered later on the consent form (e.g., to the list of the parties to be present at the surgery)? If so, was the patient informed prior to surgery?
- If surgery was performed, was there an unanticipated situation that necessitated that the procedure be "extended"?[4]
- If the procedure involved sterilization, were local, state, and federal regulations followed? (See the discussion on informed consent for sterilization in Chapter 17.)
- If the procedure involved research or an experimental project, were all institutional review board recommendations and federal regulations followed? (See Chapter 17 regarding informed consent to experimentation.)

## GASTROPLASTY

*This section is geared toward interviews with physicians. In addition, the section on all surgery cases can be referred to.*

- With regard to candidacy, did HCO policy require a psychiatric consult prior to surgery?
- What was the patient told about the surgery's risks, benefits, and alternatives?
- Was surgery a last salvage attempt to treat the patient's morbid obesity? If so, were there any alternatives?
- Was the procedure appropriate for the patient?

- What was the physician's experience with this type of procedure? How many of these procedures had he or she done? Has the surgeon experienced this type of problem before?
- Was there a referral to a more experienced practitioner?

## NOTES

1. I = no systemic disease; II = mild to moderate systemic disease; III = severe systemic disease; IV = life-threatening systemic disease; V = patient in extremis (not expected to recover). *See* U. Wolters et al., "ASA Classification and Perioperative Variables as Predictors of Postoperative Outcome," *British Journal of Anaesthesia* 77, no. 2 (1996): 217–22.
2. R. S. Lagasse et al., "Defining Quality of Perioperative Care by Statistical Process Control of Adverse Outcomes," *Anesthesiology* 82, no. 5 (1995): 1181–8.
3. Suicides can occur in any psychiatric disorder, but they are more common in depressive disorders. In addition, suicides can occur in schizophrenia, particularly if depression is superimposed and if a prominent psychosis is present. Suicides also occur in substance abuse disorders, particularly because these patients are frequently comorbid with depressive disorders. For example, alcohol is known to disinhibit depressed patients to make a suicide attempt. (Older depressed males—particularly those older than sixty-five years who are psychotic—are at high risk for suicide.)
4. Generally, courts have held that unless specified prior to surgery, a patient under general anesthesia has consented to the extension of a procedure when an unanticipated condition is noted that, in the surgeon's judgment, requires treatment. *See* S. Becker, *Health Care Law: A Practical Guide* (Chicago: Ross & Hardies, 2003), 19.02.

# Chapter 8

# Developing Interview Questions on Occurrences in Long-Term Care Facilities

---

- Documenting and Assessing the Plan of Care
- Resident Slips and Falls
- Pressure Ulcers
- Elopement
- Physical/Emotional Abuse or Neglect
- Physical or Chemical Restraints

---

There has been a significant shift in the provision of health care from acute care settings to other physical settings, particularly those providing transitional, subacute, rehabilitative, and long-term care (LTC). Consequently, as residents in LTC facilities receive more complex care, there has been an increase in the frequency and severity of malpractice claims. Investigation of such claims requires special knowledge and familiarity with the issues and risks associated with providing care in LTC settings. Familiarity with the Federal regulations (42CFR483) for LTC facilities may also be useful.[1]

Every section of this chapter applies to interviews about claims involving LTC resident injuries. The investigator should prepare for the interview(s) by following the guidelines in Chapter 6, beginning with the general questions and then adapting the questions suggested here to the specific aspects of the case he or she is investigating.

Although the questions suggested later in the chapter are geared towards nursing personnel, an interview should be included with the administrator of the LTC facility concerning *any* event. The administrator is more than likely to be named in a lawsuit. Because he or she is very much involved with day-to-day operations, it is expected that everything that occurs (whether positive or negative) must become first-hand knowledge for the administrator. Charges concerning negligence, ethical violations, Medicare/Medicaid fraud, resident abuse, and/or the management of a LTC facility that is deemed (by regulators) to provide inadequate care can result in serious licensure consequences for the administrator. Thus, the administrator is a "must-be-interviewed" person.

## DOCUMENTING AND ASSESSING THE PLAN OF CARE

LTC facilities use a multidisciplinary and interdisciplinary approach to planning care. Specialists, attending physicians, and nursing staff must coordinate their efforts by working together to communicate and document changes in the residents' condition(s) and plan of care. Failure to follow a resident's plan of care is considered a violation of state and/or federal regulations. It might also support allegations of negligent care in a medical malpractice lawsuit.

The plan of care is documented in both the *minimum data set* (MDS) and the *comprehensive care plan* (CCP), both of which are maintained for each resident. The MDS is an individualized evaluation of the physical, cognitive, and psychosocial abilities of the resident; it also focuses on the strengths and/or weaknesses of the resident, the CCP documents multidisciplinary assessments, individualized care, discharge plans, and treatment rationale. In LTC facilities, the MDS, CCP, and medical record documentation are connected to formulate the individualized plan of care, discharge plan, and to support treatment rationale. All sets of records must be consistent and up to date.

Within each LTC facility, customary documentation and assessment processes follow these steps:

1.  The resident is assessed by individual interdisciplinary team members.
2.  The individualized assessments are documented in the medical record by each team member; including the completion of the initial minimum data set assessment.
3.  The interdisciplinary team meets to discuss how to plan for the resident's care.
4.  The interdisciplinary team develops an individualized comprehensive care plan (CCP), reviews their recommendations and proceeds to address the plan with the resident.

5.  The recommendations and plan of care are formally reviewed with the resident and/or the resident's health care representative at a CCP (Comprehensive Care Plan) meeting.
6.  The resident or the resident's health care representative is able to make changes to the plan of care if they wish at this time. Changes are incorporated into the CCP and the plan is finalized.
7.  The interdisciplinary team implements the plan of care.
8.  Periodically, the plan is reevaluated by the interdisciplinary team and, if necessary, reformulated.

LTC medical records also include the Certified Nursing Assistant (CNA) accountability record. This is a flow record that documents care given (e.g., turning and positioning schedules, toileting plans, incontinence care). It may also indicate whether an assistive device such as a wheelchair, cane, or walker must be used. It is important to refer to these records when investigating a case. The information contained in the CNA accountability record is as important as the documentation provided from other licensed professional staff. The CNA accountability record should be incorporated into sections of the medical record as well. Any discrepancies or omissions could prove problematic in the defense of a lawsuit.

In general in the LTC setting, many professional disciplines document according to the "charting by exception" rule (i.e., documenting only when there is an unanticipated change in a resident's status or when the resident is not progressing toward a desired goal). Therefore, the investigator needs to review all documentation, including the CNA accountability records, in order to understand the full scope of care and treatment for individual residents.

## Patient Review Instrument

The *patient review instrument* (PRI) is another assessment tool used in LTC facilities. For example, New York State law requires that a PRI be completed for each resident prior to admission to a skilled nursing facility. Generally, PRIs are initiated in the acute care hospital, are valid for thirty days, and are used to determine the level of care and the type of LTC facility required. A PRI assessment is comprehensive and includes

- primary and/or secondary diagnoses
- treatments and medications needed

- special diets or rehabilitative therapies required
- physical and mental abilities and limitations
- ability to perform acts of daily living, such as eating, moving, and toileting
- behaviors such as aggressiveness and disruptiveness

PRIs are often used in assessing facilities as well as patients. For example, New York State aggregates PRI scores for individual residents to obtain an overall facility score. This aggregate score determines the Medicaid reimbursement rate (if the LTC facility accepts Medicaid residents) and an overall score on the acuity level for the residents living at the LTC facility. This overall acuity is also referred to as the "case-mix index" or the CMI of the facility. The CMI indicates how sick the residents are. This weight has a direct impact on the reimbursement paid by Medicaid, and is tied to the economics of this type of business.

**The Minimum Data Set**

Similar to the PRI, the MDS is primarily used as an assessment tool to identify resident care problems or strengths detailed in the individualized CCP. The MDS is made up of a core set of screening, clinical and functional status elements, including common definitions and coding categories that form the foundation of the comprehensive assessment for all residents of long-term care facilities certified to participate in Medicare and Medicaid programs. Information documented in the MDS includes a resident's diagnoses, treatments offered, and an evaluation of functional status. The goal of this assessment tool is twofold: (1) to reflect the resident's care (deficits or needs) and (2) to support evaluation of the resident's strengths. In LTC, the critical resident care goal should at all times include promoting and/or maintaining the highest level of independent functioning.

MDS data are used to classify Medicare and Medicaid residents into resource utilization groups (RUGs). Many state Medicaid prospective payment systems use RUG categories for purposes of reimbursement. The MDS evaluation data are also used to examine the quality of care (quality indicators) at LTC facilities in the United States. Individual state surveyors use quality indicator information to evaluate a LTC facility from a regulatory perspective and the data are maintained by the Centers for Medicare and Medicaid Services (CMS). Additionally, facility-specific report cards benchmark the success of care delivered by individual facilities against a similar or "like" facility. Benchmarking information for every nursing home in the country is now available for public review at the Medicare website,[2] including the following, which lists

- demographics of the LTC facility—number of residents, ownership status
- state-specific regulatory inspection findings—including any deficiencies or reports of formal complaints filed by a resident (or family member) that required a state investigation
- staffing levels
- benchmarks—concerning the quality indicators

*Rehabilitation and/or Subacute Records*

Rehabilitation records may include the daily notes from physical therapy, occupational therapy, and speech therapy departments and are usually maintained in separate areas of the LTC facility. In some LTC facilities, residents participate in a nursing rehabilitation program and not a formal physical or occupational therapy program. The nursing rehabilitation program participation is also documented and may be kept in a separate nursing section of the medical record. Initial assessments (whether an active or nursing rehabilitation program) and weekly notes are kept in the medical record. Rehabilitation documentation by physical, occupational, or speech therapies is placed in the medical record upon the patient's discharge from the therapy program.

Changes to the actual therapy program are communicated to the interdisciplinary team as required. These changes are also reflected in the CCP. It is important to note that not every resident is in an active therapy program and/or a nursing rehabilitation program.

*Residents' Rights*

Federal regulations specify that a LTC facility must notify a resident and his or her physician of an accident or incident when there is an injury or "A significant change in the resident's physical, mental, or psychosocial status (i.e., a deterioration in health, mental, or psychosocial status in either life-threatening conditions or clinical complications)."[3] In the case of a resident without mental capacity, the resident's next-of-kin or guardian must be notified. In addition, the resident may provide the facility with a written version of the occurrence/accident/incident. The investigator needs to know whether this notification procedure has been followed. Each facility may have individualized policies and procedures. The investigator should request to review the policy and procedure that was in effect at the time of the alleged occurrence.

## QUESTIONS

The following questions are geared towards nursing personnel interviews and are based on FOJP Service Corporations's (FOJP) *Long-Term Care Risk Assessment Tool.*[4]

Prior to the interview, review the various parts of the resident's medical record including the MDS, CCP, the CNA accountability records, and the PRI.

### Resident Slips and Falls

*The investigator should ask the following questions:*

- On admission, was a fall prevention or risk assessment completed? Was the assessment repeated
  - after any change in the resident's condition?
  - following an alleged or actual fall?
  - at least quarterly?
- Following a fall, were the LTC resident's medications or treatment plan reassessed?
- What medications (including over-the-counter drugs and holistic supplements) was the LTC resident on at the time of the occurrence?
- If the LTC resident was considered at risk for a fall:
  - Was a documented prevention plan implemented and revised after any previous subsequent falls?
  - Was a fall prevention bed or chair alarm used? Was this use documented?

- What was the facility's policy regarding the performance of a fall risk assessment?
- Was the LTC resident provided with an orientation to his/her environment on admission with focused monitoring for a period of time?
- Was a mini-mental status (orientation to person, place, and time; recall; ability to follow commands) examination performed?
- In retrospect, was the LTC resident's cognitive status correctly assessed?
- What activity level was ordered prior to the occurrence?
- After the fall, did the facility's rehabilitation department assess the LTC resident?
- Were there any environmental factors related to the fall?
- Was the resident on a formal bowel and bladder retraining program? Was he or she being monitored/toileted as planned?
- What was the height of the bed at the time of the fall? Was it in its lowest possible position? What alternatives were considered (e.g., mattresses on the floor, mats around the bed)?
- Was there a change in mental status or physical condition prior to the fall? If so, was the LTC resident transferred to a higher level of care promptly so that increased monitoring and supervision could be implemented?
- Was the need for side rails identified?* If so, what was their position at the time of the occurrence? Was this documented?
- Is there documentation about instructions given to the LTC resident regarding side rail use?
- Were restraints ordered? If so, were they applied prior to the occurrence?
- If the fall occurred during a lift or transfer:
  - Was facility protocol followed?
  - Was any type of device used?
- Was an occurrence report completed?

---

*LTC facilities are expected to maintain a "restraint free" environment. If restraints are used or considered, alternative to restraints must be exercised first and documented. If restraints are used, they must be monitored aggressively. Refer to federal regulations (42CFR483).

- Was the reason for the fall identified on the occurrence report or in the medical record?
- Was the LTC resident using an assistive device at the time of the occurrence?
- Was the LTC resident evaluated by a physician in a timely manner?
- Was a significant change in the patient's condition or actual injury properly evaluated and timely reported to the physician for further evaluation?
- Were follow-up tests ordered and performed on a timely basis? Does medical record documentation support that test results were reported to or reviewed by the physician?
- If bruises were noted on the resident's head, did the resident strike his or her head upon falling? Was a subdural hematoma considered?
- If bruises were noted on the resident's limbs, was a fracture considered?
- Was the resident's family notified? What was disclosed to the resident and/or the family?
- If no injury was initially noted, was the resident reassessed after the incident for signs of an injury? If the resident complained of pain after the initial assessment, was he or she reexamined?

For more questions on this occurrence type, see the "Slips and Falls" section in the previous chapter.


**Pressure Ulcers**

*The investigator should ask the following questions:*

- On admission, was a risk assessment for the potential development of pressure ulcers documented?
- Was a formal evaluation tool used to rate the risk of pressure ulcers, such as the Braden Scale for Predicting Pressure Sore Risk?
- Was a skin assessment done on admission?
- If a pressure ulcer was identified, were photographs taken?
- Was the patient suffering from incontinence on admission?

- What HCO policy and procedures address pressure ulcer prevention? Does medical record documentation support compliance with the policy and procedure? If the staff deviated from policy, is the rationale supported in the medical record or in the CCP?
- If the patient was immobilized, was a turning and positioning schedule documented?
- Was the use of any pressure-relieving device documented (including devices for the wheelchair)?
- Do weekly notes or a flow record document an ongoing assessment?* If a flowchart was used, was it consistently updated?
- Was staging recorded during the assessment?†
- Is the nursing treatment plan documented, evaluated, and updated periodically?
- Was the resident on a formal bowel and bladder retraining program?
- Were additional measures taken to maintain skin integrity?
- Is the documentation by various providers consistent regarding the pressure ulcer assessments?
- Once a pressure ulcer was identified, do the notations reflect an improvement of the wound? Were photographs taken to support the improvement?
- Was there evidence of infection?
- Is there documentation that nutritional needs were being addressed?
- Are laboratory studies, such as serum albumin, calcium, and iron levels, monitored?
- Was a pain management plan documented and updated periodically?
- Was the LTC resident's hydration addressed?
- If applicable, did the HCO's wound care management team evaluate the LTC resident? Where and how often does the team document the evaluation?

*Specific policy and procedure must be looked at. Many HCOs will perform a reassessment of the pressure ulcer wound and document this assessment on a flow record or in the progress notes.

†Pressure ulcers are graded for severity. The general scale is grade 1 through grade 4. The higher the number, the more involved or severe the ulcer. For example, 1 = blister and 4 = involvement through muscle and bone. This is recognized nomenclature.

**Elopement**

These questions are adapted from material from CNA HealthPro and the FOJP LTC Risk Assessment Tools.[5] *The investigator should ask the following questions:*

- Is there a documented evaluation of the LTC resident on admission for risk of wandering and elopement? If the resident's cognitive status changed, was he or she reevaluated?
- Did the facility lock down all external doors at night?
- Did the facility monitor all persons leaving and entering the building after hours?
- Did the facility's security department make rounds, check certain high-risk areas (rooftop exits), and/or maintain time-specific logs?
- Was camera surveillance used to monitor distant exits?
- How often were nursing rounds made for the purpose of checking on LTC residents?
- If the LTC resident was considered at risk for elopement, what security measures were taken to prevent this from happening?
  - Were these measures documented in the resident's medical record?
  - Was a photograph of the resident kept at the main entrance to alert staff? Was the photograph updated?
  - Was the resident wearing an electronic monitoring device, such as a bracelet or anklet? If so, what is the policy for testing the functioning of the monitoring device? Were the test records maintained?
  - Were the resident's family and friends educated about his or her risk of elopement? Is this education documented on a risk assessment tool?
- If the resident was in a protected unit, were exit alarms installed?
  - Is there documented evidence that the alarms were recently checked or maintained?
  - Is there keypad or "wander guard" system inside elevators and on doorways leading to stairwells or other means of egress?
  - Was the wandering guard periodically monitored for battery life or electronic failure? Is there a policy and procedure to address monitoring of LTC residents should the wandering guard system fail?

**Physical/Emotional Abuse or Neglect**

*The investigator should ask the following questions:*

- Did the LTC facility have a formal abuse/neglect and mistreatment policy?
- If an LTC resident exhibits an unexpected bruise, hematoma, or ecchymosis, does this trigger an investigation into possible physical abuse?
- If the claim involved alleged caregiver-to-resident abuse or neglect:
  - Was the investigation of alleged abuse performed in a timely manner?
  - Was an appropriate new-hire background check performed on the individual caregiver? Did it include inquiries with state registries?[6] Were background checks kept in the personnel files?
  - Was the incident reported to the proper government or state regulating agency (if appropriate) in a timely manner as required by law?
  - Was the caregiver removed from the assignment or unit, or transferred from the resident's unit?
  - Were all LTC residents routinely assessed for signs of abuse?
  - Was the incident documented in the caregiver's personnel file?
  - Did the caregiver attend staff training on resident abuse prior to the incident?
- If the claim involved LTC resident-to-resident abuse:
  - Were resident rooms reassigned to minimize roommate abuse?
  - Prior to the incident, was the LTC resident's behavior documented as being aggressive, provocative, or irritating? Are the monitoring forms kept in the medical record?*
  - Was the social service department notified of the incident? What was documented?

---

*For residents who are on "mood altering" medications, in behavior modification programs, or if staff are trying to document a particular behavior; a behavior monitoring log/form may be instituted.

- If the claim involved family-member-to-resident abuse or neglect:
    - Were any signs of abuse or neglect documented prior to the incident?
    - What did the HCO do to protect the resident from the situation?
    - Were there any contentious family issues that may have led to the incident?
    - Were potential allegations evaluated by the social service department? If so, was this allegation investigated and documented?
    - Did the investigation result in mandatory reporting to a regulatory agency?
- If the claim involved contractor-to-resident abuse:
    - Was a reference check performed? Did the facility retain copies of these records?
    - Was a criminal background check performed, if permitted? Was a copy of this check retained?
    - Were the contractor's credentials checked?
    - Does the facility require or include indemnification clauses in its contracts with subcontractors?

**Physical and Chemical Restraints**

*The investigator should ask the following questions:*

- What was the HCO's restraints policy? Does this policy distinguish between physical and chemical restraints?
- Did the policy in keeping with state and federal regulations regarding a restraint-free environment? If physical restraints were used, was a rationale and plan to assess and maintain the LTC resident's safety with the least restrictive device documented?
- If chemical restraints were used, was there a plan to monitor for extrapyramidal side effects? Was there a plan to wean the LTC resident from the medication? Was this plan documented in the CCP?
- Was a physical restraint release signed by the LTC resident or family?
- Was there a plan of care to wean the LTC resident off the physical restraint? Was this plan documented?

- Was the plan of care updated initially, with periodic evaluations? Does the documentation support periodic evaluations?*
- If wrist or waist restraints were applied, were flow sheets kept to document observation of the LTC resident's circulation and safety?
- Did the application of the restraint conform to facility policy and procedures?

## NOTES

1. 42 C.F.R. § 483B (2005), *available at* http://www.access.gpo.gov/nara/cfr/cfr-table-search.html#page1/ (accessed May 1, 2006).
2. Center for Medicare and Medicaid Services, *Nursing Home Compare,* www.medicare.gov/NHCompare/Include/DataSection/Questions/SearchCriteria.asp?version=default&browser=IE%7C6%7CWin2000&language=English&defaultstatus=0&pagelist=Home&CookiesEnabledStatus=True.
3. 42 C.F.R. § 483.10 residents rights (11) (B) (2001).
4. Jose Guzman, Jr. and Patricia Kischak, *FOJP Service Corporation's Long-Term Care Risk Assessment Tools* (New York: FOJP Service Corporation, Healthcare Risklink article–volume 3, 2004).
5. Continental Casualty Company, *Comparison of Claims Data in Long Term Care, January 1996 through March 2005,* http://www.cna.com/ (accessed January 14, 2006).
6. NCSBN Directory of Nurse Aide Registries, http://www.oregon.gov/OSBN/Pdfs/form/ana_registries_by_state.pdf/ (accessed August 1, 2006).

---

*Did the interdisciplinary team discuss the plan and did they document the plan once the team decided to use a restraint? Once this was planned and documented, did they continue to update the record to support continued use?

# Chapter 9

# Developing Interview Questions on Obstetrical Claims

---

> - Antepartum-Prenatal Period
> - Intrapartum—Labor and Delivery
> - Postpartum
> - Other Major Obstetrical Complications

Each section of this chapter guides the investigator in formulating questions to use during interviews about obstetrical claims for maternal and infant injuries. The investigator should prepare for the interview by following the guidelines in Chapter 6 beginning with the general questions and then tailoring the questions in this chapter to the specific aspects of the case being investigated.

This guideline is organized to cover all aspects of obstetrical care. Because of the high liability exposure associated with claims involving brain-damaged infants, our goal is to acquaint the investigator with risk management concerns encountered in caring for the prenatal, intrapartum, and postpartum patient. The questions in this chapter are designed to be used as a guide for both developing questions and interviewing attending obstetricians, house staff, and obstetrical nurses involved in neurologically impaired infant cases, as well as cases for other infant or maternal injuries.

## ANTEPARTUM—PRENATAL PERIOD

*The investigator should review the mother's history (obstetrical, surgical, medical, and medications) and then develop appropriate questions for the interview, including the following:*

- Early in the pregnancy, was the mother assessed for any risk factors that might be related to the development of an adverse outcome and that would have required special management?
  - Potential medical risk factors include hypertension; hemoglobinopathy; prior deep vein thrombosis or pulmonary embolism; diabetes; asthma; heart or pulmonary disease; cancer; epilepsy; renal disease; sexually transmitted disease (STD); and maternal use of alcohol, drugs, or tobacco.
- Other risk factors include a history of maternal age 35 years or older; prior Cesarean delivery; uterine scars; two or more abortions, incompetent cervix, uterine leiomyomata or malformation; prior fetal structural or chromosomal abnormality; second trimester pregnancy loss; prior premature rupture of fetal membranes (PROM), preterm delivery or low birth weight infant (less than 2,500 grams); prior neonatal or infant death.[1] If a risk factor was identified or an active problem existed, was the mother informed of the possible complications and treatments? Was the condition addressed by the obstetrician or referred to a consultant?
  - Does the mother have a history of psychiatric illness?
- The mother's family history should be reviewed. Are there any familial or genetic problems or other children with neurologic or physiologic deficits?
- The mother's menstrual history should be reviewed.
- Were any unusual findings identified in the initial physical examination?
- What was the gestational age at the time of the first prenatal visit? How was the gestational age determined? Was it based on the last menstrual period (LMP), uterine size, or sonogram findings?
- Were the routine laboratory tests recommended by the American College of Obstetricians and Gynecologists/American Academy of

Pediatrics (ACOG/AAP) performed and properly interpreted? Routine tests include:

- ○ hemoglobin and hematocrit
- ○ blood group and Rhesus (Rh) type
- ○ antibody screen
- ○ urinalysis and culture
- ○ hepatitis B surface antigen (HbsAG)
- ○ Venereal Disease Research Laboratory test (VDRL)
- ○ rubella immunity testing
- ○ human immunodeficiency virus (HIV) antibody testing
- ○ cervical cytology[2]

- Was further testing done relative to the risk assessment, for any of the following?
  - ○ Gonorrhea, chlamydia, and other STDs
  - ○ Sickle cell trait
  - ○ Maternal serum screening for congenital anamolies such as chromosomal aneuploides and neural tube defects [These tests may have a number of names including maternal serum (blood) screening test, multiple marker screening test, triple screen, quad screen, and others.]
  - ○ Diabetes
  - ○ TORCH titers (toxoplasmosis, rubella, cytomegalovirus, and herpes titers)
  - ○ Other genetic conditions such as cystic fibrosis
- Were any tests advised but refused by the mother? Was this refusal documented in the medical record?
- Were any tests and examinations performed in subsequent visits that would have indicated a fetal malformation, a problem in fetal development, or maternal complication?
  - ○ Was a sonogram performed? If so, when?
  - ○ Was an amniocentesis performed? If so, when?
  - ○ Were fundal heights, assessments of fetal heart tones, and maternal weights and blood pressures obtained at each subsequent visit as appropriate?

- ○ Was maternal urine checked for protein and sugar appropriately at these visits?
- ○ Did fetal size match gestational age? If not, was intrauterine growth restriction (IUGR) considered?
- ○ What interventions for abnormal findings, if any, was pursued? Was it documented?
- ○ Were abnormal findings discussed with the patient? Was this documented?
- Was the frequency of prenatal visits in accordance with ACOG/AAP recommendations?[3]
- Did the mother keep her appointments? If not, what was done to contact her? Were these attempts documented?
- Was the mother compliant with her prenatal instructions regarding nutrition, ingestion of any medications, and use of drugs, alcohol, or cigarettes? If not, what was done to advise the mother of the impact of her noncompliance on the pregnancy? Were these conversations documented?
- What instructions were given regarding the signs and symptoms of labor?
- What was the mother told about the signs of impending complications [e.g., decreased fetal movements, bleeding, premature rupture of membranes (PROM), headaches, dizziness, visual disturbances, pedal edema, premature contractions]?
- Was the mother told to report any of these signs to the obstetrician without delay? Does the medical record reflect this advice?
- If any of these problems were encountered, what instructions were given to the mother at that time? Were they documented?
- What active treatment was instituted? Were the risks of such treatment discussed with the mother and documented? What were the results of the treatment?
- If the mother began labor or ruptured membranes prior to 38 weeks (preterm gestation), what intervention, if any, was instituted? Was it documented?
- Once the mother passed 40 weeks of gestation, was testing (e.g., nonstress test, biophysical profile) done to establish fetal well-being? If the results were abnormal, was induction of labor (oxytocin stimulation) considered? If not, what was the rationale?

# INTRAPARTUM—LABOR AND DELIVERY

## Stage I (onset of labor to full dilatation)

*The investigator should consider the following:*

- When did labor begin? Who did the mother first contact when labor commenced, and when? What instructions were given, and by whom?
- When was the mother first assessed, examined, and triaged at the HCO?
  - Who performed the examination?
  - What were the documented findings regarding cervical dilatation and effacement, fetal presentation, station and position, status of amniotic membranes, estimated fetal weight, assessment of fetal heart strips, and quality and frequency of contractions?
  - When was the attending obstetrician informed of the examination results?
- When did the attending obstetrician arrive and first examine the mother? Was this examination done within a reasonable amount of time after the attending obstetrician was alerted that his or her patient was in labor?
- What were the other findings, including maternal blood pressure and results of the urine dip for sugar and protein?
- Were there any contraindications to labor, such as nonreassuring fetal status, maternal heart failure, transverse lie, cord prolapse, placenta previa, history of a classical Cesarean section, acute genital herpes, invasive cervical cancer, or any other condition that might have resulted in injury to the health and life of the mother or infant?
- What were the results of subsequent vaginal examinations? How often were vaginal examinations performed? The interviewee should be asked to review each set of findings with regard to effacement, dilatation and station, status of membranes, fetal position, and fetal presentation.
- When did the mother's membranes rupture? What was the characteristic of the amniotic fluid (e.g., clear, meconium-stained, frank blood, foul-smelling)? Were appropriate measures taken for unusual findings?

- The investigator should review the progress of labor.
  - Who performed the examinations?
  - Were the findings documented?
  - Was the attending obstetrician informed of any findings that might have indicated possible maternal or fetal compromise? If so, what intervention did he or she recommend?
  - How was the fetus monitored (internal or external fetal monitoring or auscultation)? What was the baseline reading? Was the monitoring done in accordance with ACOG/AAP standards?[4]
- If house staff managed the mother's labor, is there evidence of supervision by the attending physician? Are the house staffs' notes countersigned by an attending physician? Does the record documentation detail communication with the attending physician and the attending's directives regarding interventions? Is this documentation dated and timed?
- Do notations in the labor record reflect the interpretations of the fetal monitoring tracings?
- Do vaginal examinations, medications, tests, and other interventions noted in the medical record correlate temporally to notations made on the electronic fetal monitoring strips?
- Were there any examinations or bedside visits that were not documented in the labor record?
  - Was another system used for documenting and communicating the progress of labor?
- Is there evidence of monitoring of maternal vital signs? Was this monitoring done in accordance with ACOG/AAP standards?[5]
- Was physician rationale for treatment decisions and interventions documented?
- Was anesthesia administered? Is there adequate documentation regarding the administration?
  - Were the types of anesthesia available explained to the mother prior to labor or on admission? Was the mother advised of the risks, benefits, and alternatives to such medications?
  - Was an IV infusion started prior to beginning the administration of anesthesia?

- ○ Were the fetal monitoring strips examined before and after the administration?
- ○ Were the mother's vital signs and fetal heart rate monitored and assessed before, during, and after the administration of anesthesia?
- ○ What mode of administration and what medications were used?
- ○ Who administered the anesthesia—obstetrician, nurse anesthetist, or anesthesiologist?
- ○ Were there any anesthesia-related complications? What intervention was pursued?
- ○ Was a post anesthesia check done?
- After complete review of the labor record, the physician should be asked to determine whether the mother made adequate progress.
  - ○ Did he or she use the Friedman curve to track the progress of labor?[6]
  - ○ Were there any deviations from the Friedman curve norm that could have indicated complications?[7]
  - ○ How long did the mother remain in the first stage of labor? Was this an acceptable amount of time?[8]
- If the mother failed to progress, was augmentation indicated? If so, what methods were used to augment labor—surgical (amniotomy), medical (oxytocin administration), ambulation—or was a decision made to allow the mother to rest and have more time?
- If oxytocin was ordered for induction or augmentation of labor or a cervical ripener was ordered, what were the indications? Were they documented? Was the HCO's policy followed?
  - ○ What was the Bishop's score?[9]
  - ○ Who ordered the oxytocin? The physician should be asked to substantiate the indication for induction or augmentation of labor with documented clinical findings.
  - ○ What time was oxytocin administered? Who regulated the administration?
  - ○ How was the oxytocin regulated in response to fetal monitoring strips? Was there evidence of excessive uterine contractions and/or nonreassuring fetal status?[10] The interviewee should be asked to

review the results of the physician's and/or nurse's labor record, the pelvic examinations, and the fetal monitoring strips to establish whether labor was or was not progressing adequately (dilatation, effacement, descent) during oxytocin administration.

- ○ Where was the attending obstetrician during oxytocin administration? What was the HCO's policy regarding the presence of the attending obstetrician?

- The interviewee should be asked to review the fetal monitoring strips to establish the presence of fetal well-being or nonreassuring fetal status and the resulting management of the mother.

  - ○ What is their current interpretation of the fetal heart rate strips? The interviewee should be asked to comment on the presence or absence of accelerations or decelerations, the baseline of the fetal heart rate, the degree of variability, the amplitude of oscillations, and the frequency and quality of contractions.

  - ○ Is their current interpretation of the fetal monitoring strips consistent with his or her previous interpretation as documented in the medical record?

- If nonreassuring fetal status occurred, what was documented in the labor record?

  - ○ When was this status first observed during the course of labor and by whom?

  - ○ When did the obstetrician or obstetrical resident first become aware of the nonreassuring fetal status?

  - ○ Who notified the physician of the nonreassuring fetal status? What information was given to the physician?

  - ○ What measures were indicated and taken?

    - ▪ If oxytocin was being administered, was it discontinued?

    - ▪ Were any resuscitative measures taken (e.g., turning the mother on her left side, increasing intravenous fluids, administering oxygen)?

    - ▪ What were the HCO's policies for this type of situation?

    - ▪ Was a Cesarean section considered? If so, on what indications was consideration based? Were these opinions documented? Was informed consent for a Cesarean section obtained and documented?

**Stage II (full dilatation to delivery or expulsion of the fetus)**

*The investigator should consider the following:*

- Did the second stage of labor last longer than 50 minutes in a primipara? Did it last longer than 20 minutes in a multipara?[11] (These are average lengths of the second stage of labor, and exceeding this length of time is not necessarily a deviation from normal.)
- Where did the mother deliver the infant? If the mother was transferred from a labor or birthing room, was there any delay in transfer?
- What was the interviewee's role and responsibility during this second stage of labor?
- Was the attending obstetrician present throughout this stage? What other health care professionals were present?
- If no risk factors were present, was the fetal heart evaluated every 15 minutes during the second stage of labor? For patients with complications, the fetal heart should be evaluated every 5 minutes in the second stage of labor.[12]
- What treatment was given for any indication of nonreassuring fetal status?
- Was anesthesia administered during the second stage of labor? If so, what type of anesthesia, and who administered it? If an epidural was being administered already, was it "topped off" (continued or reinforced) at this time?
- Was oxygen administered to the mother?
- Were there any conditions threatening the mother or fetus that were indications for expediting a vaginal delivery by the use of forceps or vacuum extraction?
  - If so, what were these indications?
  - What type of forceps were used? What were the baby's station, position, and presentation? Application of the forceps when the leading part of the fetal skull is above +2 station (midpelvis or with head engaged) is done only in rare circumstances.[13]
- Was fundal pressure applied? If so, who applied it and for how long? What were the indications?

- Was an episiotomy done? If so, what type was performed? Was any extension of the episiotomy or a laceration documented? Was the repair documented?
- Who delivered the baby? Who assisted in the delivery?
- If a Cesarean section was performed, what was the indication? What type was done?
- Were any relatives or significant others present for the delivery?
- Was a pediatrician present?
- What was the infant's condition at birth?
  - How many weeks' gestation was the baby when delivered?
  - Were any complications noted at delivery (e.g., presence of meconium, shoulder dystocia, tight nuchal cord, or precipitous delivery)? What, if any, treatment was instituted and by whom?
  - Were any unusual findings or abnormalities, such as congenital malformations, neurological deficits (e.g., flacid extremity) noted on examination of the newborn in the delivery room? If so, could these findings be attributed to an occurrence during labor and delivery?
  - What were the Apgar scores at 1, 5, and 10 minutes?
  - What was the infant's weight? (Macrosomia is fetal growth above a specific weight, usually 4,000–4,500 grams, regardless of gestational age.)[14]
- Did the infant require resuscitation? If so, who performed the resuscitation? Was appropriate equipment available for resuscitation? Was intubation required? Were the appropriate resuscitation measures done?
- Was the infant transferred to the regular nursery or the neonatal intensive care unit (NICU) and why?
  - Was the infant stabilized before transfer to the NICU?
  - Was there a delay in treatment or transfer to the NICU?
  - What other HCO personnel were present during the transfer?
  - How was the transfer accomplished?
- Was a cord pH or a complete blood gas obtained on delivery? If so, what were the results?
- Was the cord examined, and were the findings documented?
  - What were the physical characteristics of the cord?
  - Could these findings be related to the outcome?

## Stage III (expulsion of the placenta)

*The investigator should consider the following:*

- How long after the infant's delivery was the placenta expelled?
- Were any procedures necessary to remove the placenta (e.g. manual removal, dilatation and curettage).
- What was the estimated blood loss (EBL)? What was the reason for the blood loss? Was blood replacement indicated?
- Was there excessive bleeding? How was it handled? Were medications such as methylergonovine (Methergine), oxytocin, or prostaglandin indicated?
- Were there any unusual findings on the obstetrician's physical examination of the placenta?
- Was a placenta culture performed?
- Was the placenta sent to the pathology department for examination?
- The interviewee should be asked to review the pathology report.
  - What were the results of the gross and microscopic evaluation?
  - How much did the specimen weigh? Was this significant?
  - Did the examination reveal any abnormalities (e.g., infarcts, infection, short cord, tear in the cord, knot in the cord, abnormal implantation in the placenta, small-sized placenta, meconium-stained placenta, calcified placenta, degenerative placenta)? Could any of the abnormalities be related to the outcome in this case?

## POSTPARTUM

*The investigator should review the maternal record and develop appropriate questions, such as the following:*

- Were maternal vital signs monitored appropriately?
- Was the fundus checked for firmness?
- Was vaginal bleeding checked?
- Was the condition of the perineum described?
- Were there any complications? If so, what interventions were pursued?
- Were there any complaints from the mother? If so, what action was taken?

## OTHER MAJOR OBSTETRICAL COMPLICATIONS ASSOCIATED WITH PREGNANCY, LABOR, DELIVERY, AND THE POSTPARTUM PERIOD

### Hypertensive Disorders and HELLP

The following is a brief description of hypertensive disorders that include gestational hypertension, mild and severe preeclampsia, eclampsia, and HELLP (syndrome of hemolysis, elevated liver enzymes, and low platelet count).[15] These disorders can occur in the prenatal, intrapartum, or postpartum periods.

*Gestational Hypertension* is a diastolic blood pressure of at least 90 mm of mercury or a systolic blood pressure of at least 140 mm of mercury that occurs after 20 weeks of gestation in a woman with previously normal blood pressure.

*Preeclampsia (mild)* is gestational hypertension as specified above, accompanied by proteinuria of 0.3 g or more of protein obtained in a 24-hour urine collection. It is usually associated with a 1+ or greater proteinuria on urine dipstick results obtained from a random urine specimen.

Severe preeclampsia

*In severe preeclampsia, the criteria for preeclampsia are met along with the presence of one or more of the following signs[16]:*

- *Hypertension*: diastolic blood pressure of 110 mm or systolic blood pressure greater than 160 mm of mercury, obtained twice, six hours apart, at bed rest
- *Proteinuria*: at least 5 g of protein obtained in a 24-hour urine collection or a 3+ to 4+ proteinuria based on urine dipstick results obtained from a random urine specimen
- *Oliguria:* a 24-hour urinary output of less than 400 cc
- *Cerebral or visual disturbances*: changes in consciousness, headache, scotomata (blind spots), or blurred vision, all of which are new signs
- *Pulmonary edema*
- *Epigastric or right upper-quadrant pain*

- *Abnormal liver function tests*
- *Fetal growth restriction*
- *Thrombocytopenia*
- *Elevated serum creatinine*

*Eclampsia* is defined as the presence of new-onset grand mal seizures in a woman with preeclampsia. It generally does not occur until the last trimester and is characterized by seizures in association with hypertension and the signs and symptoms of preeclampsia. The mother may exhibit a wide range of symptoms, from mild hypertension to multi-organ failure.[17]

*HELLP syndrome* is considered to be a complication of or a variant of severe preeclampsia, with hepatic involvement. Both are multi-organ disease processes. The HELLP syndrome can occur in the antepartum, intrapartum, or postpartum periods. With the HELLP syndrome, the mother exhibits hemolysis (H), elevated liver enzymes (EL), and low platelets (LP). Assessment and management are similar to those for severe preeclampsia. High doses of corticosteroids can be used to reduce the bleeding complications. However, a greater focus is on treating coagulation abnormalities, particularly DIC (disseminated intravascular coagulopathy) and identifying hepatic lesions or bleeds.

### Treatment for Hypertensive Disorders and HELLP

The treatment of preeclampsia is dependent on the severity, gestational age, maternal and fetal condition, and the presence or absence of labor. Mild preeclampsia in the preterm period is generally managed with in-hospital or careful home observation of both mother and fetus.[18] The presence of severe preeclampsia or the HELLP syndrome usually calls for management in a tertiary care setting by a maternal/fetal subspecialist. Delivery of the fetus regardless of gestational age or fetal maturity is recommended for a mother with the HELLP syndrome.[19] Magnesium sulfate is used to prevent seizures, and hydralazine or labetalol are commonly used to treat acute hypertension.[20]

Hourly intake and output monitoring is done to monitor the mother's fluid balance and to observe for oliguria.

*The investigator should review the maternal record and develop appropriate questions, such as the following:*

- How many weeks' gestation was the mother at the time of diagnosis? Was the preeclampsia severe or mild?
- Was the mother considered previously at risk for preeclampsia during her pregnancy?
- What were the mother's absolute blood pressure, trend in blood pressures, weight gain, and urine test results?
- If the mother was *not* hospitalized, was this appropriate?
- Once hospitalized, what was the course of action/intervention?
  - Was a maternal/fetal subspecialist or perinatologist consulted?
  - Were antihypertensive agents used? If so, over how long a period were they used?
  - Were there any other complications, such as abnormal renal or liver function test results, associated with preeclampsia? If so, how were these problems handled?
- If severe preeclampsia was diagnosed, how was the mother monitored?
  - Was a CVP (central venous pressure) line inserted?
  - Was cardiac output monitored via Swan-Ganz catheter?
  - Were maternal blood gases monitored?
- If the HELLP syndrome was considered, the following questions should be asked:
  - What tests were performed (e.g., uric acid, creatinine, SGOT/SGPT, hematocrit, platelets, coagulation studies)?
  - Was a liver scan performed?
  - What was the frequency of testing?
- What tests were done to evaluate fetal well-being (e.g., nonstress test, biophysical profile, Doppler blood flow test)?
  - How often were they done?
- If delivery was indicated, how was it accomplished?
- If a Cesarean section was indicated, was it performed at an appropriate time (e.g., after stabilization of the mother's condition)?
- If there was a delay in performing a Cesarean section, what was the reason for the delay?

- How many weeks' gestation was the baby when delivered? What was the condition of the baby at birth?

## Placental Abnormalities

*Placenta previa* occurs when the placenta implants over (complete) or very near (partial) the internal cervical os. It is characterized by painless vaginal bleeding in late second trimester or early third trimester.

*Placenta abruptio* occurs when the placenta separates before or during labor. Severe pain, an irritable uterus, and a lack of uterine relaxation usually accompany it.

*Placenta accreta* occurs when, following delivery of the infant, all or part of the placenta does not separate from the uterus. Maternal postpartum hemorrhage can result.

*The investigator should review the maternal record and develop appropriate questions, such as the following:*

- When was placenta previa or abruptio diagnosed?
- Did the mother have any factors associated with the diagnosis of placenta previa—such as uterine bleeding during the latter half of the pregnancy, a previous history of previa, multiparity, advanced maternal age, previous Cesarean section, tobacco use, or multiple gestation?[21] If so, were the risks (e.g., hemorrhaging necessitating a hysterectomy, blood transfusions) of placenta previa discussed with the mother?
- Did the mother have any factors associated with placenta abruption—such as hypertension, abdominal trauma or cocaine use?
- Was placenta accreta considered in a mother with a previous Cesarean section and prior placenta previa?
- Ask the interviewee to review the results of any prenatal sonograms.
- Was additional sonography or magnetic resonance imaging (MRI) performed to rule out placenta previa, abruptio, or accreta?
- If placenta previa or placenta abruptio was diagnosed prenatally, what prenatal interventions were done?

- ○ How were the mother and baby monitored?
- ○ Was bed rest instituted?
- ○ Were the appropriate personnel, blood products, medication, and equipment prepared and available for delivery?
- If active bleeding occurred, how much and what type of bleeding was the mother experiencing?
  - ○ When did the bleeding begin?
  - ○ Was it painful or painless?
  - ○ How was the case managed in relation to fetal maturity and degree of hemorrhage?
  - ○ Was blood replacement therapy instituted?
- Should a Cesarean section have been performed?
- If a Cesarean section was performed, should it have been done earlier?
- What was the condition of the infant at delivery?

### Brachial Plexus Injuries of the Neonate

Brachial plexus injuries are injuries to the brachial plexus nerves originating from C-5 through T-1 that result in either Duchenne-Erb's (C5–C6) type of upper arm paralysis or Klumpke's (C8–T1) type of lower arm paralysis.[22] The injury is usually caused by stretching, tearing or other trauma to the brachial plexus. It may occur during efforts to deliver the infant's shoulders when the shoulders do not readily deliver (shoulder dystocia). A large infant is a risk factor for shoulder dystocia.[23]

*The investigator should review the maternal record and develop appropriate questions, such as the following:*

- Was there a maternal history of previous large infants?
- Were there any prior difficult deliveries or operative deliveries? If so, what were the details?
- Did the mother have diabetes and/or a great weight gain during pregnancy?
- What were the results of the mother's glucose screens/tolerance test?
  - ○ When was the testing done?
  - ○ Was the repeat testing indicated and done?

- ○ Were urines tested routinely?
- What was the estimated fetal weight (EFW)?
  - ○ What method was used to determine the EFW?
  - ○ Who determined the EFW?
  - ○ When was it done?
- The interviewee should be asked to review the course of labor.
  - ○ In the first stage, was dilatation and descent in keeping with the Friedman curve?
  - ○ Was oxytocin used?
  - ○ How long did the second stage of labor last? Longer than two hours in a multipara and longer than three hours in a primipara are considered problematic, and cephalopelvic disproportion (CPD) should have been considered.
  - ○ When was the potential for shoulder dystocia recognized?
  - ○ At what point was the senior physician/team called?
  - ○ Was an anesthesiologist called?
  - ○ Was a pediatrician called?
- How was delivery accomplished and by whom?
  - ○ Were specific obstetrical maneuvers (e.g., McRoberts maneuver, suprapubic pressures, Woods screw maneuver, delivery of the posterior arm) applied to accomplish delivery?
- Who performed the maneuvers?
- Were instruments used?
- What was the duration of time between the delivery of the head and the delivery of the shoulders?
- What considerations were given to fracturing the clavicle if all else failed?
- Should a Cesarean section have been performed?
- What was the condition of the infant at delivery?
  - ○ When was the injury diagnosed, and by whom?
  - ○ What was done to treat the injury?
  - ○ Was a neurology or a rehabilitation consultation performed?
  - ○ What were the results and the prognosis?
- Review the infant's follow-up records to determine if there was a degree of resolution of the injury.

## NOTES

1. American College of Obstetricians and Gynecologists/American Academy of Pediatrics, *Guidelines for Perinatal Care,* 5th ed. (Washington, D.C.: ACOG/AAP, 2002), 365–66.
2. Ibid., 90–91.
3. With an uncomplicated pregnancy, a woman should be examined every four weeks for the first 28 weeks, every two to three weeks until 36 weeks' gestation, and weekly thereafter. *See* Ibid., 89.
4. If no risk factors are present, fetal heart rate monitoring should occur every 30 minutes in the first stage of labor. For patients with complications (e.g., fetal growth restriction, preeclampsia), fetal monitoring should be done every 15 minutes in the first stage of labor. *See* American College of Obstetricians and Gynecologists, *Intrapartum Fetal Heart Rate Monitoring,* ACOG Practice Bulletin no. 70 (Washington, D.C.: ACOG, December 2005), 3.
5. Vital signs should be recorded at regular intervals, at least every four hours. This frequency should be increased, particularly as active labor progresses, according to clinical signs and symptoms. *See* ACOG, *Guidelines for Perinatal Care,* 133.
6. The Friedman curve delineates the progress of labor over a period of time by graphic illustration of the results of vaginal exams, specifically descent and dilatation. (Note: Different graph patterns may be seen for nulliparas and multiparas.)
7. For example, in a nullipara, descent of less than 1 cm per hour and dilatation of less than 1.2 cm per hour are considered problematic. In a multipara, descent of less than 2 cm per hour and dilatation of less than 1.5 cm per hour could be problematic. *See* F. G. Cunningham et al., *Williams Obstetrics,* 22nd ed. (New York: McGraw-Hill Professional, 2005), 423.
8. The first stage of labor lasts 6 to 18 hours in a nullipara and about 2 to 10 hours in a multipara. *See* A. H. DeCherney and L. Nathan, *Current Obstetric and Gynecological Diagnosis and Treatment,* 9th ed. (New York: McGraw-Hill Medical, 2003), 214.
9. Bishop developed a method of evaluating a patient for elective induction by applying a score of 0 to 3 for each of the following: position, consistency, effacement and dilation of the cervix, and station of the fetal head. Generally, a score of 9 or better indicates a favorable condition for induction. *See* Cunningham et al., *Williams Obstetrics,* 471.
10. Oxytocin should be discontinued if the number of contractions persists with a frequency of more than 5 in a 10-minute period or of 7 in a 15-minute period, or a persistent non-reassuring fetal heart rate pattern. *See* Ibid., 540.
11. D. N. Danforth and J. R. Scott, *Obstetrics and Gynecology,* 9th ed. (Philadelphia: J. B. Lippincott Co., 2003), 36.
12. ACOG, *Intrapartum Fetal Heart Rate Monitoring,* ACOG Practice Bulletin no. 70, 3.
13. ACOG/AAP, *Guidelines for Perinatal Care,* 145–46.
14. American College of Obstetricians and Gynecologists, *Fetal Macrosomia,* ACOG Practice Bulletin no. 22 (Washington, D.C.: ACOG, November 2000).

15. American College of Obstetricians and Gynecologists, *Diagnosis and Management of Preeclampsia and Eclampsia*, ACOG Practice Bulletin no. 33 (Washington, D.C.: ACOG, January 2002), 1–5.

16. Ibid., 2.

17. Danforth and Scott, *Obstetrics and Gynecology*, 266.

18. ACOG/AAP, *Guidelines for Perinatal Care*, 173.

19. American College of Obstetricians and Gynecologists, *Diagnosis and Management of Preeclampsia and Eclampsia*, ACOG Practice Bulletin no. 33, (Washington, D.C.: January 2002), 4.

20. ACOG/AAP, *Guidelines for Perinatal Care*, 174–75.

21. Cunningham et al., *Williams Obstetrics*, 820.

22. A. Fanaroff and R. Martin, *Neonatal-Perinatal Medicine: Diseases of the Fetus and Infant*, 7th ed. (St. Louis: C.V. Mosby, 2001), 473.

23. United Brachial Plexus Network, Inc., Brachial Plexus Injury Awareness. Available at: http://www.ubpn.org/ubpnweb.nsf/web/information.html. Accessed May 17, 2006.

# Chapter 10

# Investigating Equipment-Related Occurrences

> - Safe Medical Devices Act
> - Products Liability
> - The Investigation

Many claims involve diagnostic, monitoring, or therapeutic equipment. The devices can range from a simple piece of disposable plastic tubing to a complex piece of equipment with computerized components that may be unfamiliar to the investigator. In addition, the device may have multiple parts, may be connected to the building's supply lines, or may be used by more than one individual during the course of a procedure. A special type of investigation is warranted for cases involving equipment-related occurrences.

The investigator should always consider the possibility of mechanical failure or manufacturer defect when reviewing a medical record for liability or devising questions for interviews. As in all investigations, the duties and responsibilities of each party must be explored fully. However, in cases of possible equipment failure, the investigator must also obtain the following information about the device in question: how the device is used, who used the device, other equipment used with this device, and whether the device was connected to the building's electrical and gas lines. The investigator should review the maintenance and service history, along with all applicable contracts and warranties, to help determine responsibility for patient injury. Finally, investigation by an outside expert may be necessary in more serious occurrences to ensure that all aspects of the device and its components are evaluated properly and thoroughly.

Equipment-related occurrences may also involve federal reporting requirements and products liability law. The following sections discuss the Safe Medical Devices Act and certain principles of the law of products liability. These sections feature specific suggestions for investigating product-related occurrences and include an outline of information to obtain about equipment involved in an occurrence. A suggested protocol for responding to equipment-related occurrences is also offered.

## SAFE MEDICAL DEVICES ACT

The Safe Medical Devices Act (SMDA)[1] of 1990 requires that all health care organizations (HCOs) file a report if information exists that reasonably suggests that a medical device or drug has caused or contributed to an adverse occurrence. Specifically, the SMDA requires all "device user facilities" to report all medical device-related deaths on a MedWatch form to the manufacturer and the Food and Drug Administration (FDA) and to report serious illnesses or injuries to the manufacturer (or to the FDA if the manufacturer is not known). The user facility must file such a report no later than ten working days after the HCO becomes aware of the situation. As of May 2005, reactions from implantation, transplantation, infusion, or transfer of human cells, tissues, and cellular and tissue-based products (HCT/P) are on the list of reportable events, and the user facility must file a report no later than 15 days after initial receipt of the information. The FDA supplies MedWatch Forms 3500 and 3500A for reporting voluntary or mandatory reportable events; both forms have been revised as of November 1, 2005, and will expire on October 31, 2008. Detailed instructions, including codes needed to complete the forms, are available on the FDA Web site (http://www.fda.gov/medwatch/). User facilities must submit semiannual summaries of previously reported incidents to the FDA. Failure to do so may result in significant civil or criminal penalties. Reports may be submitted online or by phone, mail, or fax. The Health Insurance Portability and Accountability Act Privacy Rule permits the submission of the SMDA reports by covered entities, such as hospitals and physicians, without patient authorization.

It is important for the investigator to obtain copies of any SMDA reports related to the occurrence being investigated. As well, the investigator should access "Safety Information" on the FDA Web site to review safety alerts, recalls, withdrawals, and important label changes posted since 1996.

The HCO should maintain a file on the device in question that contains only the user reporting records and other records required by the FDA. These records should be kept in a file apart from any occurrence or investigation reports relating to the incident, because any privilege against disclosure afforded the documents in litigation may be waived if they are inadvertently released to an FDA inspector. If not kept separate, they also risk public disclosure under the Freedom of Information Act.

Under the SMDA, the FDA also requires manufacturers to track devices that are (1) considered critical (i.e., whose failure would be reasonably likely to have serious adverse health consequences), (2) considered either life sustaining or life supporting, (3) used outside the device user facility, or (4) permanently implanted in the body. Certain other FDA-designated traceable devices do not fall into these categories.

The SMDA requires manufacturers to set up a mechanism for tracking devices through the market distribution chain, including identification and monitoring of the patients who receive them. The FDA maintains a list of devices that must be tracked. To facilitate that process, the law requires HCOs to notify the manufacturer upon receipt, distribution, implant, or removal of such devices. The HCO must also maintain records on all recipients of FDA-designated devices for notification if a problem arises. Certain nonimplant life-sustaining devices must also be tracked.

Clinical settings exempt from FDA MedWatch reporting include physician offices, dentists, chiropractors, optometrists, nurse practitioners, school-based clinics, employee health clinics, and freestanding care units.

In addition to the federal requirements for reporting medical device and drug-related events, some state health departments also require notification of these events.

## PRODUCTS LIABILITY

The term *products liability* generally refers to the liability of those who supply products (manufacturers, sellers, retailers) to purchasers, users, or nonpurchasers for damages resulting from alleged product defects.[2] Unlike medical malpractice cases, the plaintiff in a products liability action may recover damages by demonstrating that a defendant is "strictly liable" for the plaintiff's injuries. Strict liability often is referred to as *liability without fault*. The plaintiff does not have to prove negligence by the defendant; rather, the emphasis is on whether the product was defective, regardless of fault.

In most U.S. jurisdictions, the general rule holds that anyone who places a product in the stream of commerce (i.e., into the chain of distribution) in a *defective condition that is unreasonably dangerous* to the user or consumer, or to his or her property, is subject to strict liability (i.e., liability without proof of negligence) for harm caused to the ultimate user or consumer, or to his or her property. Strict liability may apply even if the manufacturer or seller exercised reasonable care and/or there was no contractual relationship between the manufacturer or seller and the ultimate user or consumer.

However, a strict liability standard does not make a defendant unconditionally and absolutely responsible for all injuries caused by its products. There are well-recognized defenses to strict liability actions. For example, a defendant generally is not held strictly liable if a consumer materially altered a product after it left the defendant or if the product was used in an unforeseeably dangerous manner.

Thus, under the strict liability theory of recovery, a plaintiff's burden of proof is different than in a medical malpractice claim, because the plaintiff does not have to prove the elements of negligence. In a strict liability action, the plaintiff may need only show that the product was defective and hazardous for its foreseeable use or was marketed without adequate warnings. Often there is no need for a plaintiff to show that the product was negligently manufactured or designed, or that the manufacturer had knowledge of the design defect. As stated previously, a manufacturer may be held liable under a strict liability theory of recovery even though the manufacturer is not "at fault" at all.

It is important to recognize that case law and state statutes often draw distinctions between providers of professional *services* and providers of *products*. Strict liability generally would apply to providers of products but not to providers of professional services. In a majority of U.S. jurisdictions, HCOs, physicians, and other professional health care providers are viewed as providers of professional services, not as providers of products. Therefore, they may not be held to a strict liability standard when products used in rendering professional health care treatment cause patient injuries.

In cases against providers of professional services, a plaintiff must prove negligence. For example, New York's highest court refused to allow an HCO to be held strictly liable for injuries directly related to providing defective blood.[3] A landmark New York case held that the administration of blood to a patient was a service and not the sale of a product.[4] Strict liability also has not been applied to an HCO's administration of medications, the implantation of a pacemaker, or the use of a defective needle.[5] Furthermore, if the user facility has modified the product or engaged in off-label use, this protection is not available.

Despite the majority rule that HCOs are providers of services, not products, there remains a duty to take reasonable care to provide safe and appropriate equipment and to warn of any risks. Also, if the equipment could and should have been tested prior to its use and the testing would have revealed a defect, an HCO could be held liable (on the basis of negligence) if a defect subsequently caused the patient's injury.

It is important to analyze the specific allegations being made against the HCO with regard to any product that is involved in an occurrence under investigation. It is also useful to understand the applicable state laws regarding products liability and health service providers. Such an analysis and understanding helps in identifying the type of information needed in the course of an effective investigation. However, legal counsel should review the question of whether an occurrence involving a possible "product" is a products liability case, a negligence case, or some combination of the two.

## THE INVESTIGATION

Before the investigator begins, the risk manager should make sure the device and its attachments, disposables, and packaging have been saved and sequestered. The risk manager should develop a chain-of-custody paper trail for the device. It is advisable to take photographs of the device and its position in the room before removing the equipment. Control settings should not be changed unless the patient's well-being is at stake. The clinical engineering department should be consulted before turning off, unplugging, or removing batteries from a microprocessor-controlled device, because important information may be stored in its memory.[6] The Emergency Care Research Institute (ECRI), a nonprofit organization that provides expert forensic investigators in biomedical technology, cautions against cleaning, processing, or freezing the equipment or any part of the equipment to prevent damage to important evidence.

The equipment usually can be returned to use after an inspection by biomedical or clinical engineering personnel and documentation of findings.

However, equipment deemed faulty or damaged must be taken out of service and tested by appropriate personnel.

Extreme caution should be exercised when dealing with a manufacturer if a manufacturing defect is probable and a serious injury has occurred. If the equipment-related occurrence resulted in death or serious injury, the manufacturer should not be allowed to remove the equipment or its attachments from the HCO. These cases require that a qualified HCO official be designated to deal with the manufacturer and FDA investigators.

The investigator should begin by obtaining as much information as possible about the device involved in the incident. He or she should obtain copies of the occurrence report and any reports made to the manufacturer or the FDA regarding the SMDA requirements.

*The following information and documents are essential*:

- name and address of the manufacturer
- brand name of the product
- lot and/or serial number(s)
- manufacturer and model number(s)
- description of the product (e.g., size, condition, markings, power rating)
- expiration date or "use before" date
- safety warning(s) given by manufacturer
- notation that the device was meant for single use only
- date of purchase
- last inspection date or next inspection date
- copies of lease or purchase agreements
- sales receipt
- instructional materials
- training courses offered by the manufacturer to the HCO staff

This information may be included as part of the HCO equipment program. If not, much of it can be compiled by reviewing the maintenance schedule and/or the inspection log, which should be kept by the department using the equipment. The information also may be centralized in the HCO's department of clinical or biomedical engineering, or in a SMDA-mandated report. Information on implants may be found in the implant log of the operating room or the central tracking registry.

## Analyzing the Occurrence

After completing the preliminary investigation, the investigator must analyze the occurrence in greater detail. The following steps, recommended by ECRI, may be helpful.

Virtually all equipment-related occurrences involve a system of connected devices.[7] In order to investigate the occurrences, it is important first to categorize devices in one or more of these four device classes[8]:

- *capital equipment* (anesthesia machines, defibrillators);
- *reusable equipment* (surgical instruments);
- *disposable equipment* (breathing circuits, electrodes, plastic tubing, filters);
- the *building's environment* (pipelines supplying gases, electrical power lines)

This categorization enables the investigator to focus on the proper equipment in order to pursue the possible cause(s) of the injury. For example, if an injury involved gas leakage from a piece of tubing during anesthesia, knowing whether the tubing was reusable or disposable will be a decisive factor in determining whether it had outlived its "reusable" life or was possibly manufactured defectively.

Second, the possible cause or causes of the injury should be considered. The following examples are based on ECRI research[9]:

- faulty technological or scientific foundation, in which a lack of knowledge or poorly developed theories resulted in the manufacture of a device that does not meet the intended therapeutic or diagnostic purpose
- a design or manufacturing defect due to inadequate testing of a device for its intended use by a typical health care user
- random component failure (an unpredictable malfunction of materials or components)
- packaging/labeling error
- user error—the most common cause of equipment-related occurrences (According to ECRI, user error causes more than 50% of alleged device failures.) Typical instances include:
  - ignoring of labels

- ○ improper assemblage or connection, or accidental disconnection of the device
- ○ incorrect programming or control setting of the device
- ○ failure to perform an inspection before using the device
- ○ reliance solely on automated monitoring by the device
- ○ physical abuse of the device
- ○ faulty maintenance
- nonmalicious tampering (alteration of a device due to negligence or lack of knowledge)
- sabotage (alteration of a device with the intent to harm)
- manufacturer error (failure to inspect and test components, raw materials, and/or systems prior to distribution)
- faulty repair, preventive maintenance, or calibration (whether by biomedical or clinical engineering technicians employed by the HCO, independent contractors, or personnel working for the manufacturer or distributor)
- software error (inadequate testing of device's computer components)

Third, the investigator should consider the various interfaces that may have caused an injury—between user and device, within the device itself, between device and patient, between device and attachments, and/or between device and HCO environment.

Following are *explanations of each of these interfaces,* based on ECRI research[10]:

- *Interface between user and device.* To assess the user/device interface adequately, the investigator must ascertain how the device was used and the user's level of training and experience with the device and its components. The investigator needs to know whether the user consulted instruction manuals and required any supervision. The investigator must also determine who trained the user and what information was provided.
- *Interface within the device itself.* Software used by the device's computer or microprocessor can malfunction. The investigator should question bioengineering personnel about software "glitches" if a computerized component is involved.

- *Interface between device and patient.* The investigator must determine how the device was attached to the patient and how it responded to feedback (EEG signals, temperature, respiratory volumes) from the patient. The investigator should find out whether the patient was sensitive to materials used and whether concurrent drug therapy may have been a factor in the patient's reaction. If the patient was using the device, is it possible that he or she ignored warnings and instructions?
- *Interface between device and any disposable attachments.* According to ECRI, even though disposable attachments may be responsible for an incident, this possibility is frequently overlooked during the initial phases of an investigation.[11]
- *Interface between device and environment.* A possible electrical supply interruption or failure in the medical gas supply could be a factor. An electrical engineer may need to determine whether electromagnetic or radio frequency interference from nearby transformers, electrical equipment, or communication systems, including cell phones, could have been responsible for the device malfunction. Failure in medical gas supply systems supporting anesthesia machines, ventilators and resuscitators, and oxygen delivery equipment is responsible for causing many preventable deaths, according to ECRI.[12]

Experts at ECRI caution against simply testing the device without addressing these concerns. Such tests frequently show that the device is operating as designed but fail to provide useful information as to how the patient was injured.

### Interviewing Parties Involved

In most medical malpractice cases, the parties interviewed have made entries in the patient's medical record. Some of those interviewed in equipment-related occurrences may *not* have made such entries. The record does, however, indicate key people who used the equipment and treated the patient during and after the occurrence. It is helpful to ascertain the standard procedure for preparing and operating the device.

The investigator should interview anyone directly involved in the occurrence: the technicians and other personnel who service the equipment; those responsible for sterilizing, inspecting, and maintaining it; and anyone who maintained, serviced, or in any way touched the equipment prior to or during its use. In-service educators should also be interviewed regarding the training qualifications of the parties involved in the occurrence, and a demonstration of how the equipment is set up and used should also be requested.

The investigator should "re-create" the scene by interviewing personnel who completed the occurrence report or reports to the manufacturer or FDA. The sample questions that follow can be helpful when interviewing people involved in the occurrence, those who came into contact with the equipment, bioengineering staff, and purchasing agents.

*Persons involved in the occurrence should be asked the following:*

- When was the failure noted?
- How long was the device applied before the occurrence was noted?
- When was the device removed from service or from the patient?
- Who first noted the failure?
- What was done once the failure was noted?
- How was the device being used at that time?
- Who was operating the device at the time of the occurrence?
- What was the experience of the device operator?
- What was the condition of the device while being used?
- What happened at the time of the occurrence? Was there
  - a chemical reaction?
  - a mechanical failure?
  - an electrical failure?
  - any unusual light or sound?
  - smoke?
  - a change in color or appearance of the equipment during the failure?
- Did users attend any instructional/training sessions for the equipment?
- Were instructions/maintenance manuals available for use?
- Did users have any contact with the manufacturer after the occurrence?

*HCO personnel who maintain or prepare the device for use should be asked the following:*

- Was the device previously sterilized? If so, what method of sterilization was used?

- Were any modifications made to the device before its use?
- Were the dials set properly?
- Could the device have been judged defective by inspection prior to use?
- Who was responsible for inspecting the device prior to its use?
- When was the last maintenance and inspection performed?
- Were any repairs made at that time?
- Could the device have failed because of misuse?
- Were any safety devices (alarm systems) used concurrently?
- Was any other equipment in use that could have interfered with the device?
- Was any preparation done prior to using the equipment? Were the manufacturer's instructions followed?
- Were any other items (attachments, disposables) used with the device?
- Were all disposables and their packaging retained?

*Biomedical engineering staff members should be asked the following:*

- Who was responsible for inspecting and maintaining the equipment?[13]
- What was the date of the last inspection?
- Does the biomedical engineering department receive FDA bulletins and alerts? If so, what procedure is followed within the HCO to remove or evaluate a device under alert?
- Is there a contract between the manufacturer and the HCO for the device?
- Were HCO personnel involved in assembling the equipment?
- How was the product or equipment stored?
- Were the manufacturer and/or the FDA notified of the occurrence/ equipment malfunction in accordance with the SMDA? If so, who filed the report(s)? What, specifically, was reported? How did the manufacturer respond, if at all?
- Were any other prior occurrences, similar failures, or complaints noted by HCO users? Were these problems reported?
- Were any repairs done? If so, who made them and when were they done?
- Was the equipment HCO-approved?
- If device malfunction is established, what caused the malfunction?

*The investigator may also want to review the purchasing agreement and interview the department administrator to establish the following:*

- ownership of the device (the HCO? a private physician? or is it leased from the manufacturer?). If leased, obtain the lease agreement.
- nature of the express warranty made by the manufacturer
- warranties made by the salesperson
- marketing literature claims about the product
- indemnification/hold-harmless contracts provided by or to the manufacturer
- other complaints or recalls of the product

### Assessing the Nature of the Alleged Injury

The investigator should obtain a description of the nature and extent of the patient's injuries, addressing such issues as:

- type of injury sustained by the patient and location on patient's body in relation to the attached equipment
- care rendered to the patient
- information given to the patient about the incident
- existence of any photographs of the injury

By the end of the investigation, the investigator should be able to identify the equipment in question, its type or category (disposable, reusable), the user at the time of the occurrence, and how the equipment was used. The next step is to assess the various interfaces involved and possible areas of liability. Bioengineering experts should be consulted to evaluate the product and determine whether the equipment was defective or whether the user was negligent. If the equipment is found to be defective, the investigator should comment on the causal relationship, if any, between the defective product and the occurrence and/or injury. Manufacturer's information about the equipment and how it should be used should be attached to the investigation report.

## More Information on Standards for Use and Recalls of a Product

*Many groups and agencies conduct tests and collect information on biomedical products, including:*

- ECRI—5200 Butler Pike, Plymouth Meeting, PA 19462, (610) 825-6000
- The Underwriter Laboratory, Inc.—333 Pifingsten Road, Northbrook, IL 60062-2096, (847) 272-8800
- professional engineering societies
- government inspection agencies
- the FDA—http://www.fda.gov/medwatch/

## NOTES

1. Safe Medical Devices Act of 1990, Pub L. No. 101-629, 104 Stat. 4511 (1990) (codified at 21 C.F.R. §§ 803, 807, and 1271.350 (a)).
2. W.P. Keeton et al., *Prosser and Keeton on Torts*, 5th ed. (St. Paul: West Publishing, 1984), 677.
3. S. Becker, *Health Care Law: A Practical Guide*,13.05. (Chicago: Ross & Hardies, 2003), 13.05
4. Perlmutter v. Beth David Hospital, 308 N.Y. 100, 106, 123 N.E.2d 792, 795 (1954) (codified at N.Y. Pub. Health Law § 580(4)).
5. Becker, 13.06.
6. ECRI, "Incident Reporting and Management: Risk Management Tips for Device-Related Events," *HRC (Healthcare Risk Control)*2.1 (May 2004), 3.
7. M. Bruley, "Investigating Equipment-Related Accidents" (paper presented at the spring seminar of the Association of Healthcare Risk Management of New York, New York City, 1993). Updated in interview by Nancy Acerbo-Kozuchowski on February 2, 2006.
8. Ibid.
9. ECRI, "Incident Reporting and Management: Medical Device Adverse Event Recognition and Investigation," *HRC (Healthcare Risk Control)* 2 (May 2004), 2-5.
10. Ibid., 8–9.
11. Ibid., 8.
12. Ibid., 4.
13. The Joint Commission on Accreditation of Healthcare Organizations (JCAHO) requires that medical equipment be maintained, tested, and inspected (Standard EC.6.20) and that a written management plan describe the process an HCO implements to manage the effective, safe, and reliable operation of medical equipment (Standard EC.6.10). *See* JCAHO, *Hospital Accreditation Standards, 2006: Accreditation Manual for Hospitals,* vol.1 (Oakbrook Terrace, IL: Joint Commission Resources, 2005).

# Chapter 11

## Reviewing and Maintaining the Claim File

- What Is in the Claim File?
- Glossary of Terms

This chapter discusses the claim file[1] that is set up to collect documents, reports, and correspondence relative to potential or actual lawsuits. Each risk manager organizes his or her files differently. Some use a strict chronological system; others set up categories for expert reviews, legal documents, correspondence, and bills. When a file is maintained in chronological order, the most current documents are in the front (or top) of the file, allowing easy access to the most recent information. *It is important to keep files in order so that information is readily accessible.* The risk manager and claim investigator use the claim file on an ongoing basis to evaluate discovery findings and possible significant shifts in the case value. The file must be kept up-to-date at all times for effective claim management.

### WHAT IS IN THE CLAIM FILE?

The claim file generally consists of a variety of correspondence and reports, including legal papers, defense attorney memoranda, reserve information, summaries of meetings in which claims are discussed, insurance company correspondence, investigation reports, and reports to state and federal agencies regarding the claim. All related correspondence should remain in the file so that the claim can be monitored adequately and so that the risk manager's and claim investigator's paperwork can be kept in a single location. Exactly what is contained in a particular institution's claim file depends on the flow of correspondence and the risk manager's responsibilities.

A good way to learn about the investigation and legal process is to review all of the information contained in a well-developed claim. Some redundancy may be noticed throughout the file. As the file is reviewed, the nature of the claim becomes evident. Included in the file are periodic analyses of the claim (generally by defense attorneys). These analyses are essential reading, as they focus on the pertinent medical/legal facts and issues of the claim. These reviews are based on investigation reports and discovery and enable underwriters and claim attorneys to set adequate reserves and notify appropriate excess insurance carriers of the potential need to use their layer(s) of coverage. Everything related to the medical/legal aspects of a claim should be in the file.

*The following items are listed in the usual order in which the risk manager receives them. The list may not correspond to the way specific files are set up.*

- Attorney's Request Letter or Letter of Claim
- Summons with Complaint
- Verified Answer
- First Investigation Report
- Central Index Bureau (CIB) Response Card
- Bill of Particulars
- Examination Before Trial (EBT) of Plaintiff
- Defense Expert Report or In-house Reviews
- EBT of Defense Witnesses
- Follow-up Investigation Report
- EBT of Nonparty Witness (if applicable)
- Physical Examination
- Medical Record Reviews (relevant prior or subsequent care)
- Amended or Supplemental Bills of Particulars
- Plaintiff Expert Report
- Note of Issue/Statement of Readiness
- Claim Conference

- Pretrial Conference
- Trial
- Appeal (if applicable)
- Satisfaction of Judgment
- Closing Forms

Before reviewing a file, it may help to become familiar with the following terms, which are often found in a legal file. Some of these terms are discussed in the chapters on insurance and/or medical law (Chapters 15 and 16, respectively). The terms vary from state to state. The following are those most widely used.

## GLOSSARY OF TERMS

**Affidavit**—a sworn statement setting forth facts known to the individual signing the affidavit. Because the person signing the affidavit is *under oath*, he or she must read it carefully to be certain of its accuracy. An affidavit is usually drafted by an attorney on the basis of information supplied by the signer (*affiant*). Exhibits (i.e., copies of relevant documents) may be attached to an affidavit. Both the plaintiff and the defendant can file an affidavit. The affidavit is sometimes submitted with a *memorandum of law* that supports the statements made in the affidavit.

**Appeal**—a legal procedure by which a party who loses a motion or a trial in one court seeks to have a higher court overturn the lower court decision

**Attorney's Request Letter**—a letter from a patient's attorney requesting a copy of the patient's medical record

**Brief or Memorandum of Law**—a statement submitted to a court by a lawyer summarizing the factual and legal arguments in support of an action the lawyer wants the court to take

**Case Closings**—Cases are closed after the parties come to a final agreement to resolve the case—with or without payment of damages. The agreement that ends the case can take place at any time during the life of the case. It can also occur during trial or between the judgment and an appeal.

The following is a description of the types of case closings generally used by insurers:

- **Settlement**: an out-of-court resolution of the claim agreed to by both sides. A settlement generally includes a payment of some negotiated amount. It does not necessarily indicate an admission of fault on the part of the defense or an admission of no liability on the part of the plaintiff. If the plaintiff is an infant or incompetent, or if a wrongful death action is involved, the settlement must be submitted to the court for approval by way of a *compromise* order.
- **Discontinuance**: The plaintiff decides to withdraw the lawsuit against a particular party. This results in a discontinuance by the judge.
- **Dismissal**: The defense moves to end a case, and the court grants the motion. There are two ways this can be done:
  - *Discontinuance with Prejudice*: The court dismisses the action, and the plaintiff cannot pursue the claim any further.
  - *Discontinuance without Prejudice*: The case is dismissed, but the court grants the plaintiff the right to recommence litigation against the defendant.
- **Abandonment**: Defense counsel closes the case in its internal files due to lack of legal activity on the part of the plaintiff after a sufficient amount of time. This has no legal bearing whatsoever on the case. There is a possibility that the case may "come to life" again.
- **Plaintiff's Verdict**: a trial that results in a finding for the plaintiff
- **Defendant's Verdict**: a trial that results in a finding for the defense

**Central Index Bureau Report (CIB)**—CIB is a national nonprofit organization founded by a group of insurers to store information on claims against insurance companies. All claims are filed with the CIB, for both medical malpractice and general liability. Subscribers to the CIB can obtain reports about whether a plaintiff has instituted lawsuits in the previous five years.

**Codefendant**—a party being sued who has separate insurance coverage and is represented by separate counsel. Codefendants should not be contacted other than through their respective attorneys.

**Default**—a failure by a party to respond to a summons or other legal action. Depending on the circumstances, this can have very serious consequences, including the entry of a *default judgment* awarding the case to the opposing party. Once the court enters a default judgment, an *inquest* (a type of hearing) is held to determine the award for damages. In that case, the defendant loses the opportunity to argue against liability.

**Defendant**—the party or parties being sued

**Discovery**—This term is used to denote all pretrial procedures used by plaintiff and defense attorneys to uncover information related to the case. Limited discovery also can be done by the plaintiff's attorney prior to the lawsuit to determine whether there is sufficient evidence to institute a lawsuit or to identify involved individuals. Because of the exploratory nature of the discovery process, the scope of evidence sought is wide ranging and may include hearsay and some privileged information. However, it is important to note that not all information discovered may be admitted into evidence at trial. Under current procedures, the parties ordinarily can expect to exchange discovery demands and responses among themselves without involving the court unless they are in a dispute.

Discovery procedures include the following:

- *Depositions or Examinations Before Trial (EBTs)*: This generally is the most important part of the discovery process. Each side can conduct depositions of its adversaries and of third parties with knowledge of the facts. The EBT usually takes place in a law office. Parties and other witnesses are questioned under oath with a court reporter present to transcribe the proceedings. The questioning is designed to elicit information about the strengths and weaknesses of the other side's case. The witness should be prepared in advance by his or her own attorney. The EBT is considered to be sworn testimony, and parts of the EBT may be read at trial to point out discrepancies in statements made by witnesses. In tort litigation, the plaintiff is likely to be deposed first by the defense attorney. Often, someone from the hospital's medical records department is the first person to be deposed (by the plaintiff's attorney) to verify the authenticity of the medical record.
- *Discovery Motions*: Discovery motions are filed when one of the parties declines to comply with discovery demands. In prediscovery proceedings, the plaintiff generally is seeking a copy of the medical record. During discovery, the plaintiff's attorney seeks, among other things, hospital bills, names and addresses of persons involved in the patient's care, hospital policies, and photographs. The defendant's

attorney may seek information about medical treatment the plaintiff has had, information about the plaintiff's financial position, or an order directing plaintiff's medical examinations. Before responding, the motion should be reviewed by some knowledgeable person in authority to ensure that privileged information is not released.

- *Expert Opinion*: Each party is entitled to ask physicians (or other health care practitioners) with a relevant specialty to evaluate the treatment or injury in dispute. The objective is for the party using the expert to obtain a review favorable to that party's position. Medical experts are asked to comment on the care rendered by the defendant in light of the plaintiff's allegations. Experts' opinions serve several functions. Traditionally, the goal is to obtain an honest and objective review of the medical care rendered. It should, however, also be favorable to the position of the party using the expert so that the testimony can be presented as part of that party's argument at trial. More recently, with the advent of the National Practitioner Data Bank, insurance organizations are using experts to determine the degree of responsibility of a health care practitioner involved in a case for reporting purposes. Expert reviews are usually confidential, depending on the rules of the specific court or the agreement between the parties. Generally, a verbal opinion from an expert is protected from discovery in litigation unless the expert's opinion is to be used in the litigation. In those instances in which the expert does not provide a written report, a summary of the expert's opinion, prepared by the party's attorney, is exchanged to avoid the element of surprise at trial. A written expert opinion, on the other hand, could be (depending on the court) discoverable regardless of whether the expert's opinion is to be used in the litigation. And a written expert opinion by a physician who actually examined the patient is always discoverable. Each side may depose the other's discoverable experts to determine what the testimony will be and may cross-examine those experts in court. As a practical matter, the attorneys should meet with the expert prior to the review to discuss the medical/legal aspects of the case.

- *Interrogatories*: These are questions submitted by one party to another. For example, the plaintiff may ask for the educational background of a physician. The defendant may ask for the name and expected testimony of an expert witness. A specific date should be stated for a response to interrogatories. The investigator may be asked to obtain the information needed to answer the interrogatories. Some of the information sought by interrogatories overlaps with information sought by a demand for a bill of particulars, but the two demands are used at different stages of the case.

- *Note of Issue/Statement of Readiness*: This document is filed by the plaintiff's attorney when discovery is completed and he or she is ready to proceed to trial. The case is then placed on the trial calendar.

- *Physical Examination*: This is an evaluation of the plaintiff's current physical/emotional condition, which is used by each party to determine the extent of physical/psychological damages. Each side has the right to choose a physician to evaluate the patient. Additionally, when multiple injuries are claimed, it may be possible to have different medical specialists conduct examinations. For instance, if a plaintiff alleges that negligence by an obstetrician during a delivery resulted in an Erb's palsy and developmental delays, the defense may want a pediatric neurologic examination to determine the extent of the brachial plexus injury and a neuropsychological evaluation to determine the degree of developmental delay. It is recommended that the defense counsel or their representatives be present at the physical examination of the patient.

- *Subpoena*: a legal order by which a witness is subjected to the jurisdiction of the court and required to give relevant information

  A subpoena may be of one of the following two types:

  - *Subpoena ad Testificandum*: a subpoena to appear and testify at a trial or an EBT

  - *Subpoena Duces Tecum*: a subpoena to produce documents such as medical records, pathology slides, or X-rays at the trial. When documents are requested from a nonparty, it is common practice to require an officer or employee of the nonparty to appear personally to verify the authenticity of the document. This formality can be waived if all parties agree. The rules of some courts permit parties to obtain documents by making a formal *Request to Produce* without going through all the steps required to obtain a subpoena.

The risk manager or other knowledgeable person should review all the subpoenas as they are prepared by the attorneys for the opposing parties, because these subpoenas have not necessarily been reviewed by a judge, and the health care organization may not be required to produce the information requested. In other words, care should be taken to ensure that it is legally proper to release the documents being requested. When in doubt, the opposing party may be required to obtain a court-ordered subpoena. This court-ordered subpoena is called *so ordered*.

A valid subpoena usually contains the following:

○ Names of the plaintiff and defendant

○ Case number

○ Name of the court

○ Name and address of the person ordered to attend

○ Date, time, and place of the requested appearance

○ Name and telephone number of the attorney who had the subpoena issued

○ A list of the items the recipient is ordered to bring (if it is a *subpoena duces tecum*)

• *Motion*: a written or oral application made to the court or judge to obtain a rule or order directing some action in favor of the applicant. A motion is usually made within the framework of an existing action or proceeding (e.g., motion to dismiss, motion for a protective order, motion for a new trial).

• *Notice of Motion*: This document, which can take many different forms, serves as notification that a party is petitioning the court for an order. The notice of motion usually specifies the action being sought and, if appropriate, the time frame for compliance. The other parties respond in support or opposition to the motion. Motions can be filed with respect to many different legal issues, including disputes over discovery and attempts by defendants to have the case dismissed. Accompanying the motion may be one or more *supporting affidavits* and exhibits. Many motions also are accompanied by a brief.

• *Order to Show Cause*: On the request of one of the parties, the court issues an order directing the opposing party to appear and present to the court reasons that a particular order, decree, or injunction should not be confirmed or executed. For example, a court may be petitioned to order that one's adversaries explain why a request for medical records has not been honored. An order to show cause is served in lieu of a notice of motion and is usually intended to expedite a ruling by the court.

**Judgment**—the formal and official decision of a court regarding the respective rights and claims of the parties to a lawsuit

**Letter of Claim**—This letter may be sent by a patient, a relative, the patient's attorney, or another representative to a hospital administrator or doctor. It alleges an injury and seeks a monetary settlement, compensation, or some sort of redress. Legal action may not necessarily be forthcoming if the patient is satisfied with the institution's response.

**Lien**—a claim by an interested nonparty against the recovery of damages by plaintiff. The interested nonparty is usually the health insurance carrier that paid medical expenses related to the malpractice. A common example is a Medicaid lien in which reimbursement for health care is demanded from the plaintiff and defendant; either party may be obligated to pay. Private carriers can also assert a lien. A portion of the proceeds of any recovery is generally earmarked to repay the lien.

Because the presence and amount of a lien affects settlement, it is to the advantage of all parties to monitor and investigate the presence of any liens. In many instances, it is possible to negotiate (or compromise) the amount of a lien to allow plaintiffs to receive greater compensation or lower the value of a settlement for defendants, while still repaying the carrier for services provided.

**Plaintiff**—The plaintiff is generally the patient or another claimant who has filed suit. An example of another claimant who is not a patient in a malpractice case is the administrator of the patient's estate or a parent or guardian of a patient who is a minor.

**Pleadings**—the documents submitted by plaintiff and defense counsel that contain formal allegations of their respective claims and defenses. Under the rules of civil procedure, the pleadings consist of a complaint, an answer, a reply to a counterclaim, an answer to a cross-claim, a third-party complaint, and a third-party answer. In states in which the bill of particulars is permitted, it is considered a part of the pleadings and not a discovery device. Any pleading may be amended. Here are definitions of some types of pleadings:

- *Answer*: This is the defendant's response to the complaint. The defendant admits or denies each of the plaintiff's allegations set forth in the complaint. Also contained within the Answer are any *affirmative defenses* to mitigate or provide a complete defense to the plaintiff's allegations (e.g., culpable conduct, expiration of statute of limitations)

- **Bill of Particulars**: A defense attorney obtains a bill of particulars by making a formal *demand*. In a bill of particulars, the plaintiff spells out the allegations and includes specific items, such as the names of parties involved in the lawsuit, the date and time of the occurrence, the alleged malpractice and negligence, the plaintiff's injuries, and special damages such as medical expenses already paid or lost wages. The bill of particulars must specifically answer the demands set forth by the defense attorney. A separate bill of particulars is generally required for each defendant.

- **Complaint**: a formal statement of allegations upon which the plaintiff is basing his or her claim for damages. The complaint often uses standard (boilerplate) language and usually specifies little more than the day of occurrence or day of hospitalization during which the injury occurred. Thus, the complaint may be very vague. Many of the details of the case may not be spelled out until the bill of particulars is obtained. In malpractice actions, the complaint usually states that the amount of damages cannot be determined at this time.

- **Counterclaim**: This occurs when a defendant, as part of his or her answer, makes a claim for damages of relief against the plaintiff in an independent cause of action. In malpractice cases, a counterclaim may arise when a hospital sues a patient for payment of a bill and the patient then countersues for medical malpractice.

- **Cross-claim**: This occurs when a defendant makes a claim against another defendant or when a plaintiff makes a claim against another plaintiff involved in the same lawsuit.

- **Third-Party Action**: Most often called an *impleader*, this is one of a variety of actions whereby the defendant seeks contribution and indemnification from a third party. That defendant seeking contribution is then called the *defendant/third-party plaintiff*. The new defendant is called the *third-party defendant*.

**Punitive Damages**—a claim for an award sought to punish the defendant for conduct that is considered beyond that of professional negligence. Such behavior is usually described in the pleadings as "wanton and willful" or "malicious." Because this conduct is against public policy, insurance policies do not provide coverage for its recovery and the individual defendant must be made aware of such claims as early as possible. Since the defendant's personal assets are at risk, he or she may wish to retain additional (personal) counsel to keep an eye on the progress of the case. Punitive claims are usually withdrawn or dismissed, and it is rare (but not impossible) for such damages to be awarded.

**Stipulation**—an agreement made by attorneys on opposing sides of a legal action

**Summary Judgment**—When the court grants summary judgment to a party, it has reviewed the defense and plaintiff's motion papers and found that there are no substantive issues of fact in the case; therefore, there is no case. This is a way of accelerating the judgment to finalize the case.

**Summons**—This document begins a lawsuit by giving the defendant notice that if he or she does not appear within a certain number of days, judgment will be entered against him or her. It also specifies the location of all proceedings related to the case.

**Sustainable Value**—the final value of a case after all appeals are exhausted. This is determined by a court, not the jury, and is not applicable to settlements. Sustainable values provide guidance when assessing the value of a case for setting reserves and negotiating settlements.

**Venue**—The venue is the place at which a lawsuit is brought. This is usually the county in which the patient resides, but it can also be the location of the occurrence or a defendant's residence or business.

**Verified**—If a party swears to any legal document, it is said to be *verified*.

## NOTES

1. In some institutions, the claim file is referred to as the *legal file*. In this book, however, we consistently use the term *claim file*.

# Chapter 12

# Writing the Investigation Report

---

- Objectives of an Investigation Report
- Guidelines for Using the Investigation Report Format
- Sample Investigation Report
- Guidelines for Using the Obstetrical Investigation Report Format
- Sample Obstetrical Investigation Report

---

This chapter details the step-by-step process of preparing a claim investigation report. Prior to writing the report, the investigator has already reviewed and analyzed the patient's medical record and pertinent documents, interviewed key witnesses, and identified the medical/legal issues in the case. The suggested report format given here, together with samples of appropriate phrasing, helps the investigator to organize and present the material so that the health care organization (HCO) or defense attorney can respond effectively to the claim.

The discussion of each section of the investigation report covers the information to be inserted as well as when a point requires further explanation. The first part of this chapter describes the process for preparing a

*Note: Although descriptions used throughout this chapter are drawn from the authors' experiences with actual cases, all names and personal characteristics have been created solely for purposes of illustration.*

basic investigation report (**Exhibit 12-1**). The second part is devoted to the preparation of an obstetrical investigation report (**Exhibit 12-2**).[1]

See the Appendix as well the CD-ROM included with this book for blank forms to use for investigation reports (**Appendix 12-A** and **12-B**) plus a sample test result chart (**Appendix 12-C**).

## OBJECTIVES OF AN INVESTIGATION REPORT

The investigation report provides a complete account of the events surrounding a case of alleged or potential malpractice, the results of interviews, and an evaluation of the significance of this information.

The claim investigator functions as an investigative reporter. Rather than simply reciting the facts gathered from the review of records and from interviews, the investigator uses the information to construct a coherent pattern of the facts relative to the occurrence and injury.

The report should be written in an easy-to-read style and should tell a story. The investigator should remember the report is being written for various people, including defense attorneys and HCO administrators, to use as a guide in evaluating the medical aspects of the case and for preparing a defense.

The investigation report should center on the issues of the case. Because the issues should be evident to the reader throughout the report, the investigator must identify the main area(s) of loss exposure of the case *prior to* writing the report. Such issues could include an identified breach in the standard of care, allegations made by the plaintiff, and areas uncovered during the course of the investigation that might be problematic to the defense of the case. The report should be written so these issues are adequately addressed, explored, and supported with excerpts of documentation from the medical record or from the interviews.

## GUIDELINES FOR USING THE INVESTIGATION REPORT FORMAT

The following are guidelines for writing an investigation report using a specific report format. Two sample investigation reports are included for your review (see Exhibits 12-1 and 12-2). Examples from the same cases are used throughout the guidelines to explain the type of information that should be inserted into each section of a report.

## Investigation Report Headings

The following is a list of the items included in the heading section of the report:

- *Dated*—This is the date the final draft of the report is typed.
- *Patient*—The patient's name plus "deceased" in parentheses, if applicable, should be indicated.
- *Claimant*—The name of the individual who commenced the action plus, in parentheses if applicable, the relationship to the patient (e.g., parent, administrator, executrix) should be indicated.
- *To*—This is the name(s) of the law firm and attorney or risk management professional to whom the report is being sent.
- *cc*—This is the name(s) of the individual(s) or law firm to whom the report is being copied.
- *By*—The investigator's name and title should be inserted.
- *Institution*—The name of the HCO where the occurrence took place should be inserted.
- *File #*—This is the number assigned to the claim file.
- *Defense Attorney File #*—This is the number assigned to the defense attorney's claim file.
- *Status*—How the case was investigated (e.g., as a priority alert, an attorney's request letter (ARL), a letter of claim (LOC), a summons) should be indicated.[2]
- *Severity Code*—This is the appropriate number in the Injury Severity Code of the National Association of Insurance Commissioners (NAIC).[3]
- *Interviews*—The number of interviews contained in the report should be indicated.
- *Pages*—This is the total number of pages in the report.

See Exhibit 12-1 for a sample of the heading section of an investigation report.

## Treatment Dates

The *Treatment Dates* section provides a summary of where and when the patient received treatment, including hospitalizations, outpatient department (OPD) visits, private office visits, and emergency department (ED) visits. The investigator gives the reader an overview of all known records available for review, including records from other HCOs. Records pertaining to treatment rendered before or after the occurrence may require authorization from the patient/plaintiff before the investigator can review them.

First, where the patient received treatment, followed by the corresponding medical record number and/or ED number, should be indicated. If only office records are accessible, this fact should be indicated in the report. Date(s) of *all* treatment should be listed chronologically, the earliest first. An asterisk should be placed next to the treatment date or dates that cover the actual date of occurrence. Finally, the actual date(s) of occurrence should be noted.

Sample *Treatment Dates* Section

*Treatment Dates*

| Office, Institution, or Department | Med. Record # | --Through-- | |
| --- | --- | --- | --- |
| General Hospital ED | 4,600 | *9/27/05 | 9/27/05 |
| General Hospital | 1,000 | *9/30/05 | 10/7/05 |
| Dr. Green's Private Office | N/D | 10/10/05 | 11/8/05 |
| * Relevant treatment records. | N/D = Not documented. | | |
| **Date of Occurrence** | 9/27/05 | | |

## First Reported

The *First Reported* section provides an overview of how this case first came to the attention of the risk management department. Each alerting communication, the date it was received, and the sender should be listed, in chronological order. This information is generally obtained from the claim file.

***The following list includes several possible reporting mechanisms:***

- *Alert*— The date the alert (or internal reporting mechanism) was reported should be inserted.
- *ARL*— The date the ARL was received and the name of the law firm or attorney who requested the medical record should be indicated.
- *LOC*—The date the LOC was received, along with the name of the individual or attorney who sent it, should be indicated.
- *Summons*— The date the first summons was served and the name of the attorney or law firm representing the plaintiff should be noted.

If more than one reporting mechanism was involved, the investigator should indicate the dates they were all received.

Sample *First Reported* Section

| First Reported | Date | Plaintiff's Attorney |
|---|---|---|
| Alert | | |
| Attorney's Request Letter | 11/21/05 | Jean Monte, Esq. |
| Patient Complaint/Letter of Claim | | |
| Summons | 1/9/06 | Jean Monte, Esq. |

## Parties Involved

The *Parties Involved* section identifies all of the individuals involved in the occurrence or alleged malpractice, as well as those who may become involved in the case at some point by virtue of their relationship or responsibility to the patient. This section clarifies the title, position, and employment status of all key parties who are referred to in the investigation report. For the convenience of defense counsel, individuals who are covered by the HCO's medical malpractice policy should be listed separately from those who are *not* covered. This arrangement provides an easy reference for readers needing to review an individual's title and employment status at any point during the discovery process.

*The following guidelines should be followed in completing this section:*

- The names of all the parties involved, whether insured by the HCO's policy or not, should be indicated, including
  - all named defendants and codefendants, including hospitals and corporations (available in the caption of the summons)
  - all those directly involved in the occurrence
  - prior and/or subsequent treating physicians—in particular, physicians who treated the patient *after* the occurrence for the alleged injury

- The following format should be used:
  - Names of individuals insured by the HCO should appear in boldface.
  - The parties named in the action should be listed first, followed by those individuals who were interviewed. The list should be further separated by whether or not the individual is covered by the HCO's insurance policy.
  - Full name, title, clinical status, department affiliation, and employment status *at the time of the occurrence* (i.e., employee, nonemployee) should be indicated for each individual listed.
  - For any individual no longer employed by the HCO, the last date of employment (LDE) and last known address (LKA) should be included.
  - Any unique employment/coverage agreements (e.g., residents rotating from other institutions, special fellowships, moonlighting physicians) should be indicated.
  - In order to indicate who will be involved in the legal proceedings, each named defendant and codefendant should be listed, followed by "Named Defendant" or "Named Codefendant" (underlined to highlight for defense counsel both insured and noninsured parties).
  - If any named codefendant or party involved in the case is not affiliated with the institution, this should be noted. This alerts the defense counsel that authorization may be required to review records from other hospitals and private medical offices.
  - If a defendant was named in the lawsuit but never served, "Named Defendant (named, never served)" should be inserted.
  - The names of all parties interviewed should be marked with an asterisk (*).

Sample Parties Involved Section

---

PARTIES INVOLVED

**A.  Insured**

 1.  **General Hospital**: <u>Named Defendant.</u>

 2.  **\*Phillips, Robert: MD,** PGY-1, Pediatrics, Employee.

 3.  **Jackson, Mandy: RN,** Staff Nurse, Employee. LDE: 11/30/2005. LKA: 30 Maple Drive, Smithtown, NY 11787. (516) 334-8742.

**B.  Parties with Other Insurance Coverage**

 1.  Bane, Robert: MD, Attending, Surgery, Nonemployee. Not affiliated with General Hospital. Primary: CIMLM (limits: 1 million/occurrence). Excess: SYNAH (limits: 1 million/occurrence).

 2.  Green, William: MD, Attending, Surgery, Nonemployee. Primary: HCI Insurance Company (limits: 1 million/occurrence). Excess: SYNAH Insurance Company (limits: 1 million/occurrence).

*Interview contained in this report.

---

## In-House Reviews

For in-house reviews, the names of those who performed the reviews should be listed, using the same format as in the *Parties Involved* section.

Sample In-House Review Section

---

**IN-HOUSE REVIEWS**

 1.  **\*Stone, Stanley: M.D.,** Director, Department of Surgery, Employee.

*Interview not contained in this report.

---

## Patient Demographic Information

Using documentation from the medical record, the investigator should note the patient's age, sex, race, religion, and occupation. The presence of any dependent children or any other dependents, such as an elderly parent, at the time of the occurrence should be specified. This information aids defense counsel and insurers in establishing liability exposure in terms of possible dollar payouts. If any information requested was not documented,

"N/D" should be inserted. The boxes for occupation, marital status, and dependents can be deleted from the report format in cases that involve young children.

---

*Sample Patient Demographic Information Section*

---

*Patient Demographic Information*

---

| *Age* 14 | *Sex* Female | *Race* Caucasian | *Religion* Catholic |
|---|---|---|---|
| **Occupation** | Student | | **Insurance** N/D |
| **Marital Status** | Single | | |
| **Dependents** (Specify) | N/D | | |

N/D = Not documented.

---

## Narrative Sections

Length does not determine the quality of the investigation report. It is important for the investigator to write clearly and concisely and to remember his or her work will be read!

- The report should be written in complete, grammatically correct sentences. It is generally best to write in the past tense.
- Writing to the point, the investigator should feature those facts or opinions that relate specifically to the alleged injury or occurrence.
- Slang terminology, such as "A line was put in." should be avoided. The proper wording is "An IV was inserted."

### Critical Information

The *Critical Information* section identifies significant issues that the reader should be aware of while reviewing the investigation report, such as missing or altered records (e.g., "On 1/2/2005, Jane Ryan, Director of Health Information Services, verified that the fetal monitoring strips could not be located."). If no critical information has yet been identified, "None identified at this time" should be inserted.

Guidelines for Using the Investigation Report Format

*Short Case Synopsis*

The *Short Case Synopsis* is a one-to-three sentence statement that orients readers to exactly what type of *occurrence and/or allegation(s,) injury, and outcome* the case involves. This enables readers to focus on potential issues and to recognize the relevant facts in the case. The synopsis should always begin with "This case involves..." (e.g., "This case involves the alleged failure to diagnose acute appendicitis, resulting in a ruptured appendix and peritonitis.").

*Summary of Medical Records*

The *Summary of Medical Records* section provides an *objective and factual* synopsis of the medical record documentation that clearly reveals the occurrence, injury, and outcome of the case. The summary should include all medical record documentation necessary to support or refute any liability issues identified or allegations that have been made. Clarifying facts should be added as needed. However, only information that is *relevant* to the case should be included; the investigator must determine what information is pertinent to the story and what can be omitted.

- An individual's clinical and employee status should be indicated the first time he or she is mentioned (e.g., Dr. Susan Smith (Attending, Pediatrics) or Dr. Robert Bane (Attending, Surgery, Nonemployee).
- Bold typeface should be used for the names of the HCO's insureds, and important dates and times.
- The roles of the involved witnesses should be incorporated into the summary by referencing their specific medical record entries (e.g., "According to Dr. Phillips's 10/3/2005 progress note . . ."). These attributions help defense counsel to determine the key witnesses in the case and to evaluate the witnesses' *documented* knowledge of and responsibility for the occurrence/issues in question.
- The investigator should highlight apparent deficiencies in the standard of care, such as the absence of documentation regarding necessary treatment, testing, or examination of the patient (e.g., "No temperature was recorded by the triage nurse.").
- Brief explanations and definitions should be added when needed for clarification.

- Quoting directly from the medical record should be done only when necessary to express some unusual fact. As a rule, quotations should be no longer than one or two sentences.
- The author should always be identified in referring to a particularly important note in the medical record.
- *Unusual* terminology should be identified and defined.
- Standard abbreviations should be used, and any unusual abbreviation should be defined (in parentheses) the first time it appears in the report.
- The range of normal laboratory values should be identified to facilitate the reader's understanding of the significance of abnormal findings.
- The use of tables is recommended to condense, summarize, or highlight test results, medications, vital signs, and so forth. Appendix 12-A provides a list of tables available for use, or the investigator can create a graph or table.
- When relevant entries or signatures are indecipherable, the illegibility should be mentioned in the summary. (The investigator may wish to add an annotation about the probable content of the entry.)
- Documented time of day should be included only when time is an issue in the case (e.g., in a case in which a delay in treatment is at issue).

**Admission and Initial Treatment Information**

If the patient was admitted, the investigator should indicate the admitting diagnosis and/or reason for admission, the name of the admitting physician, and whether this was a service or a private patient.

In cases that involve treatment in the ED, OPD, or private physician's office, the patient's chief complaint at the time of the initial treatment should be noted.

---

Sample *Admission and Initial Treatment Information*

---

The patient presented to the **General Hospital ED** on **9/27/2005**, complaining of abdominal pain with nausea, vomiting, and diarrhea of three days' duration.

The triage nurse's note, authored by **Mandy Jackson, RN**, indicated the patient was alert and in no acute distress. Vital signs were recorded at **9:45 P.M.**, with a temperature of 100°F rectally (normal: 98.6°F), blood pressure 90/60 (normal: 120/80), pulse 100 and regular (normal: 60–100), and respirations 20 (normal: 16–24). A triage assignment of a B priority was made.

---

## Medical/Surgical History

The medical record documentation should be used to provide a *brief* medical/surgical history relevant to the occurrence. This should include only the history of the patient's admitting complaint/disease plus the patient's pertinent past medical history. All of the histories documented in the record(s) should be combined for the summary. For example, irrelevant facts that would not be included in this case of appendicitis are a tonsillectomy at age five and a history of acne. On the other hand, if this patient had a history of colitis at age eight, it would be important to include that information.

---

### Sample *Medical/Surgical History*

---

According to the history documented by **Dr. Robert Phillips** (PGY-1, Pediatrics),the patient's pain was sharp, continuous, and diffuse but primarily localized to the right lower quadrant. The patient had vomited once two days prior, had experienced diarrhea for three days, and had intermittent low-grade temperature elevations.

---

## Physical Findings

The pertinent documented physical findings noted on admission should be highlighted. Again, the investigator should include only information that is relevant to the occurrence/issues/damages and combine the results of all pertinent physical assessments documented in the medical record(s).

---

### Sample *Physical Findings*

---

**Dr. Phillips** noted the patient appeared at ease and in no acute distress. Her abdomen was flat and soft, with diffuse tenderness, especially in the right lower quadrant. Costal vertebral angle (CVA) tenderness on the right side was also present.

---

## Laboratory Findings

Noting the pertinent admission laboratory/radiologic findings, the investigator should highlight abnormal findings when relevant and write out normal ranges, per the laboratory that reported the results, when a result is first introduced. He or she might choose to use a table to summarize pertinent findings.

### Sample *Laboratory Findings*

---

The admission work-up, which included a CBC, chemistry profile, and urinalysis, was within normal limits, except for a WBC of 12.6 (normal: 4–10). The urinalysis revealed 2+ protein (normal: 0), 2–3 WBCs (normal: rare to none), few bacteria (normal: none), 0–2 RBCs, and 2–4 epithelial cells (normal: rare to none).

---

**or**

### Admitting Laboratory Results

| Date | Type of Study | Result | Norm |
|------|---------------|--------|------|
| 9/27/2005 | CBC | WBC: 12.6 | 4–10 |
| 9/27/2005 | Urinalysis | pH: 6 | 4.8–8.0 |
| | " | Specific gravity: | |
| 1.020 | 1.003–1.030 | | |
| | " | 2+ protein | 0 |
| | " | 2–3 WBCs | Rare to none |
| | " | Few bacteria | 0 |
| | " | 0–2 RBCs | Rare to none |
| | " | 2–4 epithelial cells | Rare to none |

N/D = Not documented.

---

**Occurrence**

In telling the rest of the story, the investigator should focus on the issues and detail the facts surrounding the occurrence as found in the medical record.

- The occurrence should be identified. In certain types of cases, the occurrence may not be a single clear-cut event.
  - In cases of misdiagnosis or delayed diagnosis, the period of time *prior* to the point of correct diagnosis should be treated as the occurrence. It is important to review all clinical findings used to formulate a diagnosis and treatment plan.
  - In an ED case, generally the entire ED treatment is considered the occurrence.

- In describing the injury relative to the occurrence, the investigator should include *relevant* subsequent progress notes and consult reports, along with information from laboratory and X-ray results, operating room reports, pathology reports, autopsy reports, and consent forms if applicable.
- Medical record entries should be used to identify those directly involved in the occurrence or care of the patient (e.g., "The surgery was performed by Dr. A assisted by Dr. B." or "The patient was found on the floor by Nurse C.").
- The investigator should point out any glaring discrepancies in the record, as well as any documentation problems that relate to the case issues.
- It is important to include any information obtained from the claim file when necessary to clarify the "story" or pertinent facts (e.g., whenever these significant facts were not documented in the medical record or when the occurrence or issues are obscure.) The source of the information should be indicated.

---

### Sample *Occurrence* Section

---

**Dr. Phillips** diagnosed the patient with a urinary tract infection (UTI) and/or gastroenteritis. He documented he doubted serious pathology in the patient due to her lack of acute distress, noting her fever, pain, and CVA tenderness were consistent with a UTI and the diarrhea was consistent with gastroenteritis.

The patient was discharged to home, with a prescription for Ampicillin 250 mg orally four times a day for 10 days, and instructions to follow up with her private medical doctor if her condition did not improve within four to five days.

---

**Outcome**

The investigator should complete the story of the case as it actually happened—logically and sequentially.

- Any treatment necessitated by the occurrence should be included.
- The patient's condition/disability when last seen should be described. This description might include information obtained from the claim file or from subsequent treatment records, if allowed by statute.[4] It

may also include information from the investigator's review of subsequent records. It is important to state the source of the information (i.e., published documentation other than the patient's medical record information). Providing the source lets the reader know this information is available for review.

---

### Sample *Outcome* Section

---

On **9/30/2005** at **10:00 A.M.**, the patient returned to the emergency room with complaints of chills, vomiting, and severe abdominal pain. She was evaluated by **Dr. Arnold Mayer** (PGY-2, Surgery), who noted she was febrile with a temperature of 103°F, rectally. Examination of the abdomen yielded findings of distention, guarding, and severe palpable right lower quadrant tenderness as well as percussion and rebound tenderness. No bowel sounds were present. Rectal examination revealed gross blood.

Laboratory work-up was significant for a WBC of 17.8. An X-ray series revealed distention of the transverse colon to the region of the splenic flexure.

The patient was diagnosed with rule-out perforated appendix. She was admitted to the hospital as a private patient of Dr. William Green (Attending, Surgery, Nonemployee), to undergo exploratory laparotomy and appendectomy.

The patient's mother signed a consent. The patient underwent the procedure under general anesthesia at **9:00 P.M.** According to the dictated operative report authored by Dr. Green, the procedure was performed by him, assisted by **Dr. William Marra** ( PGY-1, Surgery). Intraoperative findings included a small amount of foul smelling yellow drainage in the abdominal cavity. The appendix was indurated and erythematous, with an obvious perforation at the base; it was noted to be retrocecal and adherent to the right gutter.

The patient tolerated the procedure well, with no complications. The pathology report confirmed the diagnosis of acute appendicitis with rupture.

Postoperatively, the patient progressed well. She was treated with IV fluids and triple antibiotics. Except for a temperature elevation of 102°F on the second postoperative day, her vital signs were stable. On **10/6/2005**, the antibiotics were discontinued. The patient was discharged to home on **10/7/2005**, with instructions to follow up with **Dr. Green** at his office in one week.

---

### *Interview(s)*

The *Interview(s)* section of the investigation report should describe—objectively—the results of the investigator's interviews and in-house reviews. (Subjective impressions about the interviewee are noted only in the second paragraph of this section.)

- The information gathered in the interview should be organized in a logical and sequential manner, regardless of the order in which it was obtained, focusing on
  - the medical record documentation
  - the issues identified
  - the occurrence and sequence of events
  - the interviewee's role and responsibilities in the patient's care
- The investigator should demonstrate that all pertinent questions were asked and thoroughly answered by the interviewee. The first paragraph should contain
  - the date of the interview
  - whether the interview was by telephone or in person
  - the interviewee's name and title, his or her role in the case, and the degree of recollection.

An example of such a beginning paragraph might be: "On 3/1/05, a personal interview was conducted with Dr. John Smith, the patient's private attending physician, who performed the surgery in question. Dr. Smith had immediate recollection of this patient."

- The second paragraph should be a description of the witness, giving the reader an idea of how the witness presents himself or herself (and thus implying what a jury would see). Subjective tactful comments are helpful in this section of the report. Areas to cover include
  - general appearance—age, race, outstanding physical characteristics, attire, whether the interviewee "looks the part" (e.g., "competent nurse," "knowledgeable physician")
  - demeanor (e.g., friendly, hostile, defensive)
  - degree of cooperation
  - ability to express himself or herself (e.g., does he or she speak with an accent that is difficult to understand?)
  - ability to understand the interviewer's questions
- In the subsequent paragraphs, the investigator should provide a *totally objective* account of what the interviewee knows about the occurrence, including
  - a precise accounting of the timing of important events related to the occurrence

- ○ any contributing factors to the occurrence
- ○ any contributing factors by the patient to the alleged injury
- ○ the physician's orders relative to the occurrence/issues
- ○ normal and abnormal test values and results, if pertinent to the occurrence
- ○ any other individual's role in the occurrence (This information is especially important when there are responsible parties or code-fendants not insured by the HCO.)
- Direct quotes should be used only when essential to capture an unusual statement (e.g., "Dr. Jones said 'Dr. Green took my hand and shoved the reamer into the medulla.'").
- The use of "I said" and "he/she said" in the interview should be limited.
- The investigator must distinguish clearly between a witness's custom and practice (i.e., what generally would have been done in similar circumstances) and his or her recall of what actually happened in this instance. Defense attorneys have to be able to differentiate between a witness who has accurate recall of an occurrence and one who does not. This should be written in the present tense.
- It is important to distinguish between what the interviewee actually said and what he or she merely implied. Words should be carefully chosen in writing up the information obtained from an interview. Because most of what is written is based on what the interviewee said, the investigator should choose words that clarify the intentions of the interviewee's statements. For example, the following words indicate that the interviewee had a good recollection of events:

| | |
|---|---|
| added | recalled |
| commented | reiterated |
| confirmed | remembered |
| explained | stated |
| indicated | pointed out |
| | remarked |

In contrast, the following words give a less affirmative tone to witnesses' statements:

| | |
|---|---|
| believed | speculated |
| hypothesized | suggested |
| implied | surmised |
| opined | theorized |

These words tell the reader that any statement that follows is not based on actual recall but is more likely conjecture. It should be noted that when properly labeled, conjecture is perfectly acceptable. In fact, in the absence of positive recall, conjecture is essential.

- The investigator should place the interview write-ups in whatever order makes the most sense in telling the story. For example, it would make sense to place a postoccurrence interview first if that witness provided a more comprehensive overview than the individuals who actually witnessed the occurrence.

### Sample *Interview* Write-Up

On 11/29/2005, I conducted a personal interview with Dr. Robert Phillips, the PGY-1 pediatric resident who examined the patient in the ED on 9/27/2005. He had excellent, independent recollection of this case.

Dr. Phillips was a moderately overweight, Caucasian male of average height in his late thirties. He was unkempt and had long, poorly managed hair. He resembled one of the Beatles. Although cooperative and fairly knowledgeable, he spoke in a callous manner. Intermittently throughout the interview, Dr. Phillips used foul language to describe the patient.

Dr. Phillips began the interview by explaining that he remembered this patient so well because there was such a difference between her initial clinical presentation and the ultimate diagnosis of a perforated appendix. Dr. Phillips stated his only contact with the patient took place while she was in the ED. He learned of her final diagnosis through another resident, whose name he could not recall.

Dr. Phillips reviewed the medical record and recalled that the patient presented to the ED in no discomfort or distress. The patient gave a history of a low-grade fever and of vomiting once, three days prior to her arrival in the ED. Dr. Phillips pointed out this was not the typical presentation seen with appendicitis. He described the typical presentation as *severe* generalized or upper abdominal pain that becomes localized in the right lower quadrant within a few hours. Instead, this patient complained of abdominal pain for three days with nausea and vomiting. He also noted patients with appendicitis generally give a history of constipation, while this patient complained of diarrhea.

Dr. Phillips stated upon examining the patient's abdomen, he found mild tenderness with no palpable mass. His initial diagnosis, based on the patient's symptoms, was gastroenteritis or urinary tract infection (UTI).

Dr. Phillips added the patient presented to the ED with a note written on a prescription pad by her private pediatrician, Dr. Bane, who was not affiliated with General Hospital. The note indicated the patient's diagnosis was rule-out acute appendicitis and that she should have a CBC and an abdominal X-ray. Dr. Phillips stated he did not know Dr. Bane and had never received a phone call to inform him that Dr. Bane was sending his private patient to the ED. Dr. Phillips did not contact Dr. Bane after examining the patient, because the patient's examination was benign.

Dr. Phillips elaborated on how he came to his diagnosis in this case. He reviewed the patient's laboratory results and noted the CBC was consistent with "someone who was sick with gastroenteritis for a few days." Based on the patient's presentation, Dr. Phillips did not believe she had appendicitis. He did not want to expose a teenage female to unnecessary radiation; therefore, he did not order an abdominal X-ray. With regard to whether a rectal examination or an examination for rebound tenderness was performed, Dr. Phillips conceded both should have been done to rule out appendicitis. However, he theorized that had he done a rectal examination in the ED, it would have been negative and nondiagnostic at that time.

In view of the absence of dysuria (frequency, or voiding in small amounts), and a urinalysis that did not seem to support the diagnosis of UTI, the patient clearly did not have a UTI. Dr. Phillips admitted this was a "weak spot in the case." In support of his decision at the time, however, Dr. Phillips stated diarrhea, right and left lower quadrant pain, and CVA tenderness are all consistent with symptoms of a UTI. He added although the urinalysis was not impressive, the 2+ protein in conjunction with the other symptoms could have been suggestive of a UTI.

Dr. Phillips commented on his documented diagnosis of a "UTI and/or gastroenteritis"— specifically, whether it was common to have these disease processes concurrently. Dr. Phillips admitted this was not one of his more "brilliant diagnoses" and generally these two processes would not occur simultaneously. Dr. Phillips stated he had limited experience with the diagnosis of appendicitis at the time. He noted he had seen approximately four cases prior to this occurrence.

With regard to the need for a surgical consultation during the patient's initial ED visit, Dr. Phillips was confident this patient's condition was benign at the time, and therefore it was unnecessary to seek a surgical opinion. He was unaware of whether any policy for obtaining surgical consultations on pediatric patients who complained of abdominal pain existed. He emphasized it would be impossible to obtain consultations on every child complaining of abdominal pain.

Finally, Dr. Phillips speculated that the damages in this case would be limited to pain and suffering. He was not of the opinion that the ruptured appendix had placed the patient at risk for the development of adhesions or possible complications associated with bowel obstruction and/or infertility. He believed had the diagnosis been made on the first ED visit, the patient still would have required surgery, but obviously her postoperative course would not have been complicated by peritonitis.

## In-House Reviews

The *In-House Reviews* section includes objective accounts of an in-house physician's assessment of the presence or absence of liability. They should be conducted and written in a format similar to that used for the interviews. In the previous example, an important issue to be addressed is: If the patient had been treated earlier, would the outcome have been any different? A review to determine whether there has been any breach in the standard of care or hospital policies should also be conducted.

## Miscellaneous Investigation

The *Miscellaneous Investigation* section of the report includes any information not previously disclosed during the review of records or the interviews that may further clarify the fact pattern of the case. Such information might include

- descriptions of HCO documents (e.g., incident reports, rules and regulations)
- relevant HCO policies and protocols
- interviews with persons not involved in the case (e.g., with an administrator to clarify a policy)
- information regarding equipment in question
- medical research notes

Where appropriate, the publication data or the name and status of the individual who provided the information should be cited.

In this section, the investigator can also address missing items (e.g., fetal monitoring strips) and list the steps taken to find them. The individual designated to sign an affidavit regarding the loss of significant items should be noted. When necessary, a list of other potential witnesses, their status, and the dates of their medical record entries should be included. The individual who confirmed an unusual insurance status of an involved party (e.g., a resident rotating from another facility who is not insured by the HCO) should be identified. The investigator for this case (failure to diagnose appendicitis) may wish to do some research on the appropriate diagnosing of this condition.

---

### Sample *Miscellaneous Investigation* Section

1. According to *Nelson Textbook of Pediatrics* (17th ed., Richard E. Behrman, ed.), when diagnosing appendicitis:

   A rectal examination is essential but should be left until the general assessment and examination are completed. Also noted is that an atypical location of the appendix—such as a location lateral to the cecum, which causes flank tenderness—makes the diagnosis of appendicitis more difficult.

2. On 11/30/2005, I met with Mr. Paul Brinn, the hospital administrator for the department of surgery. Mr. Brinn indicated there was no policy or procedure, or rule or regulation, relative to surgical consultations on pediatric patients in the ED for abdominal complaints.

---

Checklist for *Miscellaneous Investigation* Section

---

**Additional Items Considered for Investigation:**

- Relevant hospital policies and rules and regulations
- Relevant logbooks
- Information on equipment used (maintenance records)
- Occurrence reports
- Missing evidence (e.g., fetal monitoring strips, X-rays, records)

---

*Comments*

The *Comments* section *analyzes* and *evaluates* the information contained in the summary and investigation sections. At this point, the investigator integrates the facts and ideas of the case to arrive at a theory of potential liability (see "Analyzing the Facts" in Chapter 4).

When preparing comments, the investigator addresses the issues in the case and

- either supports or refutes the plaintiff's allegations, using concise statements of fact already detailed in the report
- highlights anything that may prove to be problematic in defending the case
- includes his or her own opinions and impressions

The investigator may find an outline format helpful for detailing specific investigative findings. Comments can be numbered and then listed chronologically or in order of priority.

For the reader's convenience, the text box *Issues Considered for Comment* (see below) is included in the Investigation Report format section on the CD-ROM enclosed with this book. This checklist can be used to make sure that the potential problem areas in the case have been covered. The text box should be deleted from the final draft of the report. An explanation of the categories in this checklist follows.

| Issues Considered for Comment: |
| --- |

- ❏ Medical management of the case, covering:
    - ❏ Candidacy
    - ❏ Timeliness of intervention
    - ❏ Delay in diagnosis
    - ❏ Misdiagnosis
    - ❏ Adherence to/deviation from hospital policies and procedures
    - ❏ Adherence to/deviation from AMA Practice Parameters
    - ❏ Sufficient documentation
    - ❏ Appropriate procedure, treatment
    - ❏ Supervision, experience of caregiver
    - ❏ Surgical technique
- ❏ Degree of responsibility among the involved parties
- ❏ Discrepancies/problems in the medical record, documentation or information obtained on interview
- ❏ Issues disclosed during Miscellaneous Investigation
- ❏ Damages sustained by the patient (prognosis, prolonged hospitalization)
- ❏ Plaintiff's role in contributing to the alleged occurrence and injury
- ❏ Informed consent (risks, benefits, alternative, and documentation)

**Medical Management of the Case**

The investigator should address specific *clinical* aspects of the case in terms of the "standards of care." This includes the care rendered—or not rendered—by all health care professionals involved. Medical record documentation and interview information should be used to support or refute any deviations cited.

**Degree of Responsibility Among Involved Parties**

It is necessary to determine who is responsible for—or who contributed to—the occurrence and outcome, and whether those responsible are insured or noninsured parties. Each issue identified should include the names of all parties who might be considered liable for the injury or occurrence. (This information is listed in the *Parties Involved* section.)

**Discrepancies/Problems with the Medical Record, Evidence, or Interview Information**

Problems can range from simple errors (e.g., wrong dates) to major liability issues identified in the case (e.g., missing, poor, or altered documentation or other evidence). A example of a discrepancy might be contradictory statements of interviewed parties (e.g., an attending physician claims that he was not contacted by the resident regarding the patient's deteriorating condition, whereas the resident claims to have called the attending physician and fully apprised him of the condition; no documentation of this conversation exists).

### Medical/Legal Issues (Miscellaneous)

Minor issues and factors that either mitigate or support aspects of potential liability also merit comment. Such issues may be used by a plaintiff's attorney to focus the jury's attention away from the main allegations and to discredit defense witnesses. Examples include the obliteration of medical record entries, discrepancies, inflammatory notes, writing over entries, writing in the margins, and the use of correction fluid. In addition, any other incidents or departures from accepted standards of care with or without injury and should be noted and placed in context.

### Damages

The investigator should apply the following criteria in discussing the damages sustained by the patient:

- Are the damages significant (high-exposure cases)?
- Are the damages significant to the patient's occupation or child care responsibilities?
- Does the injury have potential for significant deterioration, improvement, or resolution with treatment?
- Do subsequent records appear to refute the alleged damages?
- Is it possible that an unrelated condition or the patient's poor general health also contributed to the injury/outcome of the case?

### Plaintiff's Role in Contributing to the Alleged Occurrence or Injury

The investigator should provide an assessment of the plaintiff's culpability for the occurrence or the extent of his or her injury. Legally, this is called *comparative negligence* or *culpable conduct*. In New York State, if a jury finds that a plaintiff is guilty of comparative negligence, the damages are reduced by a percentage equal to the plaintiff's share of the fault.

**Informed Consent**

Any issues pertaining to informed consent in the case should be addressed as a separate comment (see Chapter 17 for information on this subject).

The following two examples illustrate appropriate comments.

**Case 1**

This refers to the case cited previously that involved failure to diagnose a 14-year-old girl's acute appendicitis in the ED.

---

Sample *Comments* Section for Case 1

---

**COMMENTS**

1. The failure to diagnose acute appendicitis during the patient's 9/27/2005 ED visit has been alleged. Relative to this allegation, the examination by Dr. Phillips does not appear to have been adequate to rule out appendicitis.

    a) Given the patient's three-day history of abdominal pain, a low-grade fever, and a WBC of 12.6, the absence of a documented rectal examination, abdominal Xray, and an examination for rebound tenderness by Dr. Phillips may prove problematic to the defense of the case.

    b) Although both Dr. Phillips and the admitting nurse noted the patient appeared to be in no distress, Dr. Phillips received a note from the patient's private attending physician, Dr. Bane, who opined she might have had appendicitis. Dr. Phillips' failure to consult with the private attending physician or have a surgical consultation is of concern.

    c) Dr. Phillips' diagnosis of a UTI was not well supported by the patient's history, physical examination findings, or laboratory results.

2. Dr. Bane's responsibility appears to be minimal in that he referred the patient to the ED with the diagnosis of rule-out appendicitis. Dr. Bane was not named in this suit.

3. Physical examination of the patient will be needed to assess the patient for residual damages. Although Dr. Phillips stated damages would be limited, the patient may be at risk for pelvic adhesions secondary to peritonitis. In addition, the patient had considerably more pain and suffering and a prolonged hospital stay due to the need for more extensive surgery and complications associated with peritonitis.

4. Although unrelated to the occurrence, review of the record revealed there were two incidents of IV infiltrations during the patient's postoperative course and one omitted midnight dose of an antibiotic on 10/4/2005.

---

## Case 2

This case involves a 38-year-old female who underwent gastric bypass surgery for morbid obesity. During the surgical procedure, the patient's stomach was inadvertently punctured and subsequently repaired. The patient had a very complicated postoperative course, with temperature elevations and excessive gastrostomy tube drainage. Radiology studies of the operative site initially were read as negative. However, there was a leak in the anastomosis that resulted in peritonitis, sepsis, and death.

Sample *Comments* Section for Case 2

**COMMENTS**

1. This case involves an allegation of an improperly performed gastric bypass and a failure to diagnose and treat a postoperative stomach perforation promptly. It will need to be determined whether the inadvertent entry into the stomach (as described by the resident) was a deviation from accepted surgical practice or, given the patient's condition, an accepted risk/complication of the procedure.

2. As alleged, it appears there was a delay in recognizing that a perforated viscus had occurred. Relative to this, the following should be considered:

   a) It would appear the Gastrografin studies were not performed properly in that the dye was injected via the nasogastric tube and not through the gastrostomy tube.

   b) The resident erroneously attributed free intra-abdominal air, a cardinal sign of perforation, to postoperative surgical changes. The Gastrografin studies revealed no leaks at the gastrojejunal anastomosis.

3. Investigation revealed surgical intervention was delayed by 24 to 48 hours as a consequence of the improperly interpreted Gastrografin studies. As outlined by the resident, management in this case should have been guided by the patient's clinical symptoms despite the negative radiographic studies. Although not documented, the house staff has insisted the private attending surgeon was apprised of the patient's deteriorating condition and was ultimately responsible for the postoperative surgical management of this patient.

4. The resident suggested the patient may have been "cheating" on her diet postoperatively and that this could have contributed to the postoperative complications. There is adequate medical record documentation to support this opinion.

5. Lack of informed consent also is alleged. However, a preoperative note indicates the patient understood the risks, benefits, and alternatives of the surgery. Responsibility for obtaining informed consent rests upon the private attending surgeon.

*Recommendations for Future Investigation*

The investigator should list any additional interviews or investigations that are planned. If no further investigation is warranted, this should be stated.

*Secured Items*

The purpose of the *Secured Items* section is to provide a list of all "items" (evidence) that the investigator requested the HCO or physician to sequester for possible later production in the case. The *date* the request to secure each item was sent should be indicated.

Sample Secured Items Section

Secured Items

| Items | Date Security of Original Item Requested |
|---|---|
| 1. Medical records | |
|     Inpatient | 11/30/2005 |
|     Outpatient | |
|     Emergency room | 11/30/2005 |
|     Private office | |
| 2. Bills | 11/30/2005 |
| 3. Fetal monitoring strips | |
| 4. Radiology studies | 11/30/2005 |
| 5. Pathology slides | 11/30/2005 |
| 6. Other ED Logbook | 11/30/2005 |

*Enclosures*

The *Enclosures* section lists any items included with the investigation report, including

* relevant HCO policies
* curricula vitae

- logbooks
- occurrence reports
- private office records
- fetal monitoring strips
- autopsy reports
- medical literature
- user manuals or service records for equipment in question
- photographs, videos, or audio recordings
- actual pieces of equipment or samples
- any previously missing parts of the medical record

## SAMPLE INVESTIGATION REPORT

Exhibit 12-1 is a sample investigation report based on the previously discussed case involving a missed appendicitis. It is shown in its entirety in the format suggested.

## GUIDELINES FOR WRITING AN OBSTETRICAL INVESTIGATION REPORT

Because of the high exposure associated with obstetrical claims and the complex nature of the clinical data, FOJP Service Corporation developed a separate report format for obstetrical investigations. Some of the sections in the obstetrical investigation report are similar to those in the basic investigation report format and will not be repeated here. Because awards for neurologically injured newborns can be in the multimillion- dollar range, investigation is extensive and risk managers, defense counsel, claim managers, and excess carriers are especially interested in the investigation findings. Every aspect of the case needs to be covered thoroughly.

A complete sample obstetrical investigation report (Exhibit 12-2) follows. **Exhibits 12-3** and **12-4** list commonly used abbreviations found in obstetrical and neonatal medical records.

Before describing the obstetrical investigation report, we have included a brief review of the stages of labor with their respective time durations. A deviation from these time frames may indicate a problem.

**Exhibit 12-1**  FOJP Service Corporation Sample Investigation Report

| This report is confidential and prepared solely in anticipation of, or in connection with, litigation. | Dated: 1/30/2006 |

**Patient:** Michelle Smith          **Claimant:**   Timothy   Smith   (Father)

To:   Geller and Geller, P.C.

Att: John Doe, Esq.

cc:   Team Supervisor, FOJP

By: Doris Clayton, RCC

| Institution | General Hospital | | | |
|---|---|---|---|---|
| FOJP File # | V97-0000-4991 | Defense Attorney File # | 101-145 | |
| Status | Summons | | Severity Code | 04 |
| Disposition | Opened | Interviews | 1 | Pages | 8 |

### TREATMENT DATES

| Office, Institution or Department | Medical Record # | - through - | |
|---|---|---|---|
| ED, General Hospital | 4600 | *9/27/2005 | 9/27/2005 |
| General Hospital | 1000 | *9/30/2005 | 10/5/2005 |
| Dr. Green's (VAP) Private Office | N/D | 10/10/2005 | 11/8/2005 |

\* Relevant Treatment Records     N/D = Not Documented

| DATE OF OCCURRENCE | 9/27/2005 |

| FIRST REPORTED | DATE | PLAINTIFF'S ATTORNEY |
|---|---|---|
| Alert | | |
| Attorney's Request Letter | 11/21/2005 | Jean Monte, Esq. |
| Pt. Complaint / Letter of Claim | | |
| Summons | 1/9/2006 | Jean Monte, Esq. |

**Exhibit 12-1**   continued

---

INVESTIGATION REPORT (continued)          Page 2          **FOJP SERVICE CORPORATION**

CASE OF <u>Michelle Smith</u>                                    FILE # <u>V90-0000-4991</u>

## PARTIES INVOLVED

**A. INSURED**:
1.    **General Hospital**: <u>Named Defendant</u>.

2.    **\*Phillips, Robert: MD**, PGY-1, Pediatrics, Employee.

3.    **Jackson, Mandy:   RN**, Staff Nurse, Employee.   LDE: 11/30/05.   LKA: 30 Maple Drive, Smithtown, N.Y.   11787.  (516) 334-8742.

**B. Parties with Other Insurance Coverage:**

1. Bane, Robert:  MD, Attending, Surgery, Nonemployee.  Not Affiliated with

   General Hospital.  Primary: CIMLM (limits: 1 million/occurrence). Excess:

   SYNAH (limits: 1 million/occurrence).

2. Green, William:  MD, Attending, Surgery, Nonemployee. Primary:

   HCI (limits: 1 million/occurrence).  Excess: SYNAH (limits: 1

   million/occurrence).

## IN-HOUSE REVIEWS

1.  **\*Stone, Stanley: MD**, Director, Department of Surgery,
    Employee.

\* Interview not contained within this report.

| PATIENT DEMOGRAPHIC INFORMATION | | | | | | |
|---|---|---|---|---|---|---|
| AGE | 14 | SEX | Female | RACE | Caucasian | RELIGION | Catholic |
| OCCUPATION | | | STUDENT | | INSURANCE | Oxhorn Medical |
| MARITAL STATUS | | | Single | | | |
| DEPENDENTS (SPECIFY) | | | N / D | | | |

N/D = Not Documented

**Exhibit 12-1**   continued

INVESTIGATION REPORT (continued)          Page 3          **FOJP SERVICE CORPORATION**

CASE OF <u>Michelle Smith</u>                                        FILE # <u>V90-0000-4991</u>

**CRITICAL INFORMATION:**

None identified at this time

**SHORT CASE SYNOPSIS**

This case involves the alleged failure to diagnose acute appendicitis, resulting in a ruptured appendix and peritonitis.

**SUMMARY OF MEDICAL RECORDS**

The patient presented to the **General Hospital** ED on **9/27/2005**, complaining of abdominal pain with nausea, vomiting, and diarrhea, of three days' duration.

The triage nurse's note, authored by **Mandy Jackson, RN,** indicated the patient was alert and in no acute distress. Vital signs were recorded at **9:45 p.m.** with a temperature of 100\u1d52F rectally (normal: 98.6°F), blood pressure 90/60 (normal: 120/80), pulse 100 and regular (normal: 60-100), and respirations 20 (normal: 16-24). A triage assignment of a B priority was made.

According to the history documented by **Dr. Robert Phillips** (PGY-1, Pediatrics) the patient's pain was sharp, continuous and diffuse, but primarily localized to the right lower quadrant. The patient had vomited once two days prior, had experienced diarrhea for three days, and had intermittent low-grade temperature elevations.

**Dr. Phillips** noted the patient appeared at ease and in no acute distress. Her abdomen was flat and soft with diffuse tenderness, especially in the right lower quadrant. CVA (costal vertebral angle) tenderness on the right side was also present.

**Exhibit 12-1**    continued

---

INVESTIGATION REPORT (continued)          Page 4          **FOJP SERVICE CORPORATION**

CASE OF <u>Michelle Smith</u>                                    FILE # <u>V90-0000-4991</u>

---

The admission workup, which included a CBC, chemistry profile and urinalysis was within normal limits, except for a WBC of 12.6 (normal: 4-10). The urinalysis revealed 2+ protein (normal: 0), 2-3 WBC (normal: rare-none), few bacteria (normal: none) and 0-2 RBCs and 2-4 epithelial cells (normal: rare to none).

**Dr. Phillips** diagnosed the patient with a urinary tract infection (UTI) and/or gastroenteritis. He documented he doubted serious pathology in the patient due to her lack of acute distress, noting her fever, pain and CVA tenderness were consistent with a UTI, and the diarrhea was consistent with gastroenteritis.

The patient was discharged to home, with a prescription for Ampicillin 250 mg orally, four times a day for 10 days, and instructions to follow-up with her private medical doctor if her condition did not improve within four to five days.

On **9/30/2005** at **10:00 a.m.**, the patient returned to the emergency room, with complaints of chills, vomiting and severe abdominal pain. She was evaluated by **Dr. Arnold Mayer** ( PGY-2, Surgery), who noted she was febrile with a temperature of 103°F, rectally. Examination of the abdomen yielded findings of distention, guarding and severe palpable right lower quadrant tenderness, as well as percussion and rebound tenderness. No bowel sounds were present. Rectal examination revealed gross blood.

Laboratory workup was significant for a WBC of 17.8. An x-ray series revealed distention of the transverse colon to the region of the splenic flexure.

The patient was diagnosed with rule-out perforated appendix. She was admitted to the hospital as a private patient of Dr. William Green (Attending, Surgery, Non-Employee), to undergo exploratory laparotomy and appendectomy.

**Exhibit 12-1**   continued

The patient's mother signed a consent. The patient underwent the procedure under general anesthesia at **9:00 p.m.** According to the dictated operative report authored by Dr. Green, the procedure was performed by him, assisted by **Dr. William Marra** ( PGY-1, Surgery). Intraoperative findings included a small amount of foul-smelling yellow drainage in the abdominal cavity. The appendix was indurated and erythematous, with an obvious perforation at the base; it was noted to be retrocecal and adherent to the right gutter.

The patient tolerated the procedure well, with no complications. The pathology report confirmed the diagnosis of acute appendicitis with rupture.

Postoperatively, the patient progressed well. She was treated with IV fluids and triple antibiotics. Except for a temperature elevation of 102°F on the second postoperative day, her vital signs were stable. On **10/6/2005**, the antibiotics were discontinued. The patient was discharged to home on **10/7/2005**, with instructions to follow-up with Dr. Green at his office in one week.

<u>INTERVIEW - Robert Phillips, MD</u>

On 11/29/2005, I conducted a personal interview with Dr. Robert Phillips, the PGY-1 pediatric resident who examined the patient in the emergency room on 9/27/2005. He had excellent, independent recollection of this case.

Dr. Phillips was a moderately overweight, Caucasian male of average height, in his late thirties. He was unkempt and had long, poorly managed hair. He resembled one of the Beatles. Although cooperative and fairly knowledgeable, he spoke in a callous manner. Intermittently throughout the interview, Dr. Phillips used foul language to describe the patient.

**Exhibit 12-1**    continued

---

Dr. Phillips began the interview by explaining he remembered this patient so well because there was such a difference between her initial clinical presentation and the ultimate diagnosis of a perforated appendix. Dr. Phillips stated his only contact with the patient took place while she was in the emergency room. He learned of her final diagnosis through another resident, whose name he could not recall.

Dr. Phillips reviewed the medical record and recalled that the patient presented to the emergency room in no discomfort or distress. The patient gave a history of a low-grade fever and of vomiting once, three days prior to her arrival in the ER. Dr. Phillips pointed out this was not the typical presentation seen with appendicitis. He described the typical presentation as <u>severe</u> generalized or upper abdominal pain, which becomes localized in the right lower quadrant within a few hours. Instead, this patient complained of abdominal pain for three days with nausea and vomiting. He also noted that patients with appendicitis generally give a history of constipation, while this patient complained of diarrhea.

Dr. Phillips stated upon examining the patient's abdomen, he found mild tenderness with no palpable mass. His initial diagnosis, based on the patient's symptoms, was gastroenteritis or urinary tract infection (UTI).

Dr. Phillips added the patient presented to the emergency room with a note written on a prescription pad by her private pediatrician, Dr. Bane, who was not affiliated with General Hospital. The note indicated the patient's diagnosis was rule-out acute appendicitis and that she should have a CBC and an abdominal x-ray. Dr. Phillips stated he did not know Dr. Bane and had never received a phone call to inform him that Dr. Bane was sending his private patient to the emergency room. Dr. Phillips did not contact Dr. Bane after examining the patient, because the patient's examination was benign.

**Exhibit 12-1**   continued

---

INVESTIGATION REPORT (continued)              Page 7              **FOJP SERVICE CORPORATION**

CASE OF <u>Michelle Smith</u>                                               FILE # <u>V90-0000-4991</u>

Dr. Phillips elaborated on how he came to his diagnosis in this case. He reviewed the patient's laboratory results and noted the CBC was consistent with "someone who was sick with gastroenteritis for a few days." Based on her presentation, Dr. Phillips did not believe she had appendicitis. He did not want to expose a teenage female to unnecessary radiation; therefore, he did not order an abdominal x-ray. With regard to whether a rectal exam or examination for rebound tenderness were performed, Dr. Phillips conceded both should have been done to rule out appendicitis. However, he theorized had he done a rectal exam in the ER it would have been negative and non-diagnostic at that time.

In view of the absence of dysuria (frequency or voiding in small amounts), and a urinalysis that did not seem to support the diagnosis of UTI, the patient clearly did not have a UTI. Dr. Phillips admitted this was a "weak spot in the case." In support of his decision at the time, however, Dr. Phillips stated diarrhea, right and left lower quadrant pain, and CVA tenderness are all consistent with symptoms of a UTI. He added although the urinalysis was not impressive, the 2+ protein in conjunction with the other symptoms could have been suggestive of a UTI.

Dr. Phillips commented on his documented diagnosis of a "UTI and/or gastroenteritis"—specifically, whether it was common to have these disease processes concurrently. Dr. Phillips admitted this was not one of his more "brilliant diagnoses" and generally these two processes would not occur simultaneously. Dr. Phillips stated he had limited experience with the diagnosis of appendicitis at the time. He noted he had probably seen approximately four cases prior to this occurrence.

With regard to the need for a surgical consult during the patient's initial emergency room visit, Dr. Phillips was confident this patient's condition was benign at that time and therefore it was unnecessary to seek a surgical opinion. He was unaware of whether there was any policy for obtaining surgical consults on patients who

**Exhibit 12-1**    continued

---

INVESTIGATION REPORT (continued)            Page 8            **FOJP SERVICE CORPORATION**

CASE OF Michelle Smith                                         FILE # V90-0000-4991

---

complained of abdominal pain.  He emphasized it would be impossible to obtain consults on every child complaining of abdominal pain.

Finally, Dr. Phillips speculated the damages in this case would be limited to pain and suffering.  He was not of the opinion that since the appendix had ruptured this placed the patient at risk for the development of adhesions or possible complications associated with bowel obstruction and/or fertility.  He believed had the diagnosis been made on the first ER visit, the patient still would have required surgery, but obviously her postoperative course would not have been complicated by peritonitis.

**MISCELLANEOUS INVESTIGATION**

1.      According to the *Nelson: Textbook of Pediatrics* (17th ed. Richard E. Behrman, ed.), when diagnosing appendicitis:

>       A rectal examination is essential but should be left until the general assessment and
>       examination is completed.  Also noted is that atypical location of the appendix such as a
>       location lateral to the cecum, which causes flank tenderness, makes the diagnosis of
>       appendicitis more difficult to make.

2.      On 11/30/2005, I met with Mr. Paul Brinn, the hospital administrator for the Department of Surgery.
        Mr. Brinn indicated there was no policy or procedure nor rule or regulation relative to surgical consults
        on pediatric patients in the ED for abdominal complaints.

## Exhibit 12-1    continued

INVESTIGATION REPORT (continued)          Page 9          **FOJP SERVICE CORPORATION**

CASE OF Michelle Smith                                        FILE # V90-0000-4991

### COMMENTS

1.  The failure to diagnose acute appendicitis during the patient's 9/27/2005 ED visit has been alleged. Relative to this allegation, the examination by Dr. Phillips does not appear to have been adequate to rule-out appendicitis.

    (a)    Given the patient's three-day history of abdominal pain, low grade fever and a WBC of 12.6, the absence of a documented rectal exam, abdominal x-ray and an examination for rebound tenderness by Dr. Phillips may prove problematic to the defense of the case.

    (b)    Although both Dr. Phillips and the admitting nurse noted the patient appeared to be in no distress, Dr. Phillips received a note from the patient's private attending, Dr. Bane, who opined she may have had appendicitis. Dr. Phillips' failure to consult with the private attending physician or have a surgical consult is of concern.

    (c)    Dr. Phillips' diagnosis of a UTI was not well supported by the patient's history, physical exam findings, or laboratory results.

2.    Dr. Bane's responsibility appears to be minimal in that he referred the patient to the ED with the diagnosis of rule-out appendicitis. Dr. Bane was not named in this suit.

3.    Physical examination of the patient will be needed to assess the patient for residual damages. Although Dr. Phillips stated damages would be limited, the patient may be at risk for pelvic adhesions secondary to peritonitis. In addition, the patient had considerably more pain and suffering and a prolonged hospital stay due to the need for more extensive surgery and complications associated with peritonitis.

**Exhibit 12-1    continued**

---

4.    Although unrelated to the occurrence, review of the record revealed there were two incidents of IV

infiltrations during the patient's postoperative course and one omitted midnight dose of an antibiotic on

10/4/2005.

## RECOMMENDATIONS FOR FUTURE INVESTIGATION

None planned at this time.

| SECURED ITEMS | |
|---|---|
| **ITEMS** | DATE SECURITY OF ORIGINAL ITEM REQUESTED |
| **1. MEDICAL RECORDS** | |
| INPATIENT | 11/30/2005 |
| OUTPATIENT | |
| EMERGENCY ROOM | 11/30/2005 |
| PRIVATE OFFICE | |
| **2. BILLS** | |
| **3. FETAL MONITORING STRIPS** | |
| **4. RADIOLOGY STUDIES** | 11/30/2005 |
| **5. PATHOLOGY SLIDES** | 11/30/2005 |
| **6. OTHER**          ED Logbook | 11/30/2005 |

## ENCLOSURES

None

**Review of Stages of Labor**

*First stage:* During this period, the cervix effaces and dilates. Effacement is the thinning and shortening of the cervix, measured in percent from 0 to 100. Dilatation is the opening up of the cervix measured in cm from 0-10. The cervix progresses to 100% effacement and 10 cm dilatation to allow for the delivery of the fetus. The first stage of labor lasts 6 to 18 hours in a nullipara and about 2 to 10 hours in a multipara.[5] The first stage is generally further divided into two phases[6]:

- **Latent phase**—in which the cervix dilates from 0 to 3 cm. In a nullipara, this phase averages 8 hours; in a multipara, it averages 5 hours.
- **Active phase**—in which the cervix dilates from 3 to 10 cm. In a nullipara, this phase averages 5 hours; in a multipara, it averages 2 hours.

*Second stage:* This period covers the time from complete dilatation of the cervix to the expulsion of the fetus. It averages 50 minutes for a nullipara and 20 minutes for a multipara.[7] If this stage is prolonged, it may be indicative of cephalopelvic disproportion.

*Third stage:* This stage is the delivery of the placenta. Spontaneous separation and delivery of the placenta usually occurs within 5 minutes of delivery of the infant. If there is excessive vaginal bleeding, intervention to remove the placenta may be indicated. Otherwise, manual removal of the placenta is recommended if the placenta has not spontaneously delivered within 30 minutes of expulsion of the fetus[8]

**Steps in Preparing an Obstetrical Investigation Report**

When writing an investigation report for an obstetrical case, the investigator can use the following guidelines to modify the respective sections discussed earlier in this chapter.

The initial sections are identical to those in the basic investigation report and will not be repeated here. However, the dates of treatment cover the time of pregnancy through post-delivery care (and often beyond), and there are two medical records to review— the mother's and the infant's. The report headings should specify whether the section applies to the mother or infant(s).

*Case Synopsis*

The obstetrical case synopsis provides a concise overview. Because it contains an overview of the entire case from pregnancy through post-delivery care, the obstetrical case synopsis is often the last item completed for the report. The investigator should prepare a brief description of the occurrence, injury, and outcome/allegations, and include a very brief (one or two sentences) summary of the infant's hospitalization and outcome.

**Opening Statement**

The investigator should always begin the synopsis by orienting the reader to the type of obstetrical occurrence and/or the allegations made in the case. This enables readers to focus on potential issues and recognize relevant facts in the case. This statement should not exceed three sentences and should begin with the customary *"This case involves . . .."*

**Admission and Initial Treatment Information**

Note the mother's age, parity,[9] weeks' gestation of the pregnancy, expected date of delivery (EDD),[10] and the date and time of her admission. When the patient's course of labor is an issue, the admitting vaginal examination findings, along with the initial fetal heart rate and the method used to determine it, should be noted as well.

**Prenatal Information**

Prenatal information should be noted if there are issues or allegations associated with the care of the patient during this time. If so, relevant laboratory/radiologic findings and treatment should be included.

**Course of Labor**

The investigator should summarize the progress of the mother's labor and highlight signs of non-reassuring fetal status or fetal well-being. This should include interventions or treatment as well as information significant for possible obstetrical mismanagement.

**Delivery Information**

The investigator should briefly describe by what method and by whom the delivery was managed, and summarize any problems encountered. The indication for any operative delivery (e.g., forceps, Cesarean section) should be noted. If significant, the type of anesthesia used should be included. It is also important to note the infant's Apgar scores,[11] sex, birth weight, and any need for resuscitation.

**Neonatal and Postpartum Course**

The investigator should briefly summarize the infant's hospital course and subsequent treatment (if available), noting any evidence of neurologic compromise or findings relevant to the injury or allegation. The mother's postpartum course should be noted only if it is relevant.

---

Sample Synopsis #1

---

This case involves the alleged failure to properly monitor for and diagnose fetal distress, resulting in a delay in performing a Cesarean section and a neurologically impaired infant.

This 32-year-old primipara was admitted to **General Hospital** on **6/10/2005** at **7:40 A.M.** with a full-term pregnancy in labor.. Admitting vaginal examination revealed the patient's cervix was 85% effaced, 3 cm dilated, and membranes were intact. The infant was in a vertex presentation at _1 station, and the fetal heart rate (FHR) by auscultation was 152.

At **9:40 A.M.**, an external fetal monitor revealed a FHR of 140–150. At **10:00 A.M.**, fetal heart decelerations from 140–100 were noted, and the house staff was notified. The patient was turned onto her left side, hydrated, and given oxygen via facial mask, with good recovery to the baseline FHR. Subsequently, Demerol and Phenergan were administered. At **10:25 A.M.**, the patient's membranes were artificially ruptured, and thick green pea soup meconium was noted. A scalp pH revealed fetal acidosis at 7.14 (normal: 7.25–7.35).

At **10:50 A.M.**, a female infant was delivered via Cesarean section for fetal acidosis by **Dr. Jose Francisco** (Attending physician, OB/GYN). Meconium was noted and treated by pediatrics with suctioning and intubation. The infant weighed 7 lb 8 oz, with Apgar scores of 4 at one minute and 10 at five minutes. She was quickly extubated and had an uncomplicated newborn nursery course. Neurologic examination revealed no deficits. She was discharged with her mother on **6/15/2005**.

---

Sample Synopsis #2

---

This case involves alleged negligence in diagnosing and treating prenatal toxoplasmosis, resulting in the neurologic impairment of this infant.

This 33-year-old para 5005 began receiving prenatal care in the OB clinic of St. Elsewhere Medical Center on **1/7/2005**. The patient was diagnosed as having gestational diabetes that was controlled by diet. Her EDD was **7/25/2005**. The pregnancy progressed without complication until **5/27/2005**, when the patient was hospitalized at St. Elsewhere for observation of blood sugar and for a work-up for polyhydramnios that was confirmed by sonogram. The sonogram also revealed gestational shortening of the long-bone-to-trunk ratio.

The patient was discharged on **6/1/2005**. Follow-up sonograms on **6/13/2005** and **6/30/2005** were unchanged. There was no documentation of any prenatal TORCH

titers (TORCH includes toxoplasmosis, rubella, cytomegalovirus, and herpes simplex virus) except for negative rubella testing. On **7/2/2005**, an amniocentesis was performed at St. Elsewhere. The amniotic fluid specimen was sent to **Community Hospital** for chromosomal studies; however, there was no documentation in the prenatal record concerning the results of these studies.

The patient was admitted to **Community Hospital** on **7/21/2005** in labor. **Dr. Edgar Small** (Attending, OB/GYN) delivered a male infant via spontaneous vaginal delivery. The infant, with Apgar scores of 9/9 and weighing 6 lb 7 oz, was admitted to the neonatal intensive care unit (NICU) for observation due to maternal diabetes.

On physical examination, it was also noted the infant had well-formed but low-set ears. Blood was drawn for chromosomal studies; however, no results were noted. The remainder of the infant's hospital course was uneventful. On **7/24/2005**, the day of discharge, the infant was evaluated in the radiology department for skeletal abnormalities. The formal radiology report, dated **7/25/2005,** noted the findings were suggestive of a TORCH virus.

During a postpartum clinic visit on **8/1/2005**, **Dr. Small** noted the mother and infant were positive for cytomegalovirus (CMV); however, there were no laboratory reports in the record to verify this, and subsequent urine specimens taken from the infant revealed no growth of CMV. The infant also tested negative for toxoplasmosis. The infant's current neurologic status is not known at this time.

---

*Review of Medical Records*

**Mother's Obstetrical History**
  This should include the parity and the history of prior pregnancies, including types of deliveries, complications (e.g., preeclampsia, Rh incompatibility), and size of previous infants, or a notation of "no significant history." The source of the information should be indicated.

**Mother's Medical History**
  The investigator should include a brief summary of pertinent non-obstetrical medical and surgical history, together with the source of the information.

**Review of Current Prenatal Records**
  The *Review of Current Prenatal Records* section of the investigation report captures the pertinent clinical facts obtained from the prenatal records. Most clinics and private physician offices send a copy of the prenatal records to the hospital one month prior to the due date. This copy

becomes part of the mother's labor record. The investigator should carefully review the final month of prenatal care and any other prenatal records.

Information (if available) to detail in the appropriate boxes of the *Review of Current Prenatal Records* section includes the following:

- *Clinic or Private Medical Doctor*—Where prenatal care was received should be indicated (e.g., General Hospital Prenatal OPD, Dr. John Smith's office, not determined).
- *Dates*—If relevant, the date of the mother's first visit, the number of visits, and the date of the last visit should be noted. It is also important to include the date of the mother's last menstrual period (LMP) and the EDD.
- *Estimated Fetal Weight (EFW)*—This should include the weight, the source and the date of estimate.
- *Other Information*—If relevant, the mother's total weight gain and fundal height should be indicated.
- *Vital Signs*—If relevant, pertinent vital signs should be included.

*This section of the report includes two templates for prenatal test information. Enter the following:*

- Test result, date and normal values.
- If there is no documentation indicating that the tests were done, enter N/D.

- **Template # 1—Prenatal Testing**—This template is designed to capture pertinent prenatal testing. The date, results, and location for each of the following tests should be entered:
  - Sonogram
  - Biophysical profile
  - Amniocentesis
  - Nonstress test
  - Contraction stress test
  - Chorionic villi sampling
  - Genetic counseling

- **Template # 2—Prenatal Laboratory Tests**—This optional template is designed to capture other pertinent laboratory tests. Pertinent laboratory tests may include the following (any non-pertinent test may be deleted):
  - Hemoglobin/hematocrit
  - VDRL
  - Blood group and Rh
  - Antibody screening
  - Rubella titers
  - Birth defect testing (ex: AFP , chromosomal aneuploids and neural tube defects, maternal serum, multiple marker, triple or quad screen)
  - Urine protein/glucose
  - Glucose challenge test
  - Gonorrhea culture
  - Chlamydia culture
  - Group B *Streptococcus*
  - Human immunodeficiency virus (HIV) testing
  - TORCH studies

The investigator should use the space at the bottom of the section to include any other pertinent tests as well as additional information, such as any hospitalizations during pregnancy, complications during pregnancy (e.g., vaginal bleeding, preeclampsia, premature labor), treatment for infections, , HIV exposure, or any other illness during pregnancy.

## Mother's Admission Information

The *Mother's Admission Information* section of the investigation report captures the pertinent clinical facts obtained on admission. It begins with the date and time of the mother's presentation to the hospital and the name and status of the person who performed the initial evaluation (e.g., R.N., M.D. [Attending or postgraduate year (PGY)], or certified nurse midwife [C.N.M.]).

The following information should be filled in on the template:

- Parity
- Last menstrual period (LMP)

- Expected date of of delivery (EDD)
- Weeks' gestation—the number of weeks of pregnancy (A preterm pregnancy is less than 37 weeks; a term pregnancy is greater than 37 and less than 42 weeks; a postdates pregnancy is 42 or more weeks.)
- Date and time of the onset of labor
- Frequency and duration of contractions
- Fetal heart rate (FHR)
- Mother's blood pressure, pulse, respirations, and temperature
- Estimated fetal weight (EFW)
- Time of first vaginal examination and by whom
- Cervical dilatation (the number of centimeters from zero to ten, the mother's cervix is dilated)
- Effacement (the percentage of dilatation of the cervix)
- Presentation (the fetal part lowest in the birth canal when labor begins)
  - *Vertex*—The head presents.
  - *Transverse*—A shoulder presents.
  - *Breech*—the buttocks present.
    - *Frank breech*—The hips are flexed, the knees are extended, and the feet are near the head.
    - *Complete breech*—The hips are flexed, one or both knees are flexed, and one or both feet are near the buttocks.
    - *Incomplete breech*—One or both hips are not flexed.
    - *Single-footling breech*—One foot lies below the buttocks.
    - *Double-footling breech*—Both feet lie below the buttocks.

Station (the number assigned to the level of the fetal presenting part in relation to the maternal pelvis)
  - When the widest part of the fetal head is at the ischial spines, it is considered to be zero station or "engaged."
  - When the head is above the ischial spines, it is measured in negative numbers (e.g., −1 station, each station is 1 cm).
  - When the head is below the ischial spines, it is measured in positive numbers (e.g., +1 station ).
  - When the head is above the pelvis, it is called "floating."
- Position (the relationship of the back of the fetal head [or presenting part] to the maternal pelvis)

- ○ The most common position is *occiput anterior* (abbreviated "OA"), in which the back of the fetal head (the occiput) is anterior in the maternal pelvis.
- ○ The position of the occiput is abbreviated in a clockwise fashion (e.g., *left occiput anterior* denotes that the back of the fetal head is between 12 noon and three o'clock relative to the maternal symphysis pubis [the 12 noon position]).
- Membranes—Whether the membranes are intact or, if not, the date and time they ruptured should be noted. The color of the amniotic fluid, any other description, and whether the membranes ruptured spontaneously or artificially should also be included.

The investigator should use the blank area at the bottom of this section to record any additional information, such as assessment of the FHR, admitting physical examination, abnormal admission laboratory work, or other abnormal findings. The documented plan of care, as well as when various MDs and/or CNMs saw the patient or called the hospital, should be recorded here.

*Review of Labor Records*

The *Review of Labor Records* section of the investigation report provides a chronological summary of all significant labor documentation. This documentation includes vaginal examinations, contractions, FHR, fetal scalp pH, maternal vital signs, , laboratory work, voiding, sonography, artificial rupture of membranes —including color and description, fetal monitoring, evidence of cord prolapse, and so forth. Pertinent documented impressions of fetal heart tracings (identifying author) and interventions (e.g., O2, fluid challenges, lateralization) should also be included. Any instances of the patient receiving medications including analgesics, anesthesia, or Pitocin, should always be noted. If a scalp pH was performed, this fact should be noted in bold print. This should include the result, the normal range, and who obtained the sample, followed by any documented impressions/interventions in response to the result.

This information should be presented as a *timeline*, beginning immediately after the initial evaluation and ending with the start of delivery or the time of transfer to the operating room (in the event of a Cesarean section).Each entry should cite the source and author (if possible) of all documentation.

An example of the format to be used for this section follows:

| | |
|---|---|
| 7:00 P.M. | Record of Labor (Nurse Jones, R.N.): EFM: FHR: 90–110. Resident (Dr. Thompson) informed. IV fluid increased, O2 applied via face mask, and patient positioned onto left side. |
| 7:10 P.M. | Progress Note by Dr. Smith: VE: FD/100%/+2. Patient instructed to push. Will attempt vaginal delivery. |

Any specific issues the investigator wishes to bring to the reader's attention should be placed in parentheses and italics for emphasis. He or she may want to begin with the phrase: *"Reader, please note . . ."*

## *Review of the Delivery Records*

The *Review of Delivery Records* section of the investigation report captures the pertinent clinical facts noted during a vaginal or Cesarean section delivery. For either type of delivery, the following should be noted:

- Date and time of the delivery
- Names and titles of those present
  - Who performed the delivery
  - Who assisted
  - Nurse(s) and/or C.N.M.(s)
  - Anesthesiologist (if present)
  - Pediatrician (if present)
  - Any relative or "significant other"
  - Any observers
- Type of anesthesia administered
- Time of delivery of the placenta
- Examination of the placenta (indicate the source of this information)

For a vaginal delivery, the following information should also be included:

- Presentation and position of the fetus on delivery
- Type of delivery
  - Spontaneous
  - Forceps (including type of forceps delivery and if low, mid, or high)
  - Vacuum extraction (low, mid or high)
  - Application of fundal or suprapubic pressure
  - Maneuvers for shoulder dystocia
- Description of any episiotomy or laceration

The investigator should use the area at the end of this section to record any additional information, including the indication for a forceps/vacuum extraction delivery, presence of cord around neck/nuchal cord, and any complications (e.g., shoulder dystocia, breech presentation, unusual characteristics of placenta). For all shoulder dystocia cases, the time of delivery of the baby's head and the time of delivery of the baby's shoulders should be included.

For a Cesarean section delivery, the following details of the operation should be added:

- Infant's presentation and position
- Time of the skin incision
- Type of uterine incision (e.g., low segment [or low flap], vertical [or classical], inverted T, or other type)

The investigator should use the area at the end of this section to record any additional information, including the indication for the Cesarean section, presence of cord around neck/nuchal cord, any complications, and any unusual characteristics of the placenta.

### Infant Delivery Information

The *Infant Delivery Information* section of the investigation report captures the pertinent clinical facts regarding delivery events relating to the infant.

The following information should be noted:

- The infant's Apgar scores at one, five, and ten minutes of life
- The infant's weight
- The sex of the infant
- Details of the examination of the infant at the time of delivery: Any abnormal findings such as congenital abnormalities or neuro-motor deficits and who performed the examination and authored the note should be indicated.
- Intervention/resuscitation: Any significant activities should be summarized. This includes the type and extent of the intervention(s) (e.g., suction, "whiffs" of oxygen, ambu-bagging, intubation) and the response to interventions. There should be notation of who was involved and the name of the pediatrician or neonatologist present.
- Medications given
- Cord pH
- Number of blood vessels in the umbilical cord
- Transfer of infant: This should indicate the location to which the infant was transferred after the delivery (e.g., the well-baby nursery, NICU), and when and by whom the transfer was completed.

The investigator should use the area at the end of this section to record any additional information.

## Mother's Postpartum Course

The investigator should briefly describe any significant events that took place after the delivery. This may simply be described as "uneventful."

## Review of the Infant's Medical Record

The *Review of Infant's Medical Records* section of the investigation report captures the pertinent clinical facts obtained from the records. It should briefly summarize the infant's hospital course, focusing on the documentation relating to the injury or alleged injury. For brain-damaged infants, the focus should be on the infant's neurologic status, activity, suck, cry, and so forth. The infant's condition on arrival to the nursery/NICU, and the results of any initial arterial blood gases (ABGs) and the nursery/NICU admission examination by the physician should be included. (See Exhibit 12-4 for commonly used neonatal abbreviations.)

If liability issues exist in the neonatal period, details describing the events should be included. The investigator should review the neonatal record to see if any of the following pertinent findings were noted:

- Seizures
- Cyanosis
- Respiratory distress
- Apnea and/or bradycardia
- Cephalohematoma
- Oxygen desaturations
- Bruises
- Lethargy
- Poor feeding or nippling
- Flaccidity
- Poor reflexes
- Hyperbilirubinemia
- Erythroblastosis
- Retrolental fibroplasias or retinopathy of prematurity
- Infection
- Blood in the urine
- Abnormal ABGs

If it has been alleged or the record suggests the child is compromised, if legally permissible, it may be necessary to request subsequent admissions and pediatric neurology clinic visits/other pediatric records to review for evidence of neurologic or other injuries.

## SAMPLE OBSTETRICAL INVESTIGATION REPORT

Exhibit 12-2 is an example of an investigation report for an obstetrical case resulting in a neurologically impaired infant. The report is shown in its entirety in the format suggested.

**Exhibit 12-2**     FOJP Service Corporation Sample Obstetrical Investigation Report

---

Dated:  November 12, 2005

**Patient:** Ann Flower (Infant)                **Claimant:**   Dawn Flower (Mother)

To:    Geller & Geller, Att: Mark Geller, Esq.

cc:    Team Supervisor, FOJP

By:  Doris Clayton, Risk Control Coordinator

| Institution | General Medical Center | | | | |
|---|---|---|---|---|---|
| FOJP File # | V04-0604-3910 | Defense Attorney File # | | 00000 | |
| Status | Summons | | | Severity Code | 08 |
| | | Interviews | 5 | Pages | 15 |

**Exhibit 12-2**    continued

INVESTIGATION REPORT (continued)          Page 2          FOJP SERVICE CORPORATION

CASE OF __ANN FLOWER__                                      FILE # __V04-0604-3910__

## TREATMENT DATES

| Patient | Office, Institution or Department | Medical Record # | - through - | |
|---------|-----------------------------------|------------------|-------------|--------|
| Mother  | General Medical Center            | 900-18-5713      | * 9/6/04    | 9/8/04 |
| Infant  | General Medical Center            | 900-18-5714      | * 9/6/04    | 9/25/04 |

* Relevant Treatment Records

| DATE OF OCCURRENCE | 9/6/04 |
|--------------------|--------|

| FIRST REPORTED | DATE | PLAINTIFF'S ATTORNEY |
|----------------|------|----------------------|
| Alert | | |
| ARL | 9/14/05 | Howe & Howe, Esqs. |
| Pt. Complaint/Letter of Claim | | |
| Summons | 10/15/05 | Howe & Howe, Esqs. |

**Exhibit 12-2**   continued

---

| INVESTIGATION REPORT (continued) | Page 3 | **FOJP SERVICE CORPORATION** |
|---|---|---|

CASE OF  ANN FLOWER                              FILE #  V04-0604-3910

## PARTIES INVOLVED

A   Insured:

1.   **General Medical Center.**  Named Defendant.

2.   **\* Rey, Donald: M.D.,** PGY-3, OB/GYN, Employee. Presently an Attending at General Medical Center. Named Defendant.

3.   **Gott, Michael: M.D.,** PGY-1, OB/GYN, Employee. Presently an Attending at General Medical Center. Named Defendant.

4.   **\* Koti, Patricia: M.D.,** PGY-2, Pediatrics, Employee. LDE: 6/30/05. LKA: 950 4th Street, Cross River, NY 11019.

5.   **\* Stile, Mary: R.N.,** Staff Nurse, Labor & Delivery, Employee.

6.   **\* Price, Oliver: M.D.,** Attending, Assistant Director of Neonatology, Employee.

B   Parties With Other Insurance Coverage (if possible, identify their insurance coverage):

1.   Blum, Gerald: M.D., Attending, OB/GYN, Nonemployee. Named Codefendant.

2.   Kopper, Ronald: M.D., Attending, OB/GYN, Nonemployee. Named Codefendant.

3.   Ho, Kynung Ho: M.D., Attending, Anesthesiology, Nonemployee. Named Codefendant.

4.   Joseph Hwang: M.D., Attending, Pediatrics, Nonemployee. Named Codefendant.

## IN-HOUSE REVIEWS

1.   \* Donn, Nathan: M.D., Attending, Associate Director of OB/GYN, Employee.

\* Interview contained within this report

**Exhibit 12-2**    continued

---

INVESTIGATION REPORT (continued)         Page 4          **FOJP SERVICE CORPORATION**

CASE OF __ANN FLOWER_____               FILE # __V04-0604-3910____

---

## CRITICAL INFORMATION

The medical record contains inconsistent, absent and altered documentation related to the labor and delivery.

## CASE SYNOPSIS

This case involves the alleged failure to diagnose fetal distress and the failure to perform a Cesarean section resulting in a neurologically impaired infant.

This 20-year-old primipara was admitted to **General Medical Center** on **9/6/04** at **6:30 p.m.** The patient's EDD was **10/9/04** and she was noted to be in premature labor.

The patient was not seen during the prenatal period until 20 weeks gestation and only three prenatal visits were noted. The admitting vaginal exam revealed the patient's cervix was 5 cm dilated, 100% effaced and the membranes were intact. The fetus was noted to be at the –2 station, in a vertex presentation and the fetal rate (FHR) was 142 by external monitor.

At **6:55 p.m.**, an internal monitor was applied and a FHR of 144 noted.

At **7:45 p.m.** the patient had epidural anesthesia administered by Dr. Ho. By **8:05 p.m.**, the FHR was 90-120 BPM for which the patient was turned to her left side, $O_2$ via face mask and an increase in IV fluids were administered.

At **8:32 p.m.**, the patient delivered via spontaneous vaginal delivery.* According to the delivery room log, the patient was taken to delivery room #3 where she delivered a 3 lb 14 oz female with an Apgar of 9 at one minute and 10 at five minutes. However, according to the anesthesiology record completed by Dr. Ho, the

**Exhibit 12-2**   continued

---

INVESTIGATION REPORT (continued)             Page 5              **FOJP SERVICE CORPORATION**

CASE OF  ANN FLOWER                                                        FILE #  V04-0604-3910

---

patient "delivered a girl at **8:32 p.m.** on the bed," with an Apgar score of 8 at one minute and 9 at five minutes.  Also, there is a discrepancy in the record regarding who delivered the infant, the attending or the resident.

The infant was transferred to the special care nursery where she was treated for an elevated bilirubin.  Initially, fine tremors were noted.  An NG tube was placed secondary to poor nippling.  The infant retained feedings and gained weight.  Her color, cry, activity and suck were noted as satisfactory by **9/25/04** when she was transferred to the well-baby nursery.  On **9/25/04**, the infant was discharged to her mother's care in satisfactory condition to be followed by her private MD.

*Reader: please note it was the practice of General Hospital in 2004 to allow the mother to labor in the Labor Room bed. She would then be transferred to the Delivery Room and placed on the Delivery Room table for the delivery of the infant.*

**Exhibit 12-2**    continued

INVESTIGATION REPORT (continued)               Page 6          **FOJP SERVICE CORPORATION**

CASE OF  ANN FLOWER                                            FILE #  V04-0604-3910

## REVIEW OF MEDICAL RECORDS

| MOTHER'S DEMOGRAPHIC INFORMATION | | | | | | | |
|------|------|------|--------|------|-------|----------|-----|
| AGE | 20 | SEX | Female | RACE | Asian | RELIGION | N/A |
| OCCUPATION | | | Housewife | | INSURANCE | N/D | |
| MARITAL STATUS | | | Married | | | | |
| DEPENDENTS (SPECIFY) | | | One newborn | | | | |

N/D = Not Documented

**OBSTETRICAL HISTORY** One abortion - 2003

**MEDICAL HISTORY**  No significant PMH documented.

## REVIEW OF CURRENT PRENATAL RECORDS

| | |
|---|---|
| Clinic or PMD: Dr. Ronald Kopper | |
| Dates: | First Visit: 6/4/04 |
| | No. of Visits: 3 |
| | Last Visit: N/D |
| LM P: 1/2/04 | EDD: 10/9/04 |
| EFW: N/D | |
| Total Weight Gain: 10 lbs per prenatal record; | |

**Exhibit 12-2**    continued

| | | |
|---|---|---|
| INVESTIGATION REPORT (continued) | Page 7 | **FOJP SERVICE CORPORATION** |
| CASE OF _ANN FLOWER_ | | FILE # _V04-0604-3910_ |

20 lbs per documented weights (pre-

preg:134lbs; admission wt: 154lbs)

Vital Signs:

| DATE | VITAL SIGNS |
|---|---|
| 7/8/04 | BP 100/60 |
| 8/9/04 | BP 115/70 |
| | |
| | |

**PRENATAL TESTING**

| | Date | Results | MD/Location |
|---|---|---|---|
| Sonogram | N/D | N/D | N/D |
| Biophysical Profile | N/D | N/D | N/D |
| Amniocentesis | N/D | N/D | N/D |
| Non-Stress Test | N/D | N/D | N/D |
| Contraction Stress Test | N/D | N/D | N/D |
| Chorionic Villi Sampling | N/D | N/D | N/D |

Genetic Counseling: N/D

**Exhibit 12-2**    continued

| INVESTIGATION REPORT (continued) | Page 8 | FOJP SERVICE CORPORATION |
|---|---|---|
| CASE OF  ANN FLOWER | | FILE #  V04-0604-3910 |

## MOTHER'S ADMISSION INFORMATION

Date and Time of Initial Presentation and Evaluation: 9/6/04 6:21 p.m. per record of L&D; 6:33 pm per

admission record

Evaluated By: Dr. Gott

| Parity: 0010 (0000 per L&D record) | | Weeks Gestation: 36 weeks (Labor record) | |
|---|---|---|---|
| LMP: 1/2/04 | | EDD: 10/9/04 | |
| Date/Time of Onset of Labor: 9/6/2004 10:30 am | | Membranes: intact | |
| Contractions: q6 min/30 sec (L&D record); q4min/90 sec (admission record) | | | |
| FHR: 142 MLQ by EFM | | EFW: 2400 gm | |
| BP: 118/78 | T: N/D | P: 120 | R: N/D |
| Time of First Vaginal Exam: 9/6/04 6:21(am or pm not noted) per L&D record | | By MD/CNM: Dr. Gott | |
| Cervical Dilation: 5 cm | | Effacement: 100% | |
| Station: -2 | Presentation: Vertex | Position: N/D | |

**Exhibit 12-2**   continued

INVESTIGATION REPORT (continued)                Page 9            **FOJP SERVICE CORPORATION**

CASE OF  _ANN FLOWER_                                              FILE #  _V04-0604-3910_

## REVIEW OF LABOR RECORDS

6:55 pm    Nurse's Note (M. Ollie RN):  Sterile vaginal exam by Dr. Gott for AROM.  Clear fluid noted and
           IFM (Internal Fetal Monitor) applied.  FHR 144.

7:12 pm    Record of L&D (Dr. Gott):  VE: cervix dilated to 6 cm.

7:45 pm    Nurse's Note (V. Zip RN):  Epidural anesthesia started by Dr. Ho.

8:00 pm    Record of L&D (Dr. Gott):  Fully dilated, station 0, vtx presentation (*Reader please note: the time
           noted as 8:00 pm appears to have been written over and altered. The documented FHR also appears
           altered and can be interpreted as 105 ,125, 185, or 195 BPM.*)

8:05 pm    Nurse's Note (M. Stile RN) *(time appears written over and altered from 8:15 pm):* FHR 90-120.
           Dr. Rey notified.  IV fluid increased and O$_2$ applied by face mask.

8:10 pm    Nurse's Note: Patient on left side. (*There was no indication on the nursing labor records of when
           the patient was taken to the delivery room.*)

**Exhibit 12-2**    continued

---

## REVIEW OF DELIVERY RECORDS

### VAGINAL DELIVERY

| | |
|---|---|
| Date & Time of Delivery: 9/6/04 8:32 pm<br>*(However, the anesthesia record notes the patient<br>arrived in the delivery room at 8:40 pm.)* | Delivered by: Dr. Blum (attending) assisted by Dr.<br>Rey (resident) (per the physician's delivery record)<br>or Dr. Rey assisted by Dr. Blum (per the nurse's<br>delivery record). |
| | Pediatrician(s) present: Dr. Koti saw the infant in<br>DR (per M. Stile's nurse's note in infant's record).<br>Dr. Hwang (Attending Pediatrics) was present per<br>L&D record. |
| | Anesthesiologist(s): Dr. Ho |
| | RN(s)/CNM(s): M. Stile |
| | Significant Other Present: N/D |
| Presentation/Position: Vertex/OA | Anesthesiology Type: Epidural |
| Type of Delivery: Spontaneous (NSVD) | Episiotomy/Laceration: First degree paracervical<br>laceration (repaired). |
| Time of Delivery of Placenta: 8:40 pm per nurse's<br>record of delivery; 9:40 or 9:46 per MD record of<br>delivery | Pathology Exam of Placenta: N/D |

Additional Information:

1.  According to Dr. Ho's anesthesiology record, the patient "delivered girl at 8:32 pm on the bed."

2.  According to the DR log – the patient delivered at 8:32 pm in DR #3 and that pediatrics was present
    although the room # appears to have been altered.

**Exhibit 12-2**   continued

| INVESTIGATION REPORT (continued) | Page 11 | **FOJP SERVICE CORPORATION** |
|---|---|---|

CASE OF __ANN FLOWER__     FILE # __V04-0604-3910__

## STAGES OF LABOR

Length of First Stage of Labor: 9 hours 30 minutes

Length of Second Stage of Labor: 32 minutes

Length of Third Stage of Labor: 8 minutes

## INFANT DELIVERY INFORMATION

Apgars     One Minute: OB/9; Anesthesia /8

Five Minutes: OB/10; Anesthesia /9

Ten Minutes: N/D

Weight: 1770 gm (3 lb 14 oz)

Sex: Female

Infant Exam at Delivery: No apparent abnormalities per M. Stile, RN

Intervention/Resuscitation: Suctioned with a DeLee by Dr. Rey

Cord pH: N/D

Medications given: N/D

Number of Vessels: N/D

Infant Transferred to: special care nursery

## MOTHER'S POSTPARTUM COURSE

Received RhoGAM  (Patient O negative); otherwise uneventful

**Exhibit 12-2**   continued

## REVIEW OF INFANT'S MEDICAL RECORD

The infant was admitted to the special care nursery at **9:00 p.m.** on **9/6/04**. The nurse's notes revealed the infant's color was pink and her cry lusty and strong. An admission physical was performed by **Dr. John Merchant** (PGY-1 Pediatrics) and revealed no abnormalities.

By **9:15 p.m., Staff Nurse Edna Nixon** documented the infant was slightly jaundiced. A **10:30 p.m.** nurse's note revealed **Dr. Susan Sony** (PGY-2, Pediatrics) was made aware of the infant's jaundice and of fine tremors of the extremities. Additionally, the infant was noted to have strange facial features.

A **9/7/04** note by Dr. Joseph Hwang (Attending, Pediatrics, Non-employee) revealed the infant's bilirubin was 6.5 (normal [less than 1 day old] 6). Dr. Hwang had phototherapy initiated for the infant and blood for an exchange transfusion was kept available should the bilirubin levels rise. A hematology consult was performed on **9/7/04** by a physician who signed the note "O.R." According to this physician, the infant could be maintained on phototherapy and the exchange transfusion could be canceled. Subsequently, the hyperbilirubinemia resolved.

The infant remained in an incubator and required the placement of a nasogastric feeding tube on **9/10/04** for poor nippling.

By **9/12/04**, the infant was sucking well, taking and tolerating formula and the nasogastric tube was discontinued.

On **9/25/04**, the infant was transferred to the well-baby nursery in preparation for discharge. She was discharged that same day at a weight of 4 lb 8 oz. Physical examination was done at discharge by the pediatric

## Exhibit 12-2   continued

attending, **Dr. Alan Rose** (Attending, Pediatrics), who was covering for Dr. Hwang. **Dr. Rose** documented the discharge physical findings as "negative" and the discharge diagnosis as pre-term infant and hyperbilirubinemia.

### INTERVIEW – Donald Rey, M.D.

On **11/1/05**, I conducted a personal interview with Dr. Donald Rey, the PGY-3 in OB/GYN who was noted on the nurse's delivery record as having delivered the infant on **9/6/04**.

Dr. Rey was a well-groomed physician in his mid-thirties. Although Dr. Rey had a South African accent, he was easily understood. Dr. Rey was extremely pleasant. Dr. Rey was intelligent and cooperative. He had an excellent recollection of infant and Ms. Flower.

Dr. Rey recalled examining Ms. Flower and noted upon vaginal examination the patient was fully dilated and under epidural anesthesia. Dr. Rey stated he called Dr. Blum to inform him of the patient's progress. Dr. Blum advised Dr. Rey not to transfer the patient to the delivery room until he (Dr. Blum) arrived on the unit. Dr. Rey recalled that subsequent to his conversation with Dr. Blum, he (Dr. Rey) returned to the patient's bedside and noted the patient already delivered the infant spontaneously in the bed with no physician in attendance at the time of the infant's delivery. Dr. Rey stated he was unable to recall whether a nurse was present in the room at the time of the infant's delivery.

Dr. Rey remembered the infant's color was pink. Dr. Rey stated the infant's Apgar scores were 9 and 10. Dr. Rey recalled Ms. Flower and the infant were transferred from the Labor Room to the Delivery Room for further care, where they were met by Dr. Blum.

**Exhibit 12-2**    continued

Dr. Rey could not recall whether he or Dr. Blum delivered the placenta and performed the repair of the paracervical laceration. Dr. Rey also was unable to recall if a pediatrician was present in the delivery room. Dr. Rey stated if the infant had required resuscitation, either he (Dr. Rey) or one of the nurses would have resuscitated the infant until the pediatrician arrived.

Dr. Rey reviewed the mother's record and stated the patient's prenatal history and course were uneventful. Dr. Rey noted, although the patient was at 35 weeks' gestation, the patient was in "good labor" when she was admitted.

Dr. Rey stated artificial rupture of membranes was performed in order to apply an internal fetal monitor. Dr. Rey noted the amniotic fluid was clear when the patient's membranes were ruptured.

Dr. Rey reviewed the fetal monitor tracing and observed some variable decelerations when the patient was pushing. Dr. Rey stated variable decelerations are common when a patient is pushing. He stated these decelerations signified a short period of non-reassuring fetal heart patterns prior to delivery.

Dr. Rey stated at 35 weeks gestation and weighing three pounds and 14 ounces, the infant was small for gestational age. Dr. Rey stated the average weight of a fetus at 34 weeks gestation is 4½ to 5 pounds. Dr. Rey suggested the possibility of intrauterine growth restriction (IUGR). Dr. Rey remarked IUGR can be caused by placental insufficiency or as a result of congenital anomaly.

With regard to the plaintiff's allegations of brain damage, Dr. Rey stated intrauterine growth restriction can cause mental retardation.

**Exhibit 12-2**   continued

---

INVESTIGATION REPORT (continued)          Page 15          **FOJP SERVICE CORPORATION**

CASE OF _ANN FLOWER_                                       FILE # _V04-0604-3910_

Dr. Rey was graduated from New York University in June 2000. From July 2000 to June 2002, Dr. Rey was a surgical resident at St. Mary's Hospital. From July 2002 to June 2005, Dr. Rey was a resident in obstetrics/gynecology at General Medical Center.

Dr. Rey resides at 425 Nepperhan Avenue, Yonkers, NY 10024.

**INTERVIEW – Oliver Price, M.D.**

On **10/30/05**, I conducted a personal interview with Dr. Oliver Price, Assistant Director of Neonatology at General Medical Center. At the request of Dr. Hwang, Dr. Price was a consulting physician for infant Flower on **9/7/04**. Dr. Price had no independent recollection of infant Flower.

Dr. Price was a tall, handsome man in his mid-fifties. He spoke with a Spanish accent but was easily understood. Dr. Price was cooperative and articulate.

In reviewing the record, Dr. Price noted the infant's Apgar score was 9 after one minute and 10 after five minutes and observed the infant was not depressed. However, Dr. Price remarked the infant was on the small side for her gestational age of 35 weeks.

Dr. Price stated although the infant appeared jaundiced, the infant was Coombs negative. Dr. Price explained this is significant since it means that the maternal antibodies are not hemolyzing (destroying) the baby's blood. Dr. Price commented the infant's jaundice could have been due to her prematurity. Dr. Price stated an exchange transfusion was unnecessary because at the time he saw the infant, which was the day

**Exhibit 12-2**    continued

---

INVESTIGATION REPORT (continued)              Page 16              **FOJP SERVICE CORPORATION**

CASE OF  ANN FLOWER                                                FILE #  V04-0604-3910

following birth, the bilirubin was dropping.  Dr. Price stated phototherapy was used to break down the bilirubin in the infant's blood.

Dr. Price opined the infant's jaundice was not due to infection.  Dr. Price noted although the white blood count was elevated, the cultures performed on the infant were negative.

Since tremors were observed in the infant, Dr. Price reviewed the calcium and glucose levels in the infant's blood.  Dr. Price explained tremors in infants can be the result of low calcium and low glucose levels.  Dr. Price noted infant Flower's calcium and glucose levels were normal and stated the tremors could be due to prematurity.  In evaluating other laboratory tests, Dr. Price noted the hematocrit was stable and the electrolytes were normal.

Dr. Price stated the infant was not tested for antenatal intrauterine infection.  Dr. Price stated titers for TORCH should have been performed.  Swabs from the infant's throat and rectum, along with a blood specimen from the infant should or could have been sent to the Board of Health, where the TORCH test is performed.

**Exhibit 12-2**   continued

INVESTIGATION REPORT (continued)       Page 17       **FOJP SERVICE CORPORATION**

CASE OF  ANN FLOWER                           FILE #  V04-0604-3910

The TORCH test is utilized in diagnosis of the following intrauterine antenatal viral infections:

1. T – toxoplasmosis
2. O – other viral infections
3. R – rubella
4. C – cytomegalovirus
5. H – herpes

In conclusion, Dr. Price stated, although infant Flower had an elevated bilirubin initially, the bilirubin dropped in a short time. Dr. Price noted the infant was feeding well and gaining weight. Dr. Price remarked he saw no problem in the neonatal care rendered to the infant except for the omission of the titers for TORCH test.

Dr. Price was graduated from New York Medical College in 1995. He completed his residency at Washington University Medical Center in 1999. He began employment at General Hospital in 2000.

**INTERVIEW – Patricia Koti, M.D.**

On **10/13/05**, I conducted a personal interview with Dr. Koti, the PGY-2 pediatric resident who examined the infant in the delivery room.

Dr. Koti was a small, attractive physician in her early thirties. Dr. Koti spoke with a heavy East Indian accent but could be easily understood. Dr. Koti was cooperative and pleasant.

**Exhibit 12-2**    continued

---

Dr. Koti had no recollection of the infant. In reviewing the record, Dr. Koti stated a pediatrician is usually notified by the delivery room personnel when the birth of a premature infant is anticipated.

In reviewing her initial physical examination documentation, Dr. Koti stated her findings were normal. Dr. Koti was not able to explain why the Apgar score (9 and 10) she gave the infant differed from the Apgar score given by the anesthesiologist (8 and 9). However, Dr. Koti remarked the difference in the scores was not significant.

Dr. Koti noted the infant was small for gestational age. Dr. Koti explained although by dates infant Flower was 36 weeks, physical examination of the infant revealed a gestational age of 34 weeks.

Dr. Koti stated the low birth weight could have been the result of IUGR, malnutrition or maternal smoking during pregnancy. Dr. Koti commented tremors are fairly common in premature infants. Dr. Koti noted the infant's glucose and calcium levels were "okay." Dr. Koti stated the infant's bilirubin was high for the age of the infant. Dr. Koti noted the infant was treated with intravenous therapy and phototherapy. Exchange transfusion was scheduled, but canceled because the bilirubin level dropped.

Dr. Koti declined to comment on the fetal heart rate decelerations noted during the mother's labor.

When I asked Dr. Koti why the titers for TORCH had not been performed, Dr. Koti responded this test is done when an infant is small or any problems are suspected. Dr. Koti was unable to explain why the test had not been performed upon infant Flower.

Dr. Patricia Koti graduated in 1999 from the Lee Medical College, India. From 1999 to 2000, Dr. Koti was a resident 1 OB/GYN in Somalia. From 2001 to June 2003 Dr. Koti did not practice medicine.

## Exhibit 12-2  continued

| | | |
|---|---|---|
| INVESTIGATION REPORT (continued) | Page 19 | **FOJP SERVICE CORPORATION** |
| CASE OF  ANN FLOWER | | FILE #  V04-0604-3910 |

In July 2004, Dr. Koti began a pediatric residency at General Medical Center.

### INTERVIEW – Mary Stile, R.N.

On **10/7/05**, I conducted a personal interview with Staff Nurse Mary Stile, one of the nurses who cared for Dawn Flower and the infant in the labor and delivery room on **9/6/04**.

Mary Stile was a well groomed, Black nurse in her late thirties. Ms. Stile spoke with a West Indian accent. Although somewhat shy, Ms. Stile spoke intelligently and was cooperative.

Ms. Stile did not recall the patient. In reviewing her notes, Ms. Stile noted she first saw the patient in the labor room at **8:05 p.m.** She remarked when she observed the FHR, it had fallen from 128 beats per minute to 90 BPM. Ms. Stile stated according to her custom and practice, she administered oxygen to Ms. Flower, increased the intravenous drip and turned the patient on her left side. Ms. Stile explained these are the usual measures taken by the nurses when a fetal deceleration is first noted. Ms. Stile noted that she also notified the resident, Dr. Rey. She commented the patient was probably examined by Dr. Rey, although Ms. Stile was unable to explain why she had not documented this examination on the patient's record.

Ms. Stile noted the infant was delivered in the mother's labor room bed. Although Ms. Stile stated when a patient delivers in the labor room bed she (Ms. Stile) usually documents that fact on the record, she did not know why she had not in this case. She then explained the procedure that is followed when a patient delivers in bed. A nurse or physician remains with the mother and infant. One of the nurses obtains a delivery room instrument tray and brings it to the labor room. The infant's umbilical cord is clamped and cut. The infant and mother are transferred across the corridor to a delivery room. The infant is suctioned

**Exhibit 12-2**    continued

---

INVESTIGATION REPORT (continued)                    Page 20                    **FOJP SERVICE CORPORATION**

CASE OF  ANN FLOWER                                                            FILE #  V04-0604-3910

and oxygen is administered if it is required. A pediatrician is notified to examine the infant in the delivery room. If the infant is having difficulty, the infant is transferred immediately to the special care nursery.

Subsequent to the pediatrician's examination, the infant is checked by the nurses. Eyedrops are placed in the infant's eyes. Identification bracelets are placed on the infant, and the infant's footprints are taken.

Ms. Stile explained that the obstetrician, pediatrician, anesthesiologist and nurse evaluate the infant for an Apgar score. Ms. Stile stated the Apgar score given by the pediatrician is the final one which is used on the nursing records.

In conclusion, Ms. Stile noted the infant's Apgar score was 9 and 10, and the infant did not require oxygen or resuscitation.

Mary Stile graduated from the Colony Hospital in Grenada in 1987. From 1987 to 1988 she studied midwifery. From 1988 to 1998 Ms. Stile worked in Grenada as a district nurse. Ms. Stile has been employed at General Medical Center as a staff nurse working in the labor room since 1998.

Ms. Stile resides at 439 Bremsen Avenue, Katonah, NY 11012. Her telephone number is 941-225-1482.

**Exhibit 12-2** continued

---

## IN-HOUSE REVIEW – Nathan Donn, M.D.

On 10/24/05, I conducted an in-house review with Dr. Nathan Donn, the Associate Director of OB/GYN at General Medical Center.

In reviewing the patient's labor and delivery room record, Dr. Donn stated Ms. Flower's history was unremarkable, and the patient's labor and delivery room record did not merit concern.

However, Dr. Donn noted the infant's birth weight and stated infant Flower's birth weight was small for dates. Dr. Donn indicated according to the gestational age sheet, "Infant Flower would be categorized in the lower ten percentile." Dr. Donn stated this was a premature infant with severe symmetrical growth retardation.

As well, when Dr. Donn reviewed the fetal monitor tracings, he noted marked late decelerations, mixed atypical latent and variable decelerations, and fetal tachycardia. Dr. Donn felt these tracings were indicative of fetal hypoxia and stress. Dr. Donn stated the overall score of infant Flower's tracing was 4 on a scale of 10.

Dr. Donn stated as soon as fetal tachycardia and late decelerations were evident (approximately 20 minutes after Dawn Flower's admission), a cesarean section should have been performed upon the patient. Dr. Donn noted a delay of 2¼ hours from the time of admission to the time of delivery.

**Exhibit 12-2**   continued

---

INVESTIGATION REPORT (continued)          Page 22          **FOJP SERVICE CORPORATION**

CASE OF _ANN FLOWER_                                            FILE # _V04-0604-3910_

When questioned about the infant's Apgar score of 9 and 10, Dr. Donn explained a good Apgar score can result following fetal hypoxia since "the body compensates and restores itself." He noted cord bloods could have confirmed this.

In conclusion, <u>Dr. Donn stated in his opinion this case is indefensible.</u>

Dr. Donn was graduated from University of Texas, Austin, in June 1985. From July 1985 to June 1987, he was an OB/GYN resident at Columbia-Presbyterian Hospital. From August 1987 to September 1990, he was an OB/GYN practicing at St. Luke's Roosevelt Hospital. Dr. Donn has practiced at General Medical Center since October 1990 and has served as Associate Director of OB/GYN since January 2000.

## COMMENTS

1. Dawn Flower delivered an infant girl spontaneously at 35 weeks' gestation weighing 3 lb 14 oz. According to Dr. Rey, a fetus of 34 weeks gestation weighs 4½ to 5 lb. According to Dr. Donn, Dr. Rey and Dr. Koti, infant Flower's low birth weight may have been as a result of intrauterine growth restriction. Dr. Rey noted that this can result in brain damage and that IUGR suggests placental insufficiency or a congenital anomaly as the etiology of the infant's problem.

2. According to the nurse's delivery room record, infant Flower was delivered by Dr. Rey (resident) assisted by Dr. Blum (attending). According to Dr. Ho's anesthesia record, the infant was delivered in the labor room bed. Dr. Rey's recollection was that there was no physician in attendance. The absence of a physician at the delivery, and the inconsistent and contradictory documentation regarding who delivered the infant, may be problematic for the defense of the case.

## Exhibit 12-2   continued

| | | |
|---|---|---|
| INVESTIGATION REPORT (continued) | Page 23 | **FOJP SERVICE CORPORATION** |
| CASE OF __ANN FLOWER__ | | FILE # __V04-0604-3910__ |

3.  It appears the times and fetal heart rates were changed on the physician's and nurse's records of labor and delivery. This may be problematic as it points to a possible deliberate alteration of the record and deception on the part of the staff.

4.  Dr. Donn's review of the fetal heart tracings revealed evidence of non-reassuring fetal heart rate for 2½ hours prior to delivery. Dr. Donn stated a Cesarean section should have been performed as soon as fetal tachycardia and late decelerations were evident. This will make it difficult to defend against the plaintiff's allegations of failure to diagnose fetal distress and the failure to perform a Cesarean section.

5.  It should be noted, although the infant was given scores of 8 and 9, and 9 and 10, Dr. Donn stated it was possible the infant's brain damage occurred during labor. Dr. Donn explained a good Apgar score can result following fetal hypoxia since "the body compensates and restores itself by delivery."

6.  According to Dr. Price, except for the omission of titers for TORCH test, infant Flower received proper and adequate neonatal care. Whether or not this is significant remains to be determined.

### RECOMMENDATIONS FOR FUTURE INVESTIGATION

An interview with Dr. Michael Gott will be scheduled.

**Exhibit 12-2**    continued

INVESTIGATION REPORT (continued)           Page 24          **FOJP SERVICE CORPORATION**

CASE OF  ANN FLOWER                                          FILE #  V04-0604-3910

| SECURED ITEMS | | |
|---|---|---|
| ITEMS | MOTHER | INFANT |
| | DATE SECURITY OF ORIGINAL ITEM REQUESTED | |
| 1.  MEDICAL RECORDS | | |
| INPATIENT | 11/14/04 | 11/14/04 |
| OUTPATIENT | | |
| EMERGENCY ROOM | | |
| PRIVATE OFFICE | | |
| 2.  BILLS | 11/14/04 | 11/14/04 |
| 3.  FETAL MONITORING STRIPS | 11/14/04 | |
| 4.  RADIOLOGY STUDIES | | 11/14/04 |
| 5.  PATHOLOGY SLIDES | 11/14/04 | |
| 6.  OTHER | | |
| | | |

ENCLOSURES

Copy of labor & delivery log for 9/06/04.

KAK/ja

Q:\WP\JCA\FEMINELL.OB

**Exhibit 12-3**    Obstetrical Abbreviations Seen in Records

| | |
|---|---|
| 0000 or P0000 | No Previous Deliveries, No Full Term Deliveries, No Premature Deliveries, No Abortions, No Living Children |
| 1° C/S | Primary (1st) Cesarean Section |
| AF | Amniotic Fluid |
| AFI | Amniotic Fluid Index |
| AFV | Amniotic Fluid Volume |
| AI | Amnioinfusion |
| AMA | Advanced Maternal Age |
| ARM | Artificial Rupture of Membranes |
| AROM | Artificial Rupture of Membranes |
| BBT | Basal Body Temperature |
| BPD | Biparietal Diameter |
| BPP | Biophysical Profile |
| BTBV | Beat to Beat Variability |
| CAN | Cord Around Neck |
| C/S | Cesarean Section |
| CPD | Cephalo-Pelvic Disproportion |
| CST | Contraction Stress Test |
| CTX | Contractions |
| CX | Cervix |
| DIU | Death In Utero |
| EDC | Expected Date of Confinement (Due Date) |
| EDD | Expected Date of Delivery (Due Date) |
| EFF | Effacement |
| EFM | External Fetal Monitor |
| EFW | Estimated Fetal Weight |
| EXT | External |
| FD | Fully Dilated |
| FM | Fetal Monitor |
| FS Ph | Fetal Scalp pH |
| FTP | Failure to Progress |
| FTP | Full Term Pregnancy |
| G | Gravida (number of pregnancies) |
| GDM | Gestational Diabetic Mother |
| HELLP | Hemolysis, Elevated Liver Function Test and Low Platelets |
| IFM | Internal Fetal Monitor (the same as ISE) |
| IUD | Intrauterine Demise |

**Exhibit 12-3**    continued

| | |
|---|---|
| IUPC | Intrauterine Pressure Catheter |
| ISE | Internal Scalp Electrode (the same as IFM) |
| IUPC | Intrauterine Pressure Catheter |
| IUPT | Intrauterine Pressure Transducer (the same as IUPC) |
| L/C/P | Long, Closed, Posterior (referring to the cervix) |
| LF | Low Flap |
| LMP | Last Monthly Period |
| LOA | Left Occiput Anterior |
| LOP | Left Occiput Posterior |
| LOT | Left Occiput Transverse |
| L/S Ratio | Lecithin-Sphingomyelin Ratio (measurement of fetal lung maturity) |
| LTV | Long Term Variability |
| MLE | Mid Line Episiotomy |
| NRFHT | Non-reassuring Fetal Heart Tones |
| NST | Non Stress Test |
| NSVD | Normal Spontaneous Vaginal Delivery |
| OA | Occiput Anterior |
| OCT | Oxytocin Challenge Test |
| OP | Occiput Posterior |
| P | Para |
| PIH | Pregnancy Induced Hypertension |
| PP | Postpartum |
| PPH | Postpartum Hemorrhage |
| PROM | Premature Rupture of membranes (Prior to Labor) |
| PPROM | Prolonged Premature Rupture of Membranes |
| PTL | Preterm Labor |
| PUBS | Percutaneous Umbilical Blood Sampling |
| RML | Right Medial Lateral Episiotomy |
| ROA | Right Occiput Anterior |
| ROM | Rupture of membranes |
| ROP | Right Occiput Posterior |
| ROT | Right Occiput Transverse |
| S=D | Size Equal Dates (fetal size correctly corresponds to gestational age) |
| SE | Scalp Electrode |
| SSE | Sterile Speculum Exam |
| ST | Station |
| STV | Short Term Variability |

**Exhibit 12-3**   continued

| | |
|---|---|
| SVE | Sterile Vaginal Examination |
| TOL | Trial of Labor |
| TOLAC | Trial of Labor After C-Section |
| TOP | Termination of Pregnancy (Abortion) |
| UA | Uterine Activity |
| US | Ultrasound |
| UT | Uterus or Uterine |
| VBAC | Vaginal Birth After C/Section (the same as VDAC) |
| VDAC | Vaginal Delivery after C-Section (the same as VBAC) |
| VE | Vaginal Exam |
| VTX | Vertex |

(To assist the investigator, this list includes variations as well as standard abbreviations.)

*These may not be officially-approved abbreviations, but they may be helpful to refer to when reviewing a record.

**Exhibit 12-4**   Neonatal Abbreviations Seen in Infant's Records

| | |
|---|---|
| AFOF | Anterior Fontanel Opened and Flat |
| AGA | Average for Gestational Age |
| A & B | Apnea and Bradycardia |
| ASD | Atrial Septal Defect |
| Bili T & D | Bilirubin Total and Direct |
| BPD | Bronchopulmonary Dysplasia |
| CAN | Cord Around Neck |
| CPAP | Continuous Positive Airway Pressure |
| DOL | Day of Life |
| EBM | Expressed Breast Milk |
| ECMO | Extracorporeal Membrane Oxygenation |
| GFR | Grunting Flaring and Retracting |
| EBM | Expressed Breast Milk |
| HA | Hyperalimentation |
| H/B | Hematocrit and Bilirubin |
| HB | Head Box |
| HC | Head Circumference |
| HFV | High Frequency Ventilation |
| HIE | Hypoxic Ischemic Encephalopathy |

**Exhibit 12-4**   continued

| | |
|---|---|
| HMD | Hyaline Membrane Disease (the same as RDS) |
| IDAM | Infant of Drug Abusing Mother |
| IPPB | Intermittent Positive Pressure Bagging or Breathing |
| IUGR | Intrauterine Growth Restriction |
| IVH | Intraventricular Hemorrhage |
| LGA | Large for Gestational Age |
| L/S Ratio | Lecithin-Sphingomyelin Ratio (measurement of fetal lung maturity) |
| NC | Nasal Cannula |
| NEC | Necrotizing Enterocolitis |
| PDA | Patent Ductus Arteriosus |
| PEEP | Positive End Expiratory Pressure |
| PFC | Persistent Fetal Circulation (the same as PPH) |
| PFOF | Posterior Fontanel Opened and Flat |
| PPH | Persistent Pulmonary Hypertension (the same as PFC) |
| PVL | Periventricular Leukomalacia |
| RDS | Respiratory Distress Syndrome (the same as HMD) |
| RLF | Retrolental Fibroplasia (the same as ROP) |
| ROP | Retinopathy of Prematurity (the same as RLF) |
| SGA | Small for Gestational Age |
| TPN | Total Parental Nutrition |
| TTN | Transient Tachypnea of the Newborn |
| UA | Umbilical Artery |
| UAC | Umbilical Artery Catheter |
| UV | Umbilical Vein |
| UVC | Umbilical Vein Catheter |
| VSD | Ventricular Septal Defect |

(To assist the investigator, this list includes variations as well as standard abbreviations.)

*These may not be officially-approved abbreviations, but they may be helpful to refer to when reviewing a record.

## NOTES

1. Although descriptions used throughout this chapter are drawn from the authors' experiences with actual cases, all names and personal characteristics have been created solely for purposes of illustration.
2. See Chapter 1 for definitions of these terms.
3. For an explanation of NAIC codes, see Chapter 19.
4. See Chapter 14 for information on confidentiality of medical records.
5. A woman who has never delivered a baby is a *nullipara*. For subsequent pregnancies, she is a *multipara*. *See* A. DeCherney and L. Nathan, *Current Obstetrics and Gynecology Diagnosis and Treatment*, 9th ed. (New York: Lange Medical Books/McGraw Hill, 2003), 214.
6. J. R. Scott et al., *Danforth's Obstetrics and Gynecology,* 9th ed. (Philadelphia: Lippincott Williams & Wilkins, 2003), 398.
7. Ibid., 36.
8. Ibid., 45–46.
9. *Parity* is the number of deliveries a woman has had. *Primipara* or "primip" is often used to refer to a woman experiencing her first delivery. In the maternal medical record, the number of prior pregnancies is usually denoted by four numbers: the first is the number of prior full-term births; the second is the number of prior premature births; the third is the number of prior abortions (spontaneous or induced); the fourth is the number of currently living children. *Gravida* refers to the total number of pregnancies including the current one. Sometimes you may see both terms combined as an abbreviation (e.g., G2_P1).
10. Expected date of delivery (EDD), is sometimes written as expected date of confinement(EDC).
11. The Apgar score is a quick method to access the newborn at delivery. It is the sum of a zero-to-two-point rating for each of the following: heart rate, respirations, reflexes, muscle tone, and color. A low Apgar score does not always indicate brain damage and, conversely, a high score does not necessarily mean that labor and delivery were trouble free.

Appendix 12-A

# FOJP Service Corporation
# Investigation Report (Blank)

| This report is confidential and prepared solely in anticipation of, or in connection with, litigation. |
|---|

Dated _____

Patient: _____     Claimant: _____

To: _____

cc: _____

By: _____

| Institution | | | |
|---|---|---|---|
| FOJP File # | | Defense Attorney File # | |
| Status | | | Severity Code |
| Disposition | | Interviews | Pages |

### TREATMENT DATES

| Office, Institution or Department* | Medical Record # | - through - |
|---|---|---|
| | | |
| | | |

\* Relevant Treatment Records   N/D = Not Documented

| DATE OF OCCURRENCE | |
|---|---|

| FIRST REPORTED | DATE | PLAINTIFF'S ATTORNEY |
|---|---|---|
| Alert | _____ | _____ |
| ARL/NOM | _____ | _____ |
| Pt. Complaint/Letter of Claim | _____ | _____ |
| Summons | _____ | _____ |

232

INVESTIGATION REPORT (continued)          Page 2          **FOJP SERVICE CORPORATION**

CASE OF *_____                    FILE # *__

## PARTIES INVOLVED

A   Insured(s):

    1.

    2.

B   Parties With Other Insurance Coverage (if possible , identify their insurance coverage)

    1.

    2.

    3.

## IN-HOUSE REVIEWS

    1.

\* Interview contained within this report.

| PATIENT DEMOGRAPHIC INFORMATION | | | | | | |
|---|---|---|---|---|---|---|
| AGE | | SEX | | RACE | | RELIGION |  |
| OCCUPATION | | | | INSURANCE | | |
| MARITAL STATUS | | | | | | |
| DEPENDENTS (SPECIFY) | | | | | | |

N/D = Not Documented

## CRITICAL INFORMATION

## SHORT CASE SYNOPSIS

This case involves...

INVESTIGATION REPORT (continued)          Page 3          **FOJP SERVICE CORPORATION**

CASE OF *_____          FILE # *

## SUMMARY OF MEDICAL RECORDS

## INTERVIEW

## INTERVIEW

## IN-HOUSE REVIEW

## MISCELLANEOUS INVESTIGATION

REFER TO INVESTIGATION REPORT GUIDELINES
**ADDITIONAL ITEMS CONSIDERED FOR INVESTIGATION:**
    Relevant Hospital Policies, Rules and Regulations
    Relevant Patient Logbooks
    Information on Equipment used, Maintenance Records
    Occurrence Reports
    Missing Evidence (FM strips, x-rays, records, etc.)

INVESTIGATION REPORT (continued)          Page 4          **FOJP SERVICE CORPORATIC**

CASE OF *_____                          FILE # *__

COMMENTS

1.

---

**ISSUES CONSIDERED FOR COMMENT:**

**Medical management** of the case, covering:

| | |
|---|---|
| Candidacy | Sufficient documentation |
| Timeliness of intervention | Appropriate procedure, treatment |
| Delay in Diagnosis | Supervision, experience of caregiver |
| Misdiagnosis | Surgical technique |

Adherence to/deviation from hospital policies and procedures

**Degree of responsibility** among the involved parties

**Discrepancies/Problems in the medical record**, documentation or information obtained on interview

**Issues** disclosed during Miscellaneous Investigation

**Damages** sustained by the patient (prognosis, prolonged hospitalization)

**Plaintiff's role** in contributing to the alleged occurrence and injury

**Informed Consent** (Risks, benefits, alternative and documentation)

INVESTIGATION REPORT (continued)            Page 5            **FOJP SERVICE CORPORATION**

CASE OF *_____                                FILE #  *

## RECOMMENDATIONS FOR FUTURE INVESTIGATION

1.

| SECURED ITEMS | |
|---|---|
| **ITEMS** | DATE SECURITY OF ORIGINAL ITEM REQUESTED |
| 1.  MEDICAL RECORDS | |
| INPATIENT | |
| OUTPATIENT | |
| EMERGENCY ROOM | |
| PRIVATE OFFICE | |
| 2.  BILLS | |
| 3.  FETAL MONITORING STRIPS | |
| 4.  RADIOLOGY STUDIES | |
| 5.  PATHOLOGY SLIDES | |
| 6.  OTHER | |

## ENCLOSURES

1.

# FOJP Service Corporation Obstetrical Investigation Report (Blank)

| This report is confidential and prepared solely in anticipation of, or in connection with, litigation. |
|---|

Dated:_____

Patient:_____     Claimant: _____

To: _____

cc: _____

By: _____

| Institution | | | | |
|---|---|---|---|---|
| FOJP File # | | Defense Attorney File # | | |
| Status | | | Severity Code | |
| Disposition | | Interviews | Pages | |

### TREATMENT DATES

| Patient | Office, Institution or Department | Medical Record # | - through - | |
|---|---|---|---|---|
| Mother | | | | |
| Infant | | | | |

Relevant Treatment Records

| DATE OF OCCURRENCE | |
|---|---|

| FIRST REPORTED | DATE | PLAINTIFF'S ATTORNEY |
|---|---|---|
| Alert | | |
| ARL/NOM | | |
| Pt. Complaint/Letter of Claim | | |
| Summons | | |

INVESTIGATION REPORT (continued)          Page 2          **FOJP SERVICE CORPORATION**

CASE OF _____                          FILE # _____

## PARTIES INVOLVED

1.  Insured(s):

    A.

    B.

    C.

2.  Parties With Other Insurance Coverage and if possible, identify their insurance coverage.

    A.

    B.

    C.

## IN-HOUSE REVIEWS

1.

Interview contained within this report.

## CRITICAL INFORMATION

## CASE SYNOPSIS

This case involves

CASE OF _____          FILE # _____

# REVIEW OF MEDICAL RECORDS

| MOTHER'S DEMOGRAPHIC INFORMATION | | | | | | | |
|---|---|---|---|---|---|---|---|
| AGE | | SEX | Female | RACE | | RELIGION | |
| OCCUPATION | | | | INSURANCE | | | |
| MARITAL STATUS | | | | | | | |
| DEPENDENTS (SPECIFY) | | | | | | | |

N/D = Not Documented

## OBSTETRICAL HISTORY

## MEDICAL HISTORY

## REVIEW OF CURRENT PRENATAL RECORDS

Clinic or PMD:

Dates: (**optional**)          First Visit:

No. of Visits:

Last Visit:

LM P:          EDD:

EFW:

Total Weight Gain: (**optional**)      Fundal Ht: (**optional**)

Vital Signs: (**optional**)

           **DATE**                              **VITAL SIGNS**

INVESTIGATION REPORT (continued)          Page 4              FOJP SERVICE CORPORATION

CASE OF _____                                   FILE # _____

## PRENATAL TESTING

|  | | Date | Results | MD/Location |
|---|---|---|---|---|
| Sonogram | 1. | | | |
|  | 2. | | | |
| Biophysical Profile | 1. | | | |
|  | 2. | | | |
| Amniocentesis | | | | |
| Non-Stress Test | 1. | | | |
|  | 2. | | | |
| Contraction Stress Test | | | | |
| Chorionic Villi Sampling | | | | |
| Genetic Counseling: | | | | |

## PRENATAL LAB TESTS (optional)

|  | Date | Results | Normal Value |
|---|---|---|---|
| Hbg/Hct | | | |
| VDRL | | | |
| Group & Rh | | | |
| Antibody Screening | | | |
| Rubella Titers | | | |
| Birth Defect Testing* | | | |
| Urine Prot/Glucose | | | |
| Glucose Challenge Test | | | |
| GC Culture | | | |
| Chlamydia Culture | | | |
| Group B Streptococcus | | | |
| HIV Testing | | | |
| Other (Indicate) | | | |

Additional Information: (optional)

## MOTHER'S ADMISSION INFORMATION

Date & Time of Initial Presentation & Evaluation:
Evaluated By:

| | |
|---|---|
| Parity: | Weeks Gestation: |
| LMP: | EDD: |
| Date/Time of Onset of Labor: | Membranes: |
| Contractions: | |
| FHR: | EFW: |
| BP:          T: | P:                 R: |
| Time of First Vaginal Exam: | By M.D./CNM: |
| Cervical Dilation: | Effacement: |
| Station:     Presentation: | Position: |

Additional Information: (optional)

*Birth Defect Testing (i.e., AFP, chromosomal aneuploides and neural tube defects screen. May also be called maternal serum, multiple marker, triple or quad screen.)

## REVIEW OF LABOR RECORDS

## REVIEW OF DELIVERY RECORDS
### VAGINAL DELIVERY

| | |
|---|---|
| Date & Time of Delivery: | Delivered by: |
| | Pediatrician(s) present: |
| Time Head Delivered: **(optional)** | Anesthesiologist(s): |
| Time Shoulders Delivered: **(optional)** | RN(s)/CNM(s): |
| | Significant Other Present: |
| Presentation/Position: | Type of Anesthesia: |
| Type of Delivery: | Episiotomy/Laceration: |
| Time of Delivery of Placenta: | Pathology Exam of Placenta: |
| Additional Information: **(optional)** | |

### CESAREAN DELIVERY

| | |
|---|---|
| Date & Time of Delivery: | Delivered By: |
| | Pediatrician(s) present: |
| | Anesthesiologist(s): |
| | RN(s)/CNM(s): |
| | Significant Other Present: |
| Presentation/Position: **(optional)** | Type of Anesthesia: |
| Time of Skin Incision: | Type of Uterine Incision: |
| Time of Delivery of Placenta: | Pathology Exam of Placenta: |
| Additional Information: | |

### STAGES OF LABOR

| |
|---|
| Length of First Stage of Labor: |
| Length of Second Stage of Labor: |
| Length of Third Stage of Labor: |

INVESTIGATION REPORT (continued)              Page 6            **FOJP SERVICE CORPORATION**

CASE OF _____                                     FILE # _____

**INFANT DELIVERY INFORMATION**

| Apgars | One Minute: |
|--------|-------------|
|        | Five Minutes: |
|        | Ten Minutes: |

| Weight: |
|---------|
| Sex: |
| Infant Exam at Delivery: |
| Intervention/Resuscitation: |
| Cord pH: |
| Number of Vessels: |
| Infant Transferred to: |
| Additional Information: **(optional)** |

## MOTHER'S POSTPARTUM COURSE

## REVIEW OF INFANT'S MEDICAL RECORD

## INTERVIEW

## IN-HOUSE REVIEW

## MISCELLANEOUS INVESTIGATION

INVESTIGATION REPORT (continued)     Page 7     **FOJP SERVICE CORPORATION**

CASE OF _____     FILE # _____

REFER TO INVESTIGATION REPORT GUIDELINES
**ADDITIONAL ITEMS CONSIDERED FOR INVESTIGATION:**
    Relevant Hospital Policies, Rules and Regulations
    Relevant Patient Logbooks
    Information on Equipment used, Maintenance Records
    Occurrence Reports
    Missing Evidence (FM strips, x-rays, records, etc.)

## COMMENTS

1.

INVESTIGATION REPORT (continued)          Page 8              FOJP SERVICE CORPORATIO

CASE OF _____                          FILE # _____

---

REFER TO INVESTIGATION REPORT GUIDELINES
**ISSUES CONSIDERED FOR COMMENT:**

**Medical management** of the case, covering:

| | |
|---|---|
| Candidacy | Sufficient documentation |
| Timeliness of intervention | Appropriate procedure, treatment |
| Delay in Diagnosis | Supervision, experience of caregiver |
| Misdiagnosis | Surgical technique |
| Adherence to/deviation from hospital policies and procedures | |

**Degree of responsibility** among the involved parties

**Discrepancies/Problems in the medical record**, documentation or information obtained on interview

**Issues** disclosed during Miscellaneous Investigation

**Damages** sustained by the patient (prognosis, prolonged hospitalization)

**Plaintiff's role** in contributing to the alleged occurrence and injury

**Informed Consent** (Risks, benefits, alternative and documentation)

---

## RECOMMENDATIONS FOR FUTURE INVESTIGATION

INVESTIGATION REPORT (continued)          Page 9          **FOJP SERVICE CORPORATION**

CASE OF _____                              FILE # _____

| SECURED ITEMS | | |
|---|---|---|
| ITEMS | MOTHER | INFANT |
| | DATE SECURITY OF ORIGINAL ITEM REQUESTED | |
| 1.  MEDICAL RECORDS | | |
| INPATIENT | | |
| OUTPATIENT | | |
| EMERGENCY ROOM | | |
| PRIVATE OFFICE | | |
| 2.  BILLS | | |
| 3.  FETAL MONITORING STRIPS | | |
| 4.  RADIOLOGY STUDIES | | |
| 5.  PATHOLOGY SLIDES | | |
| 6.  OTHER | | |
| | | |

## ENCLOSURES

\#

# Appendix 12-C

# Blank Form for Test Results

| Arterial Blood Gases | | | | | | | |
|---|---|---|---|---|---|---|---|
| Tests | Normal Range | Dates/Times | | | | | |
| pH | | | | | | | |
| $pCO_2$ | | | | | | | |
| $PO_2$ | | | | | | | |
| $HCO_3$ | | | | | | | |
| $O_2$ Sat. | | | | | | | |
| | | | | | | | |
| | | | | | | | |

| Potassium Administration | | | | | |
|---|---|---|---|---|---|
| Date | Potassium Levels Time Value | | Potassium Administered Time        Amount | Ordering Physician | Date/Time Written |
| | | | | | |
| | | | | | |
| | | | | | |
| NOTES: | | | | | |

| Admitting Laboratory Results | | | |
|---|---|---|---|
| Date | Type of Study | Result | Normal Range |
| | | | |
| | | | |
| | | | |
| | | | |
| All other laboratory work was within normal limits. | | | |

| Hematology | | | | | |
|---|---|---|---|---|---|
| Date | Pre-transfusion Hematocrit | Name of Ordering MD | Amount and Product Administered | Person Who Administered | Post-Transfusion Hematocrit |
| | | | | | |
| | | | | | |
| | | | | | |
| | | | | | |
| | | | | | |
| | | | | | |

| Cardiac Catheterization | | | | | | |
|---|---|---|---|---|---|---|
| Date | T | B/P | P | Rhythm | RR | Procedure/Comments |
| | | | | | | |
| | | | | | | |
| | | | | | | |
| | | | | | | |
| | | | | | | |
| | | | | | | |
| | | | | | | |
| | | | | | | |
| | | | | | | |
| | | | | | | |
| | | | | | | |
| | | | | | | |

# Chapter 13

# Additional Investigation

---

- Investigation During the Discovery Phase
- Responding to Defense Attorneys' Requests for Information
- Preparing Follow-up Investigation Reports
- Sample Follow-up Investigation Report Form

---

## INVESTIGATION DURING THE DISCOVERY PHASE

The investigation of a claim continues virtually until the case is settled or results in a jury verdict. Throughout the discovery phase of a lawsuit, the investigator may be required to obtain a variety of items.

*The following list covers some of the things an investigator might be asked to do during discovery*:

- Gather pertinent films or photographs taken by the defendants (e.g., films taken during surgery, "before and after" photographs)
- Request pathology slides, X-rays, and other items for expert physicians to review
- Obtain surveillance films and private investigation reports
- Locate other pertinent documents, such as logbooks, reports, and rules and regulations
- Obtain certain pieces of equipment or medical or surgical devices
- Locate and review medical records involving prior or subsequent treatment of the patient by the institution. The investigator should consult

in-house counsel to assess the possible need to obtain a release from the patient for such records before accessing the records and before they are provided to defense counsel. Defense counsel is generally responsible for obtaining permission from the plaintiff for copies of records from other institutions or physicians involved in treatment prior to or subsequent to the occurrence. However, it also may be necessary under the Health Insurance Portability and Accountability Act (HIPAA) (see Chapter 14, Confidentiality of Medical Records and Other Documents) to obtain permission from the plaintiff for subsequent treatment records from within the health care organization (HCO). The investigator should consult in-house counsel or a privacy officer.

As the claim approaches trial, the investigator may want to begin verifying the whereabouts of witnesses expected to testify. Considering the length of time it takes for a claim to reach trial, the investigator may find that witnesses have relocated, married, divorced, or just plain disappeared! Therefore, it is important to allow enough time to complete this essential task. A good time to start is when the note of issue (NI) is filed by the plaintiff. (For explanation of a note of issue, see Chapter 11, "Reviewing and Maintaining the Claim File.")

## RESPONDING TO DEFENSE ATTORNEYS' REQUESTS FOR INFORMATION

The investigator generally is responsible for responding to defense attorneys' requests for information relative to a lawsuit. These requests are usually for additional interviews or copies of medical documents, X-rays, or HCO policies or contracts.

*The investigator should evaluate each request carefully to make sure that*

- he or she understands exactly what is being requested
- it is actually possible to obtain the information requested
- the information has not already been provided to defense counsel and misplaced or simply crossed in the mail

Verbal communication with defense counsel is recommended, to clarify the request so the investigator does not lose time in obtaining wrong or unnecessary information. It is best to document these conversations.

## PREPARING FOLLOW-UP INVESTIGATION REPORTS

After completing the initial investigation, defense counsel may request additional information, or the investigator may want to move forward with the investigation plans outlined in the initial report. Follow-up reports should be prepared using the same format as the original investigation report (i.e., addressed to the defense attorney) so as to help provide protection from disclosure (**Appendix 13-A**).

*Guidelines for preparing a follow-up report are as follows:*

- Fill in the headings, beginning with the patient's name and ending with the investigator's name. (These reports need not include a *First Reported* section or information pertaining to the date of admission, date of discharge, or medical record number.)
- The first paragraph of the *Short Case Synopsis* section should indicate clearly that the report is a follow-up to an initial investigation report, with the date of the initial report being included.
- The second paragraph of this section provides a brief (three- to five-sentence) synopsis of the case. This should include the patient's age, sex, and admitting diagnosis; the occurrence; the injury; and the allegations. The synopsis is followed by the *Parties Involved* section, which includes only the names of the individuals interviewed for the follow-up report or those newly identified as having been involved in the occurrence. This section is followed by the interviews. The remainder of the format is unchanged.

## SAMPLE FOLLOW-UP INVESTIGATION REPORT FORM

### Sample *Short Case Synopsis* Section

This report is for the first follow-up investigation to the initial report dated 1/30/06.

The case involves a 14-year-old female treated and released from the emergency department (ED) on 9/27/05 for gastroenteritis/urinary tract infection (UTI). Three days later, she returned to the ED with a ruptured appendix and peritonitis. She required an exploratory laparotomy, during which an appendectomy was performed. Allegations of a failure to diagnose properly have been made.

# Appendix 13-A

# FOJP Service Corporation Investigation Report

| This report is confidential and prepared solely in anticipation of, or in connection with, litigation. |
|---|

Dated:_____

Patient:_____     Claimant: _____

To: _____

cc: _____

By: _____

| Institution | | | | |
|---|---|---|---|---|
| FOJP File # | | Defense Attorney File # | | |
| Status | | | Severity Code | |
| | | Interviews | Pages | |

| DATE OF OCCURRENCE | |
|---|---|

### CRITICAL INFORMATION

### SHORT CASE SYNOPSIS

This is the follow-up investigation report to the initial report dated ___.

FOLLOW-UP INVESTIGATION REPORT #          Page 2          **FOJP SERVICE CORPORATION**

CASE OF _____                              FILE # ___

## PARTIES INVOLVED

A   Insured(s):

   1.

   2.

   3.

B   Parties With Other Insurance Coverage & if possible , identify their insurance coverage.

   1.

   2.

   3.

## IN-HOUSE REVIEWS

1.

Interview contained within this report.

## INTERVIEW

## MISCELLANEOUS INVESTIGATION

1.

FOLLOW-UP INVESTIGATION REPORT #          Page 3               FOJP SERVICE CORPORATI(

CASE OF _____                                    FILE # __

REFER TO INVESTIGATION REPORT GUIDELINES
ADDITIONAL ITEMS CONSIDERED FOR INVESTIGATION:
    Relevant Hospital Policies, Rules and Regulations
    Relevant Patient Logbooks
    Information on Equipment used, Maintenance Records
    Occurrence Reports
    Missing Evidence (FM strips, x-rays, records, etc.)

## COMMENTS

1.

REFER TO INVESTIGATION REPORT GUIDELINES
ISSUES CONSIDERED FOR COMMENT:

Medical management of the case, covering:

| | |
|---|---|
| Candidacy | Sufficient documentation |
| Timeliness of intervention | Appropriate procedure, treatment |
| Delay in Diagnosis | Supervision, experience of caregiver |
| Misdiagnosis | Surgical technique |
| Adherence to/deviation from hospital policies and procedures | |

Degree of responsibility among the involved parties

Discrepancies/Problems in the medical record, documentation or information obtained on interview

Issues disclosed during Miscellaneous Investigation

Damages sustained by the patient (prognosis, prolonged hospitalization)

Plaintiff's role in contributing to the alleged occurrence and injury

Informed Consent (Risks, benefits, alternative and documentation)

FOLLOW-UP INVESTIGATION REPORT #          Page 4          **FOJP SERVICE CORPORATION**

CASE OF _____          FILE # ___

## RECOMMENDATIONS FOR FUTURE INVESTIGATION

1.


## ENCLOSURES

1.

# Part II

# Additional Topics Related to Medical Malpractice Claim Investigation

Once the claim investigation process is mastered, the investigator may want to broaden his or her knowledge base about the risk management, insurance, legal, and claim management fields. In Part II, we have included subjects that a medical malpractice investigator should become familiar with to interact effectively with legal, insurance, claim, and risk management professionals. For instance, the investigator should be familiar with the HIPAA privacy rules governing confidentiality of medical information so that he or she can contact legal counsel in order to obtain guidance on handling such information during the investigation. Similarly, legal definitions and the course of a malpractice claim are covered so that the investigator can follow the proceedings and assist the defense attorney. The risk management response to adverse occurrences and the claim management theories and processes are included to help the investigator understand the behind-the-scenes activities to which he or she will contribute. Finally, we conclude with some advice on how best to write the investigation report effectively and in a professional manner.

# Chapter 14

# Confidentiality of Medical Records and Other Documents

- Health Insurance Portability and Accountability Act (HIPAA), State Regulations, and Personal Health Information (PHI)
- Releasing PHI without Patient Authorization
- Patient Access to PHI
- Releasing Records of Psychiatric, Substance Abuse, and/or HIV-Related Treatment
- Sharing Confidential Information with Government Agencies
- Protecting Confidentiality during Litigation
- Additional Practices that Safeguard Confidentiality

This chapter deals with some of the most common issues surrounding the confidentiality of patients' medical records and other health care organization (HCO) documents.

## HEALTH INSURANCE PORTABILITY AND ACCOUNTABILITY ACT (HIPAA), STATE REGULATIONS, AND PERSONAL HEALTH INFORMATION (PHI)

With the implementation of the privacy regulations for the Health Insurance Portability and Accountability Act (HIPAA) of 1996, came new requirements for the safeguarding of health information. Although most states have statutes that protect the confidentiality of a patient's medical records, HIPAA sets the minimum standard. It is advisable to check specific state statutes, which may be stricter than HIPAA, and to confer with legal counsel on these matters.

Both HIPAA and state statutes are based on the concept that confidentiality of patient information is essential to the development and maintenance of the unique physician-patient relationship. As a result, information related to physician-patient interactions is generally "privileged," or immune from discovery during legal proceedings. This privilege protects the health care provider from being compelled to testify about confidential communications pertaining to the patient, unless either the patient waives the privilege or a specific statute overrides the privilege.

In the past, this immunity applied to all oral communication between parties, as well as written information contained in the patient's medical record, including X-rays, electrocardiogram strips, laboratory results, and other details about the patient's condition. With the advent of HIPAA, coverage is expanded to include any information that is, or could be, maintained in electronic form as well. HIPAA also set new parameters for the privacy of personal health information (PHI), which is defined as *any health information that identifies, or could reasonably be expected to identify, an individual.*

## RELEASING PHI WITHOUT PATIENT AUTHORIZATION

A patient can waive the confidentiality of the physician-patient privilege at any time. However, there are occasions when—even under HIPAA and without the patient's authorization or waiver—the public interest outweighs the privilege, requiring the physician to disclose confidential information. Some examples include mandated reporting of communicable diseases and suspected child abuse or neglect.

In addition, HIPAA regulations permit access to information to facilitate both the timely and appropriate delivery of care and the management of operations, while protecting PHI from disclosure under other circumstances. The rules apply to "covered entities," including health care providers (e.g., physicians, hospitals, clinics), health plans, and health care clearinghouses. In most instances, a covered entity is permitted to use or disclose PHI *without the consent* of the individual for purposes of *treatment, payment, or operations (TPO)*. Release of this information must be limited to the *minimum necessary* to meet the need or request; however, the "minimum necessary" standard does not apply to

- Disclosures to or requests from a provider for treatment purposes
- Disclosures to the individual who is the subject of the PHI
- Disclosures accompanied by an individual's authorization
- Disclosures to the Department of Health and Human Services required by the Privacy Rule
- Other disclosures as required by law

Disclosure of PHI for any purpose other than TPO must be tracked by the use of a log, and patients may request an accounting of where their PHI has been sent. Because the penalties for the unauthorized disclosure of PHI can be severe, organizations are wise to have policies and procedures in place to guard against any improper release of information without the patient's consent. The law mandates that organizations designate a Privacy Officer to oversee the implementation of these policies and procedures and to monitor compliance. Covered entities are required to maintain security processes to protect PHI, whether stored in a record room or on a hard disk, with access limited on a "need-to-know" basis.

Although these rules do not alter the unique protection provided under the physician-patient privilege, they can affect the flow of patient information in the course of litigation. Patient consent may be required for the release of certain information to certain individuals (i.e., attorneys or other parties). The investigator should consult the Privacy Officer at his or her institution about any questions.

## PATIENT ACCESS TO PHI

The medical record and PHI contained therein—generated by the HCO or individual provider—is the property of the HCO or provider. However, under HIPAA, a patient or other legally authorized individual may submit a written request to access, inspect, and/or copy the patient's PHI. Such a request may be denied if

- The information contains psychotherapy notes (see definition page 263)
- A physician determines that such access is not in the patient's best interests
- The information could endanger the safety or life of an individual

- The information was prepared for a legal proceeding
- Such access is prohibited by law

Patients may request, in writing, to amend or correct their PHI if they believe it contains incorrect or incomplete information. A request may be denied if

- It is not in writing
- The information was not created by the facility or provider
- The provider verifies that the information is accurate and complete

If a request is denied, the patient must be notified in writing and be given the opportunity to submit a Statement of Disagreement.

Patients may authorize the release of all or some of their PHI to any party, or refuse to have records released to specific parties or entities—even in the process of a lawsuit. If the patient is deceased, incapacitated, or a minor, the authorization (or refusal to authorize) should be signed by the parent, estate administrator, health care agent, or legal guardian. If a plaintiff refuses to authorize the release of records necessary to defend a claim, defendants may take legal action.

## RELEASING RECORDS OF PSYCHIATRIC, SUBSTANCE ABUSE, AND/OR HIV-RELATED TREATMENT

Because of the stigma associated with mental illness, substance abuse, and human immunodeficiency virus (HIV), plus the concern that fear of prosecution would keep people from seeking treatment, records related to health care for these conditions have been treated with additional protection from disclosure. As a result, an HCO should have safeguards in place to prevent the incidental release of such PHI and to ensure that such sensitive information is disclosed only in compliance with HIPAA guidance and applicable state laws.

Although the HIPAA regulations do not supersede more stringent state or federal rules, they have standardized the minimum requirements for release of this type of PHI. In addition to a patient's general consent to the release of records, a specific authorization to release mental health, substance abuse, and/or HIV-related information—even for TPO—must be obtained from the patient or the patient's legal guardian. A patient can revoke or limit this authorization at any time. If authorization is not forthcoming, legal action may be necessary to obtain the needed information. However, unauthorized disclosure is permitted when a therapist learns that the patient is at risk of harming himself or a specific individual. The therapist may then breach the physician-patient privilege to warn and protect the patient or the person at risk.

Psychotherapy notes are a unique type of PHI. They are notes prepared by a mental health professional during counseling that document or analyze discussions with the patient and are kept separate from the medical record. A patient's authorization is required for their release except under certain conditions(e.g., if requested by the originator for treatment purposes, if necessary to defend a legal action brought by the patient, if required by law). Although a patient may not be able to prevent the disclosure, under HIPAA he or she has the right to request an account of all such releases made without authorization. A log of these disclosures must be maintained.


## SHARING CONFIDENTIAL INFORMATION WITH GOVERNMENT AGENCIES

### Release of Information to Law Enforcement Agencies

An HCO may release PHI to law enforcement agencies if the patient consents. In addition, there are many situations in which PHI can be disclosed to law enforcement agencies without authorization:

- If required by law
- Pursuant to a court order, search warrant, or grand jury or other subpoena
- If there is a good faith belief that the disclosure is necessary to prevent or decrease a serious and immediate threat to the health or safety of the public or an individual

Patient authorizations, subpoenas, and other legal documents (i.e., search warrants presented by law enforcement officers) must be thoroughly reviewed by the appropriate administrator and/or by HCO counsel prior to the release of any PHI.

## Professional Reviews, Regulatory Agencies, and Access to PHI

Disclosure of confidential PHI to professional review agencies generally does not require patient authorization or waiver, when pursuant to the applicable statutes. Such statutes specify that reports submitted for review should be written in statistical form, obscuring any implicit or explicit identification of patients.

## PROTECTING CONFIDENTIALITY DURING LITIGATION

### Attorney-Client Privilege and Documents Prepared in Anticipation of Litigation

Generally, when an attorney is consulted on an issue and advice is given, this communication is considered confidential unless the client waives the privilege. In the health care setting, the privilege protects communication between HCO personnel and HCO counsel (in-house or outside) concerning incidents and adverse events that have taken place and about which legal advice is sought. These discussions are privileged attorney-client communications—particularly if it is believed that there is a strong possibility that litigation will arise. If counsel attends a risk or quality management meeting dealing with such an adverse event, the attorney should keep the minutes and prepare memos containing advice to the client with legal opinions about the committee's deliberations and actions to follow. It is advisable to use outside counsel for this type of activity, to avoid any confusion about whether legal counsel is acting as an administrator (which might happen with in-house counsel) or as counsel. Documents prepared in anticipation of litigation should be labeled as such, with the caveat that these documents may be discoverable if the plaintiff can demonstrate substantial need for them or undue hardship in obtaining the information without them.

### Reviews of Patient Records by Risk Managers or Claim Investigators Before a Lawsuit Is Filed

Although the content of the medical record belongs to the patient, the physical document belongs to the HCO. As such, before litigation begins, risk managers or other agents of the HCO—including internal claim investigators—may review the record to investigate an adverse occurrence, a patient complaint, or other matter. Many of these investigations are conducted under the umbrella of an HCO's quality review process for purposes of improving care and, as such, the results are protected from disclosure. If the claim investigator is an outside agent of the insurance company, access may be permitted under the TPO exception to patient authorization, especially if the investigation is being conducted based on a patient claim.

### Release of PHI During the Discovery Phase of a Lawsuit

After the filing of a lawsuit, a pretrial process follows whereby documents and other information are exchanged between parties. During this *discovery* phase, lawyers for each side begin to prepare their case and develop a defense strategy. Requests for various documents are exchanged in the course of discovery. In a medical malpractice suit, one of these requests will most certainly be for the medical record. The HCO or provider should verify that the request is appropriate and the correct authorization has been received. Defense counsel may decide to release copies of the requested records, may arrange for the requesting party to inspect the records, or may go to court and ask for a protective order if the medical record contains information perceived to be confidential and thus requiring special authorization. Only the *minimum necessary* information to fulfill the request may be released under HIPAA. Therefore, records or other information pertaining to medical treatment that took place prior to, or subsequent to, the treatment period at issue in the lawsuit may not be released without appropriate authorization.

### Physician-Patient Privilege and Litigation

As discussed above, the physician-patient privilege protects the confidentiality of medical information exchanged between a physician and patient. In the course of discovery, attorneys frequently seek copies of records of care and treatment not directly related to the subject of the litigation. The theory is that patients who have put their health history at issue by filing a lawsuit have waived the right to the privilege. However, this waiver has limits, and the party seeking to overcome the claim of privilege must establish that the waiver applies to the additional records sought. Although filing a lawsuit might waive the privilege covering information relating to the injuries claimed in the litigation, the waiver does not necessarily apply to *all* of a patient's records.

Although the records of the care at issue are more easily obtained by the defense, HIPAA has tightened access to records generated by prior or subsequent providers without specific authorization by the patient, or through court action. This restricted access can lead to a delay in preparation of the defense of a claim. When considering a request for records not directly related to the care at issue, the court examines whether the request is too broad and involves medical information that is not relevant to the injuries in the suit at hand. This review conforms to the HIPAA standard requiring that, in response to a request, a "covered entity" may release only the *minimum* amount of information *necessary* to accomplish the intended purpose.

### Interviewing Parties, Nonparties and Subsequent Treating Physicians

Parties who are named together in the caption of a lawsuit (the heading at the top of legal documents) (e.g., John Doe v. Hospital A, Dr. B, Nurse C) may not necessarily share the same interests. Therefore, the risk manager's or claim investigator's first task should be to identify the time period at issue in the lawsuit. Next, the parties who were employees of the HCO and/or covered by the HCO's insurance at the time the events took place should be determined. If the HCO currently employs one or more of these individuals and employed them at the time in question, the investigator should confirm who was covered by the HCO's insurance. If an individual was covered, it is permissible for the investigator to conduct an interview with him or her regarding the details of the care and treatment of the patient. If the HCO does not currently employ the individual, having the investigator try to locate and speak to the person can reduce defense costs. If not, the HCO's defense counsel will need to do so.

Nonparties to the lawsuit who were employed by the HCO and covered by its insurance at the time in question should also be located when possible and interviewed. Because HIPAA relates to PHI in any form—including verbal—it is necessary to wait for a patient's authorization before approaching subsequent treating physicians.

## Plaintiff's Requests for Discovery of Information on Other Patients

There are many instances within hospital operations in which one patient's name may appear on a list along with the names of and identifiable information about other patients (e.g., operative logs, schedules for tests or procedures). On occasion, a plaintiff's attorney may request copies of log-books or other items that would include information not only about the plaintiff, but also about other patients as well. Legal counsel must analyze the propriety of releasing these documents prior to disclosure. There are instances when all other patient names can be redacted (blacked out), leaving only the plaintiff's name. However, in cases in which the information sought relates only to other patients and plaintiff is not mentioned at all, the court may have to decide whether disclosure should occur. The judge could review the documents at issue for relevancy before allowing plaintiff's counsel to see them (in-camera inspection) and may decide to edit out any information that might identify other patients. With the advent of HIPAA, judges are increasingly sensitive to the release of the PHI of other patients in the course of litigation and are more likely to require a solid showing of need before authorizing it. The HCO must advocate for the confidentiality of the records of these uninvolved patients before the court.

## Confidentiality of Quality Review Documents Maintained by the HCO

The Health Care Quality Improvement Act (HCQIA) of 1986 was enacted by the federal government to encourage health care professionals to participate in meaningful peer review by providing them with immunity from claims for monetary damages arising from these activities. Most states have enacted similar legislation to protect quality or peer review records from discovery. Because state laws and court decisions are not consistent, no peer review material or documents prepared during the course of an HCO's quality review process should be produced pursuant to any discovery request without consultation with the risk manager or legal counsel.

Generally, the law protects only the peer review or quality process itself and not the nonprivileged records (e.g., incident reports, personnel records, administrative records prepared in the ordinary course of business) used in the process. Documents and records that have been prepared specifically for the peer review or quality committee and minutes of these meetings

may be protected, although actions taken as a result of these deliberations—such as disciplinary actions—may not be protected.

Peer review organizations (PROs), are independent regional organizations empowered by the federal government to perform quality assurance
and utilization reviews of health care services rendered to Medicare beneficiaries. To protect confidentiality, they must produce reports in the form
of statistical data that do not implicitly or explicitly identify any individual
patients, practitioners, or reviewers and do not contain confidential information. Special regulations govern the confidentiality of data collected by
the PRO.

The National Practitioner Data Bank (NPDB) was created when
Congress recognized an increase in medical malpractice litigation and the
need to improve the quality of care on a national level. It was intended to
encourage state licensing boards, hospitals, other health care entities and
professional societies to identify and discipline physicians, dentists, and
other practitioners who act unprofessionally or incompetently. Intended to
be an alert or flagging system, NPDB further serves to restrict the ability of
these professionals to move from state to state without disclosure or discovery of prior medical malpractice or adverse action history. Medical
malpractice insurers are required to report to the NPDB and their state
licensing boards all payments made on behalf of health care practitioners
in settlement or satisfaction of a claim or judgment against them.

HCOs and other health care entities must report to the state medical
board all professional review actions that adversely affect clinical privileges or appointments. State medical boards must report all disciplinary
and professional review actions to the NPDB. HCOs are obligated to obtain
information from the NPDB when conducting initial credentialing reviews
or reappointment activities. All information reported to the NPDB is considered confidential and not available to the general public. Disclosure is
limited to the practitioner involved, medical boards, and any health care
entity engaged in professional review activities.

The Safe Medical Devices Act (SMDA) requires HCOs, nursing homes,
diagnostic, and other facilities to report device-related incidents to the
Food and Drug Administration (FDA) and the manufacturer within 10
working days after medical personnel become aware of the event. The
report submitted directly to the FDA is protected from disclosure and may
not be used in a civil action unless the information submitted was pur-
posely false. However, information submitted to the FDA via the manufac-

turer's device-reporting procedure *is* discoverable under the Freedom of Information Act (FOIA).

## ADDITIONAL PRACTICES THAT SAFEGUARD CONFIDENTIALITY

### Protecting What Is Not Protected

There are precautions that an organization can take when generating and handling sensitive material that may not specifically fall within any of the privilege categories. All documents prepared during quality review should be stamped with a statement indicating that they were created for quality or peer review purposes. Such a statement alerts everyone that the information should be handled discreetly.

The distribution of such documents should be limited to those with a need for access. Once a meeting ends, only the original document should be maintained; all other copies should be collected and shredded. Care should be taken when preparing minutes to assure that only essential information is disclosed. Nothing derogatory or judgmental should be recorded. In the course of peer review or quality meetings, information discussed should be factual and objective. Decisions made based on hearsay or innuendo can lead to future liability.

### Occurrence or Incident Reports

State statutes and case law vary regarding the discoverability of occurrence reports. Plaintiffs' counsel want them disclosed because of the possibility that they contain damaging information. Occurrence reports prepared in the ordinary course of business to document minor occurrences like falls or minor medication errors may not be protected. For this reason, forms with boxes that can be checked to indicate the type of occurrence and injury are safer than a narrative report in which the entire story, including editorial comments, can be read. When an HCO's form allows for a narrative, staff should be educated to stick to the facts and avoid judgmental or negative remarks directed at an individual or institution. Objective details of the incident should be charted in the medical record. The fact that an incident report was prepared *should not* be charted. To make sure that a copy does not end up in the wrong hands, there should, if possible, be only one copy of the incident report—the original.

### Protecting Documentation of Serious Occurrences

Most of the time, the risk manager or claim investigator can sense when information surrounding a serious occurrence requires special handling. In such cases, the original medical record should be sequestered, if possible. A file should be opened, in anticipation of litigation. No copies of the contents should be made or distributed without the consent of the risk manager. Access to these files should be limited to those with a need to know, including the attorney handling the claim or litigation. The discoverability of electronically stored information is a new and potentially troublesome area for medical malpractice litigation.

### Protecting the Actual Investigation Report from Discovery

An investigation report is a detailed account of an adverse occurrence or the details of the care and treatment rendered to a patient. Such a report can be generated in the course of exploring what happened, or when a patient has either filed a lawsuit or requested his or her records. Often prepared in anticipation of litigation, the report includes interviews with witnesses, a review of the clinical information in the medical record, and further analysis. Public policy considerations that encourage complete and candid disclosure to a liability carrier favor the protection of reports about prelitigation events. Reports involving an investigation of an event resulting in a legal claim that are addressed to defense counsel should be protected under the attorney-client privilege.

### Physician Credentialing Files

Protection of physician credentialing documents varies with the law in each state. These files are required by the Joint Commission on Accreditation of Healthcare Organizations to contain information on licensure, (re)certification and training, NPDB queries, competency determinations, any sanctions against the provider (i.e., exclusion from Medicare, state licensing actions), and other sensitive information. A physician generally has access to his or her own credentialing file and should be aware of what it contains. The physician is also responsible for updating the file as new information of significance becomes available, such as proof of additional training to support a request for new or expanded privileges. In some lawsuits, plaintiffs will allege that the HCO is liable for harm because of faulty credentialing of a physician. They subpoena the credentialing file to prove their claim. The risk manager and/or legal counsel should be consulted prior to release of any part of one of these files.

# Chapter 15

# What the Investigator Needs To Know about Insurance

- Insurance Mechanisms
- Glossary of Insurance Terms

## INSURANCE MECHANISMS

Insurance is the transfer of risk from one party to another. A risk can be defined as a possibility that an untoward occurrence will result in bodily injury, property damage, or economic loss that will require financial compensation. Therefore, the major function of insurance is to provide security against potential monetary loss or losses. A traditional insurance agreement usually takes the form of a contract called an *insurance policy*, whereby the insurer accepts the risk in consideration for the payment of a fee by the insured. The fee is called a *premium*.

Aside from the risk control methods of risk avoidance, loss reduction, and prevention, the risk manager must consider other means of protecting the institution's assets.

A risk manager can use any of the following mechanisms to deal with potential losses:

- **Risk retention**—assuming the risk by partially or fully self-insuring
- **Transfer of risk**—purchasing insurance to cover all risks
- **Transfer of liability**—negotiating a hold harmless agreement with another party

Over the past 25 years, many health care organizations (HCOs) have found it difficult or too expensive to purchase commercial insurance. As a result, various forms of risk retention and self-insurance have been used with increasing frequency. The methods vary according to such factors as the HCO's financial condition and the regulatory structure of the state in which the HCO is located.

*Common vehicles for self-insuring include the following:*

- **Setting up a self-insurance trust fund:** This involves an HCO setting aside funds to pay for anticipated losses. It usually requires the HCO to administer its own claims or to contract out for this service.
- **Setting up a captive insurance company:** A captive is a limited-purpose insurance company established by a single-parent institution or by a group engaged in a similar business to cover actuarially determined insurable losses. It is often based outside the United States. Captives allow administrative and regulatory flexibility and, in certain situations, may also offer favorable tax benefits.
- **Joining a pool:** A pool is a group of organizations that share their exposure to one or more areas of risk without establishing a formal insurance company. If properly managed, pools provide for savings through economies of scale.
- **Joining a risk retention group:** The United States Liability Risk Retention Act of 1986, Public Law 99-660, allows for the formation of interstate groups comprised of entities with similar liability risks for the purpose of self-insuring.

It is important that the risk manager understand the institution's insuring mechanisms so that he or she can interact effectively with insurance or administrative representatives.

## GLOSSARY OF INSURANCE TERMS

The following insurance terms are helpful to claim investigators, because they are often used in discussions with insurers and attorneys and in claim files.

*Actuarial science*—a scientific technique by which mathematical principles are used to project an insurance program's future liabilities in order to determine insurance rates. Actuaries consider such factors as an HCO's individual loss history, industry-wide losses, the HCO's total number of beds, interest rates on investments, and other costs in the projection of future liabilities.

*Aggregate limit*—the total amount an insurer will pay under the insurance policy for all covered losses occurring during a given policy period (usually a year).

*Certificate of insurance (COI)*—a document that serves as evidence of insurance coverage and indicates, in general, the basic terms and nature of the coverage (e.g., applicable policy periods and limits of coverage). A certificate may be sent to a third party at the request of the insured. For example, HCOs require physicians to submit COIs as part of the credentialing process. A COI is used for reference purposes only and is not a binding document.

*Claim evaluation/examination*—a process of evaluating the facts, damages, and potential total liability of a case to arrive at the monetary value of a claim. The HCO's insurance carrier generally performs this analysis, but the evaluation also can be a joint effort of the HCO risk manager, insurance claim examiner, and defense counsel.

*Claims-made coverage*—a type of insurance that covers claims reported during the policy year, as long as the underlying incidents occurred after the policy's inception date (or an earlier negotiated "retro" date) and before the termination date. Incidents reported or claims made *after* the policy expires are not covered unless the policy is renewed each year with the same carrier; unless the incident occurred during the policy period and is reported during the "discovery period" (usually withing 3 months after policy expiration); or unless tail coverage is purchased. (See definition of *tail coverage* under **Extended reporting endorsement**.)

*Covered person/insured person (or organization)*—refers to an individual or organization named or otherwise indicated as an insured under the insurance contract. Depending on the policy, "covered" persons also may include certain employees. For example, a policy for a physician might extend coverage to his or her nurses and physician's assistants.

*Defense*—It is generally the insurer's duty and obligation to provide legal defense against a claim. The insurer pays the attorney's fees and other legal costs involved in the litigation. Depending on the policy, defense costs may or may not be included in the policy limits. In a "no-consent" policy, the insurance company reserves the right to make the sole decision as to the settlement of any claim. Conversely, a "consent to settlement" policy allows the insured to participate in the decision-making process.

*Effective date*—the date and time that insurance coverage commences.

*Endorsement*—an attachment to an insurance policy used to clarify, extend, or restrict coverage with regard to perils, locations, insureds, or exposures.

*Excess insurance*—a type of policy that provides limits above the amounts covered by one or more primary policies. Excess limits are used after primary limits are exhausted.

*Extended reporting endorsement (tail coverage)*—This coverage is purchased when an insured leaves a claims-made carrier and wants to cover claims resulting from services rendered during the claims-made policy period but not as yet reported. A "tail" policy is often purchased if an insured switches from a claims-made policy to an occurrence policy.

*Fiduciary*—an individual or other entity entrusted to act for the benefit of another, usually with respect to a financial responsibility. Examples of fiduciary obligations include those of an insurer to the insured and of an attorney to his or her client.

*First-dollar coverage*—a term used in connection with any form of insurance that pays a covered loss without a deductible.

*Hazard*—A "material increase in hazard" is a condition that may increase the frequency or severity of a potential loss; e.g., a hazard premium may be imposed on institutions that add additional services or on insureds who pose new or increased risks to the insurance program. One example would involve an HCO that opens a cardiac surgery program and employs several new cardiac surgeons. The new cardiac surgery program increases the HCO's risk of patient injury and may result in an additional premium (hazard) charge.

*Hold harmless/indemnification agreement*—One party assumes the liability of another party during the period of time a specific activity is taking place. As a result, the second party is held harmless (not liable) for any claims encompassed by the hold harmless clause based on incidents during that period. HCO risk managers and/or HCO counsel should review each contract entered into by the institution for hold harmless and indemnification clauses. In most cases, they also should request hold harmless agreements that shift their liabilities to others when appropriate (see *Indemnity Agreement*).

*Incurred losses*—an insured loss that occurs within a specific period of time. Incurred losses include both paid losses and anticipated losses reserved on claims (see *Reserves*).

*Indemnification*— (see *Hold Harmless/Indemnification Agreement*)

*Indemnify*—to make "whole" or restore financially after a loss

*Indemnity or indemnification agreement*—an agreement by which one party agrees to indemnify or make whole a second party for losses suffered by the second party

*Insurance*—a means of transferring the risk of financial loss from one party to another. The insurer agrees to indemnify each insured for covered losses.

*Types of insurance coverage include the following:*

- **Directors and officers' (D&O) liability insurance**—covers directors and officers for certain claims arising out of wrongful acts or omissions committed in their capacities as directors or officers. For example, HCO trustees can be held liable for negligently carrying out their fiduciary responsibility to the institution. D&O insurance is designed to provide protection against claims of economic loss not ordinarily covered by other types of insurance. D&O insurance excludes coverage for bodily injury, such as medical malpractice or non-medical bodily injury, which is generally covered by professional or general liability insurance. D&O policies for non-profit organizations often cover employment practices, discriminatory and other types of lawsuits, and other types of claims, and often insure employees (not just directors and officers).
- **Errors and omissions insurance (E&O)**—a form of professional liability insurance that protects an insured party from liability for economic loss caused to third party as a result of an error or omission made in the practice of a particular profession.
- **General liability**—provides coverage for losses caused by the negligent acts of an insured that result in bodily injury to or the destruction of the tangible property of another. In this case, the negligent act is not judged by a professional standard.

- **Liability insurance**—indemnifies the insured for third party injuries for which the insured is legally liable
- **Products liability insurance**—affords bodily injury and property damage coverage for the insured's legal liability if the proximate cause of the loss arises out of goods or products manufactured or sold by the named insured. Coverage is provided only if the bodily injury or property damage occurs away from the premises owned by or rented to the named insured and after such goods or products have been relinquished to others. Coverage is limited to the insured's resulting legal liability. Damage to the product out of which the occurrence arose is not covered.
- **Professional liability (malpractice)**—provides coverage for liability resulting from injury or damage to a client allegedly due to a professional's departure from a standard of practice for that profession. The professional may be required to pay monetary damages to the injured party.
- **Workers' compensation acts**—state statute that holds that employers have strict liability for the death of or injury or illness to any employee, arising out of or in the course of employment, regardless of possible employee negligence. Workers' compensation insurance generally provides benefits in scheduled dollar amounts (reimbursement of medical bills and income benefits for employees) for personal injury or death caused by accidents arising out of, or in the course of, employment. Under Workers' Compensation Law, the employee is generally limited to workers' compensation benefits as his or her exclusive remedy against the employer.

*Insurance agent*—representative of an insurance company or group of companies

*Insurance broker*—an agent of the insured who facilitates obtaining insurance coverage by locating insurance companies to write policies covering risks for which the insured wants coverage. For certain purposes, a broker could also be an agent of the insurer (e.g., by giving the policy to the insured and receiving premiums for the insurer). Typically, a broker receives a commission that is a percentage of the premium for the insurance that the broker placed.

*Insurance company or insurer*—a company that is in the business of making insurance contracts

*Occurrence coverage*—Unlike claims-made coverage, occurrence coverage covers claims arising from incidents that occur while the policy is in force—regardless of when the actual claim is reported and whether the insured still maintains the policy. An alleged injury that occurs during the policy period but does not result in a claim until some time after the policy period would be covered under such a policy (see *Claims-made coverage*).

*Policy*—a written document that contains the terms and conditions of the insurance arrangements between the parties.

The various components of a policy include the following:

- **Conditions**—provisions that set forth certain duties and responsibilities of the parties to an insurance contract (e.g., a requirement that the insured give the insurer notice of a claim "as soon as is practicable"). Conditions may be found anywhere in the contract. Failure to fulfill a condition may reduce or eliminate coverage.
- **Declaration page or "dec page"**—insurance policy cover sheet. The declaration page sets forth basic details about the specific coverage purchased (e.g., the name of the insured, the policy limits, the premium, and the time period of the coverage).
- **Exclusion**—a restriction limiting the scope of policy coverage. Common exclusions include criminal acts, punitive damages, and undue familiarity (e.g., unauthorized physical contact by the insured physician with a patient during the insured's performance of professional services).

*Policy limit*—the maximum amount of coverage provided for the policy period (usually annual) under the terms of the insurance policy. Limits may be on a per-occurrence or an aggregate basis, or a combination of both.

*Policy period*—the time period a policy covers. Medical malpractice and commercial general liability policies generally are renewed each year.

*Premium*—the amount paid by the policyholder to the insurance company to procure the insurance policy

*Present value*—This is a computation of the amount of money that, if invested today at a set interest rate, will generate a given dollar amount by a specified date. For example, if $1,000 is needed to pay a claim in two years, assuming a 7% interest rate, you would need $873.00 set aside now. The present value of $1,000 is $873.00. Calculating the present value of funds has many implications in both risk control and risk financing decisions.

*Primary insurance*—the first layer of insurance coverage. In cases in which there is excess insurance coverage, the primary policy pays first.

*Punitive damages*—damages awarded by the court to penalize the at-fault party to deter others from similar activities or conduct. Punitive damages are generally uninsurable.

*Reinsurance*—method whereby an insurance company purchases coverage, from another insurer, that wholly or partially indemnifies the original insurance company against the risk it has assumed. An insurer then can underwrite higher limits in a single contract without retaining the entire limit of liability. The insured usually cannot recover directly from the reinsurer.

*Reporting*—Most insurance policies provide coverage for claims that are reported according to procedures set forth in the insuring agreement. In some cases, the first notice that a claim has been made comes when the HCO receives a subpoena or a summons, which it then turns over to the insurer.

*Reserves*—funds set aside to cover the expected amount of future loss

*Self-insurance*—A formal insurance program established by an individual or organization. Instead of buying insurance commercially, the insured sets aside a predetermined amount of funds to cover projected losses.

*Structured claim settlement*—a method of paying awards over a period of time rather than in a lump sum. The defendant's insurance carrier typically purchases an annuity or a series of annuities to cover the claimant's expected lifetime damages and expenses associated with the injury. The annuity company guarantees the claimant periodic tax-free payments over the course of the structured period. The advantage is twofold: the defendant pays out a smaller amount at the time of settlement, and the plaintiff does not have the responsibility of handling a potentially large sum of money intended to last the rest of his or her life.

*Umbrella excess liability policy*—provides high excess limits of liability beyond those of primary liability policies for catastrophic losses and, in some cases, for losses not covered by underlying policies

*Underwriting*—a process for evaluating an applicant against preestablished criteria for insurability. Underwriting determines whether an applicant will be accepted or rejected for coverage and at what rates (standard or modified). For instance, underwriters might review the HCO's activities and exposures, loss experience, and hold harmless contracts to evaluate the risks involved in insuring the HCO.

*Underwriting syndicate*—a group of individuals and/or companies that collectively provides insurance coverage through an underwriting agent. The underwriter usually is responsible for accepting or declining risks, using appropriate policy forms and claims settlements.

*Warranty*—an assurance by one party to a contract of the existence of a fact upon which the other party can rely. In insurance, an applicant may provide a warranty (usually as part of the application) regarding the nature of loss exposure to be insured. If warranted information is not true, coverage may be voided.

# Chapter 16

# The Life of a Medical Malpractice Claim

- Malpractice Defined
- Commencement of a Medical Malpractice Lawsuit
- Pleadings
- Pretrial Discovery
- Motion Practice
- The Trial
- Verdicts/Damages
- Post-Trial Motions
- Appeals

## MALPRACTICE DEFINED

Malpractice is a type of *tort*, which is a civil (as opposed to criminal) wrong to a person's physical well-being or property. An *intentional tort*, such as assault or battery, occurs when a person *intends* to bring about a particular result. In contrast, *negligence* occurs when there is *no* intent to create harm; rather, the actor's conduct falls below the standard of care established by law to protect others against unreasonable risk or harm.

Medical malpractice is one example of a negligence tort. It is the failure of a health care provider to exercise the degree of skill or care required of a professional in the same type of practice rendering comparable care under similar circumstances *and* that proximately causes injury to a patient (see definition of *proximate cause*, page 16:3). A medical malpractice action generally is brought by the patient (*plaintiff*) against one or more health care professionals or corporate entities (*defendant[s]*). If the patient is deceased, his or her legal representative may bring a *wrongful death action* as well as a malpractice action.

Ordinarily, a person or entity is responsible for his or her own negligence. There are, however, certain circumstances in which an entity or person may be held liable for the actions of another. Under the principle of vicarious liability, a physician or health care organization (HCO) may become liable for the medical malpractice or negligence of others. For example, a person in a partnership may be held liable for the actions of the other partners. Further, pursuant to the principle of *respondent superior* (a type of vicarious liability), an employer is automatically liable for the negligence of his or her employees. Thus, HCOs, professional corporations, medical partnerships, and private doctors legally are responsible for the malpractice of their employed doctors, nurses, and technicians.

In certain instances, an HCO also may be held liable for the acts of its nonemployed attending physicians or other health care professionals either (a) under a theory of direct *corporate negligence* for failing properly to review the credentials or monitor the performance of its attending staff or (b) under a theory of *apparent or ostensible employment or agency*, in which the patient reasonably may infer that the physician is an employee or agent of the HCO. Such cases arise when the physician is rendering institutional-type services by working in the radiology, anesthesiology, or emergency department.

*For there to be a finding that malpractice occurred, the plaintiff must demonstrate the existence of a legal duty, the breach of that duty, proximate cause, and damages.*

- **The existence of a legal duty:** The relationship between the parties must be examined to determine whether a physician-patient relationship exists. If such a relationship does exist, a physician then owes a legal duty to his or her patient to possess the requisite skills and knowledge, to exercise reasonable care and diligence, and to use his or her best judgment in the application of his or her skills and knowledge.
- **Breach of duty:** A breach of duty is a departure from the applicable standard of care resulting either from

- ○ **nonfeasance**—the failure to act when a situation imposes a duty to act or the failure to do what a reasonably prudent physician would do under the same or similar circumstances or
- ○ **malfeasance**—performing an act improperly or negligently

*Experts identify the standard of care and existence of departures from that standard.*

- **Proximate cause:** This refers to a legal principle that the defendant's negligence must have been a substantial contributing factor in bringing about the injury for a plaintiff to recover an award of damages. *Proximate cause* is sometimes defined as the foreseeability of a particular injury.
- **Damages sustained:** An actual injury must result from the health care provider's breach of duty, generally with some *physical* harm being shown. In many jurisdictions, a plaintiff cannot recover for an emotional injury that is not accompanied by physical injury.

A bad outcome does not in itself indicate malpractice. In such cases, however, a plaintiff may attempt to use the principle known as *res ipsa loquitur* ("the thing speaks for itself"). *Under this principle, there is an inference of negligence based on the mere fact that the injury occurred. A plaintiff may initially establish defendant's liability without calling a medical expert at trial to comment on the medical departure by showing that*

- the injury is of a type that ordinarily does not occur without someone's negligence
- the instrument causing the injury was in the exclusive control of the defendant
- there was no contributory negligence by the plaintiff

The *res ipsa* doctrine may be applied in those cases in which the defendant is better able than the plaintiff to explain the cause of an injury. For example, if an injury occurred while the plaintiff was under anesthesia and thus was unaware of what happened, this doctrine may apply. Another typical situation in which the doctrine is used is when a "foreign object" (e.g., a lap pad during surgery) is left in the patient.

## COMMENCEMENT OF A MEDICAL
## MALPRACTICE LAWSUIT

The service of a *summons* upon a defendant marks the initiation of the litigation process and serves as notice that a defendant is a party to a lawsuit. The summons is a one-page legal document that, when properly served, obtains personal jurisdiction over a party so that a court can compel a defendant, if found liable, to pay money to a plaintiff. A summons sometimes may contain a statement as to the nature of the action.

A process server who is not a party to the litigation may personally deliver the summons to a defendant. Specific jurisdictional rules regarding service must be followed. Failure to do so may result in the dismissal of a lawsuit. It is therefore important to apprise HCO defense counsel and the HCO risk manager of the details of service in order to evaluate whether service was proper.

The plaintiff must commence a medical malpractice action through the proper service of a summons within a relevant time period. This time period, called the *statute of limitations*, is set by state law and varies from state to state. In general, the statute of limitations for adult plaintiffs ranges from one to three years. Statutes of limitations also vary in the case of minors or individuals with specific disabilities (i.e., incompetence). Statutes of limitation also may differ in cases involving *continuous treatment* and the *discovery of foreign objects*.

Many plaintiffs' attorneys tend to utilize a shotgun approach in medical malpractice case by listing many of the health care professionals whose names appear in a patient's medical record as defendants in the lawsuit. By using this approach, a plaintiff may obtain pertinent information from all named defendants during the course of discovery. Serving multiple defendants also gives the plaintiff an opportunity to obtain inconsistent and/or contradictory information, which bolsters the plaintiff's case. If it is then determined that a certain defendant was not involved primarily in the patient's care or responsible for the alleged injury, the plaintiff may discontinue the action against that defendant, but usually not until after he or she is deposed.

The top of a summons ordinarily indicates which court has jurisdiction over the case, as well as the venue of the case. *Venue* refers to the county in which the trial of the plaintiff's claim will take place. The choice of venue is based on the residence of the plaintiff or defendant (s). Certain counties may be considered to have jurors favorably disposed towards plaintiffs, so plaintiff's attorney will choose a venue that is most favorable to his or her client.

## PLEADINGS

The *complaint*, which is often served upon the defendant along with the summons, is the first pleading in a lawsuit and contains the plaintiff's allegations and causes of action (e.g., negligence, lack of informed consent). The allegations and causes of action are listed in numbered paragraphs, usually in the form of vague, generalized statements.

An *answer* filed on a defendant's behalf must respond, within a statutorily defined time period, to the various allegations in the complaint. The answer to the complaint may deny allegations known or believed to be untrue, deny knowledge or information sufficient to form a belief, or admit the truth of certain facts. The answer also may contain *counterclaims* by the defendant against the plaintiff on any cause of action, to which the plaintiff then must respond in the plaintiff's *reply*.

The running of the statute of limitations, or lack of personal jurisdiction due to improper service of the summons, may be included in the defendant's answer. These affirmative defenses may also be raised in a *motion to dismiss*, which a defendant's attorney may choose to file prior to filing an answer. A motion to dismiss also may be made on the grounds that the plaintiff has failed to state a legally viable cause of action.

If there is more than one defendant, an answer may contain *cross-claims* by one defendant against other defendants in the lawsuit.

Culpable conduct may be raised in an answer as a defense to a medical malpractice claim. Culpable conduct defenses are usually stated in terms of *contributory negligence* or *comparative negligence* and allege that the plaintiff's injuries are, in whole or in part, his or her own fault. If a culpable conduct defense is successful, any damages awarded to the plaintiff will be reduced, usually by an amount equal to the plaintiff's contributing fault.

At any time after the service of a defendant's answer, a defendant may utilize a procedure called *impleader*, by which the defendant may proceed against a person or entity who is not a party to the original lawsuit but who may be liable for all or part of the amount demanded by the plaintiff. The impleading defendant takes on the role of a plaintiff (as well as the continuing role of defendant) and has the same responsibilities and requirements of a plaintiff, since he or she is now suing a new defendant. The impleading defendant is now known as a *third-party plaintiff* and is required to serve upon the third-party defendant a summons, a third-party complaint, and all prior pleadings exchanged by parties to the action. He or she also provides a copy of the third-party complaint to the plaintiff in the original action. As part of or after the service of an answer, the defendant's attorney may ask the plaintiff for a more specific statement of the facts and circumstances surrounding the claim. This request is sometimes referred to as a demand for a *bill of particulars*. The plaintiff's response to such a demand gives the defendant a better picture of what the lawsuit is about so that a defense posture may be formulated. The response answers questions regarding the date, time, and location of the alleged occurrence, the specific injuries allegedly sustained by the plaintiff, and the theories of liability upon which the plaintiff is basing his or her case.

A defendant may also be required to provide a bill of particulars, in response to plaintiff's demand, relating to certain *affirmative defenses*. For instance, if the defendant asserts a culpable conduct affirmative defense, the plaintiff may demand clarification of what the defendant claims the plaintiff did or did not do to contribute to his/her injury.

## PRETRIAL DISCOVERY

The period of *discovery* is a fact-finding process that begins some time after an answer is served and continues until a case is ready for trial and placed on the trial calendar. Discovery takes place under the supervision of a judge and enables the parties to prepare their cases in the most thorough and informed manner possible and to avoid any surprises at trial that would prejudice a party's rights or interests. During discovery, each party must disclose to the other all evidence that is material and necessary, provided that such evidence is not exempt from discovery by virtue of a *legal privilege*.

Material that falls under an absolute *privilege* need not be disclosed to an adversary. For example, a client's professional relationship with an attorney creates a bond of confidence, and matters discussed pursuant to such a relationship are not discoverable. In addition, an attorney's work product prepared in connection with pending or anticipated litigation is privileged and protected from discovery.

Patients' medical records, whether maintained by a private physician or an HCO, are privileged and generally may not be released unless the patient has consented or has waived the privilege (as is the case when the plaintiff commences a lawsuit concerning the treatment that is the subject matter of the record). In rare cases, where there are countervailing state interests to be weighed against the physician-patient privilege, records may be released without the patient's consent pursuant to a subpoena or court order. In addition, special rules may apply to records containing drug- and alcohol-related or AIDS-related information.

Some states require HCOs to increase their activities in areas of peer review, quality assurance, risk management, and credentialing. Records maintained as part of these activities have been granted increased protection from discovery in many jurisdictions.

When parties disagree about what material is privileged, and thus protected from discovery, a judge may require production of the material in court for an *in camera* inspection. The judge then reviews the documents to determine whether a privilege applies.

One commonly used discovery device is the *examination before trial* (EBT) or *oral deposition*. A deposition may take place in an attorney's office and is attended by the party or witness to be deposed, his or her attorney, the deposing party's attorney (who asks the questions), and a court stenographer, who transcribes all that is said at the deposition. Depositions are given under oath. Deposition testimony makes a record of facts in the event memories fade before trial or witnesses disappear or die.

Each witness (plaintiff, defendant, or nonparty) is usually prepared for the deposition by an attorney. The physician may refer to the patient's medical records during the deposition and, if necessary, base his or her responses entirely on simultaneous reference to the records.

*The deposition may be used at the trial in any of the following situations:*

- For impeachment purposes, if the same question asked of the same person at trial elicited a different response at the deposition
- When a nonparty witness is deceased, aged or infirm, unavailable, or unobtainable by subpoena
- For its probative or evidentiary value to support allegations or defenses

Other elements of discovery include document discovery, written interrogatories, and medical examinations. In *document discovery*, through written authorization or subpoenas to the appropriate parties, the opposing parties request such items as HCO records, charts, tax returns, school records, and other documents that have bearing on questions concerning the alleged injuries and damages suffered by the plaintiff.

*Written interrogatories* are questions submitted in writing by one party to another. Answers also are written and are given under oath. Written interrogatories are generally used to obtain information that is not readily available during oral depositions. For example, a plaintiff's attorney might use written interrogatories to ask about a specific HCO protocol.

*Medical examinations* are used by the defense in a medical malpractice lawsuit to ascertain the actual extent of the plaintiff's injuries. The defense may require that the plaintiff submit to a physical or mental examination by a physician chosen by the defense. The examining physician reports on the extent and possible causes of the injuries and may render an opinion as to the merits of the plaintiff's allegations.

## MOTION PRACTICE

Motion practice, which consists of written or oral applications made by either or both parties to the court, can occur at any time during the progress of a lawsuit. A motion asks the judge for a ruling or order directing some action in favor of the applicant. One common motion is the motion for *summary judgment*, which is often brought when discovery is complete. A summary judgment motion asks the court for a determination that there are no material issues of fact presented in the case and, therefore, there is no need for a trial. If the judge agrees, he or she makes a ruling on issues of law that decide all or part of the plaintiff's claim without going before a jury. A summary judgment motion may be partially granted or granted in full.

Once all the pretrial motions have been decided and all discovery is complete, the case is ready for trial.

## THE TRIAL

If a case is not disposed of by way of settlement or dismissal prior to the trial date, it proceeds to trial.

Jury selection commences with a process that is known as *voir dire*, in which the attorneys ask prospective jurors questions, under oath, that are designed to evaluate a juror's ability to be fair at trial. An attorney may excuse, through *challenges*, any jurors who are in any way related to anyone connected with the case or in whom there is any indication of possible bias or prejudice.

Sometimes, before the actual trial begins, issues on the presentation of evidence still need to be resolved. When either party requests a ruling from the judge at the time of trial, that party makes a *motion in limine*. Once the judge disposes of pretrial motions, the trial then proceeds.

After a jury is chosen, sworn in, and seated, each attorney makes opening statements to the jury. Following opening statements, the parties present their respective cases by calling witnesses to the stand. The plaintiff presents his/her case first and may call defendants as witnesses. Medical experts may also be called to testify "with a reasonable degree of medical certainty" why a physician's actions were or were not negligent, and may be cross-examined by the adversary's attorney. If the defense believes the plaintiff failed to present all the elements necessary to prove medical malpractice, the defense makes a motion for a directed verdict. If the judge agrees with the defense, he or she directs the verdict for the defense, and the trial is over. If the judge rules against the motion, the trial proceeds. The defense has another opportunity to make this motion at the end of the case.

When all the parties and witnesses have finished their testimony, the attorneys conclude the trial with *summations* in an effort to highlight, for the jury, the evidence that is most favorable to their client.

The attorneys then submit to the judge their requests to charge the jury. These requests consist of suggestions as to the instructions he or she should give to the jury to serve as guidelines during deliberations. Once the judge has evaluated these requests, he or she determines how the jury should be charged and reads the charge in open court. The charge tells the jurors the rules they must follow in weighing the evidence presented at trial. Following the reading of the charge, the jury retires for deliberations.

## VERDICTS/DAMAGES

Where a jury determines that it finds for the plaintiff, some state laws require the jury to render an *itemized verdict*, which includes *special damages* (objective damages such as medical expenses and lost earnings) and *general damages* (subjective damages such as pain and suffering and loss of enjoyment of life). The jury must assign a dollar amount to each element of damages and must itemize the amounts intended to compensate for past damages and the amounts for future damages. A plaintiff is responsible for paying his or her attorney's fees out of any awarded damages. These fees often are capped by applicable state legislation.

In wrongful death actions, the heirs of the deceased patient may recover additional damages for the *pecuniary* loss they have suffered. Compensable damages include loss of financial support and services, medical and funeral expenses, and the loss of prospective inheritance.

Most states have legislation regarding the use of structured settlements or periodic payment of damages. In these methods of payment, the defendant purchases an annuity contract and the plaintiff receives periodic checks over a number of years rather than a single lump payment.

Damages awarded to the plaintiff are reduced in some jurisdictions by sources of collateral payments, such as the insurance available to the plaintiff. Damages may be reduced further by the amount of taxes the plaintiff would have paid, if he or she had earned the lost-wages portion of an award through actual employment.

The plaintiff's damages also are reduced by the percentage, if any, that his or her fault contributed to his or her overall damage. If more than one defendant is found liable, liability is apportioned by the jury according to the defendants' respective degrees of fault. Under the legal theory of *contribution*, each of several defendants is required to pay a share of the plaintiff's damages. Under the doctrine of *joint and several liability*, a defendant may be required to pay damages owed by another defendant and then seek repayment from the codefendant. This situation may arise when a particular defendant does not have adequate insurance limits and is unable to pay his or her own share of a jury award. Limitations on the application of the joint and several liability rule may be imposed by state law.

## POST-TRIAL MOTIONS

Prior to submitting a case to a jury for its deliberations, either party may move for a *directed verdict*. Such a motion requests the judge to direct that judgment be entered on behalf of the moving party because the evidence at trial is so clear that, as a matter of law, the jury has no issues on which to deliberate.

Once the jury has returned a verdict, either party may move for a *judgment notwithstanding the verdict (JNOV)*. Such a motion requests that the judge set aside the jury verdict or reduce the amount of damages awarded, because such verdict or damages do not conform to the evidence introduced at trial.

Defendants may make other common motions at the end of a trial to reduce the amount of damages, or the plaintiff may make a motion to increase the amount of the award. If either side is dissatisfied with the final results, that party may appeal the case to a higher court.

## APPEALS

After a trial, a case may be appealed to a higher court. The higher courts have the power to modify jury verdicts, raise or lower the amount of damages awarded by juries, or order a new trial because of mistakes made by the judge during the trial. Quite often, medical malpractice defendants pay far less in final damages than the initial jury verdict because of a reduction by appellate courts.

# Chapter 17

# Informed Consent

- General Principles
- Documentation of Informed Consent
- Consent by Other Parties for an Adult Patient
- Consent for Treatment of Minors
- Special Situations Involving Consent
- Advance Directives
- Practical Implications for Claim Investigation

Physicians are expected to obtain the permission of their patients before treatment. This expectation is based on common law and on case law. In the words of Justice Cardozo, who authored a relevant landmark judicial decision in 1914, "Every person of adult age of sound mind has a right to determine what shall be done to his or her body; and the surgeon who performs an operation without the patient's consent commits an assault for which he is liable in damages."[1]

Thus, if a physician fails to obtain consent from a patient before performing a surgical or other procedure, he or she may have committed an assault (and battery). But even if the physician clearly obtains the patient's *consent* to treatment—and thus does not commit an assault and battery upon the patient—he or she may not have obtained the patient's *informed* consent. Failure to obtain *informed* consent may amount to negligence; that is, malpractice.

The concept of *informed* consent began with legal developments in the 1950s, when the consent concept was expanded to require not only the fact of consent by the patient but also that the consent be informed. The legal principles governing informed consent derive from negligence law in that the physician who fails to obtain informed consent has breached a professional duty by failing to inform the patient as to the risks and benefits of, and alternatives to, the medical care offered.

In short, a physician is responsible not only for obtaining the patient's permission but for obtaining an informed consent based upon the sufficient, relevant information provided to the patient.[2]

## GENERAL PRINCIPLES

Informed consent is a *process* whereby the patient and the physician engage in a dialogue that results in the patient's decision to accept or decline treatment.[3]

The patient must be able to make an informed choice regarding the proposed treatment based on information provided by his or her physician. *Most courts have held that the patient must be apprised of the*

- nature and purpose of the proposed treatment and the expected benefits
- risks of the proposed treatment
- alternatives available, including the consequences of no treatment

In addition, the patient must be given an opportunity to ask questions.

Prepared videotapes or audiotapes that impart information about the procedure, including its risks, benefits, and alternatives, can be a valuable adjunct to the informed consent process but should not be used as a substitute for an informed consent discussion between the physician and patient.

### How Much Should a Physician Disclose?

There are two general standards on which the various states have based their disclosure requirements. Most jurisdicitions follow the physician-based standard; however, a substantial minority adheres to the reasonable-patient standard.[4] The physician-based standard requires the disclosure of what a reasonable physician would disclose in the same or similar circumstances.[5] The patient-based standard requires the physician to disclose information that is material and significant to the patient's decision-making process.[6] This is also called the *materiality standard.* In the landmark case *Canterbury v. Spence*, the court defined a material risk as one to which "a reasonable person . . . would be likely to attach significance . . . in deciding whether or not to forego the proposed therapy."[7]

### Exceptions to the Informed Consent Requirement

There are several exceptions to the informed consent doctrine in which the physician generally need not obtain the patient's informed consent. *The most notable exceptions include the following:*

- **Situations involving medical emergencies**—if the delay necessary to obtain informed consent would result in serious harm or would be life threatening to the patient
- **Commonly known risks**—risks that the ordinary person would be expected to know and that are not associated with substantial injury (e.g., the risk of pain after a tooth extraction)
- **Remote risks**—obscure risks that are extremely unlikely and are not associated with grave injury
- **Waiver by the patient**—if a patient tells the physician that he or she will have the procedure "regardless of the risks" involved
- **Therapeutic privilege**—a situation in which the physician reasonably believes that providing the information necessary to make an informed decision would be extremely harmful to the patient, mentally or physically

### Communication of Consent by the Patient

Once the patient has the necessary information, he or she must communicate his or her consent to complete the informed consent process. The patient may give either express consent (verbally or by signing a consent form) or implied consent (as by submitting to the described medical treatment). Implied consent theoretically may be sufficient; however, it is advisable to obtain the patient's express consent so that it is clear that consent was given.

As a practical matter, implied consent is generally accepted for such minor procedures as a needle-stick for a blood test, insertion of a throat swab for a culture, and a physical examination. In fact, because the risks associated with such procedures (e.g., a bruised arm from a needle-stick or vomiting from insertion of a throat swab) often are "commonly known" or "remote" (see earlier descriptions of these terms), in practice the patient may receive little or no information concerning the procedure before he or she impliedly consents by submitting to the procedure.

### Who Should Obtain Informed Consent?

The health care provider who will perform the procedure should be the person to obtain the informed consent from the patient after discussing the procedure's risks, benefits, and alternatives. However, another physician or nurse can obtain the patient's signature on the consent form, in accordance with the health care organization's (HCO's) policy. The consent form merely provides evidence that the discussion took place. The physician or nurse is simply witnessing the patient's signature in this instance.

If a patient is capable of consenting to the procedure, then only the patient may sign the consent form. When a consent form is signed in the physician's office, the original form should be sent to the institution's admitting office and a copy kept in the office chart.

### How Long Is Consent Valid?

Consent remains valid for a reasonable amount of time after disclosure—as long as there is no material change in the patient's condition. However, HCOs may vary in their policies on the length of time consent is considered valid. Usually, this period is no longer than a few weeks if the patient is not discharged or readmitted and if his or her condition does not change. The investigator should be aware of the specific HCO's policy in this regard.

Consent need be obtained only once at the commencement of a series of the same procedures or treatments. The consent form should indicate that the patient consented to a continuing course of treatment. Any change in circumstance that alters the risk to the patient necessitates obtaining a new consent.

## DOCUMENTATION OF INFORMED CONSENT

Although the consent process involves a dialogue between the patient and the physician regarding the proposed treatment or procedure, most state laws and most HCOs require written consent in the patient's medical record. As noted earlier, the consent form should be signed by the patient receiving treatment. However, the consent form itself is merely written evidence that the consent was granted. A signed form is *not* a substitute for the consent process.

One widely used method is the preprinted consent form. This standard form has blank spaces for the name of the physician performing the procedure, the patient's name, the type of procedure, the date and time of the consent, and the signatures of the patient and a witness. The form states, in general terms, that the patient is aware of the risks and benefits of and alternatives to the procedure, understands the nature of the procedure, has been given the opportunity to ask questions, and has received satisfactory answers. *Some forms include clauses that read:*

- *I understand that during the course of the operation unforeseen conditions may arise that necessitate procedures different from those contemplated. I therefore consent to the performance of additional operations and procedures that the above-named physician or his/her associates or assistants may consider necessary.*
- *I have also been informed that there are other risks, such as loss of blood, infection, cardiac arrest, damage to teeth, etc., that are attendant to the performance of any surgical or anesthetic procedure.*
- *I am aware that the practice of medicine and surgery is not an exact science, and I acknowledge that no guarantees or assurances have been made concerning the results of the above operation, treatment(s), or procedure(s).*
- *I consent to the administration of such drugs, infusions, transfusions of blood or blood components, or any other treatment deemed necessary or desirable in the judgment of the medical staff, and I further consent to the administration of such anesthetics as may be considered necessary or advisable by the physician or dentist responsible for this service, with the exception of _____.*
- *I also consent to the admittance of observers to the operating room, and to the photographing or televising of the operation or procedure*

*to be performed, including appropriate portions of my body, for the purpose of advancing medical education and for other medical or scientific purposes, provided my identity is not revealed by either the pictures or the descriptive texts accompanying them.*

- *I consent to the retention or disposal by the HCO authorities of any tissue that may be removed during the operation/procedure.*

Some physicians use customized forms written for specific procedures.

In addition to the consent form required by an HCO, it is helpful from a liability standpoint to have the physician make an entry in the patient's medical record that the patient understands the proposed procedure and its risks, benefits, and alternatives and has had the opportunity to ask questions of the physician performing the procedure. This note should be dated and timed, and any witnesses to the conversation should be listed. There is, however, debate within the legal community regarding just how specific the documentation should be regarding the risks imparted to the patient. On the one hand, listing every risk described to the patient would be helpful in the defense of a claim should one of these risks materialize into an injury. However, if the patient suffers an injury from a risk that has been stated but not documented in the list of risks, the claim of lack of informed consent may be more difficult to defend.

### Telephone Consent

Telephone consent may be necessary when the patient cannot consent to treatment and the next of kin or another person who legally can provide consent for that patient is not present. Some HCO policies require that a second individual witness the consent by listening to the conversation on an extension.

*Documentation for telephone consent should include*

- date, time, and telephone number called
- identity of the person called to provide consent and his or her relationship to the patient
- name and title of the health care provider who obtained the consent
- information given to the consenting party about the patient's condition, recommended treatment, and the attendant risks, benefits, and alternatives, as well as a brief summary of questions posed and answers given

- whether consent was obtained
- signature of the health care provider

## Videotaped Consent and Information about the Procedure

There has been much debate concerning the use of audiotaped and videotaped informed consent conversations between patients and health care providers. Some risk management experts believe that taping enhances the consent process because the physician is thorough and thoughtful and will consider more carefully what to disclose and what not to disclose. In addition, if properly performed, electronic documentation can strengthen the defense against a claim of lack of informed consent, particularly for high-risk procedures or litigation-prone patients. Opponents of taped consent object that the storing of the tapes is impractical and that the recording can be used against the defendant if the consent is arguably found to have been performed improperly.

## CONSENT BY OTHER PARTIES FOR AN ADULT PATIENT

When a physician obtains informed consent, he or she has judged that the patient has the ability to understand the proposed treatment and its risks, benefits, and alternatives. However, when a patient clearly does not have the capacity to consent because he or she is senile, unconscious, or severely retarded, consent from another party is required. In some cases, a competent adult's ability to give an informed consent is impaired temporarily, as may occur when a patient's mental status has been altered by trauma or substance abuse. In the case of substance abuse—if the situation is not an emergency— the physician generally should wait for the effects of the substance to wear off before assessing the patient's capacity to provide an informed consent.

Patients with psychiatric symptoms and those who are mentally retarded do not necessarily lack capacity to consent. That is, although they may be deemed to be in need of commitment to a psychiatric setting, they may still have capacity to understand some aspects of their care and to consent to such treatments as medications and medical procedures.

When there is any doubt about decisional capacity, the treating physician should make the initial assessment of the patient. If there is still doubt, he or she needs to obtain a second opinion from a physician with appropriate clinical expertise who is not involved with the patient's care. If doubt still persists, and the physicians are unable to agree about the patient's capacity, the matter should be discussed with legal counsel and perhaps submitted for judicial review.

When a patient is determined to lack capacity, surrogate consent must be obtained from a legally appointed guardian, designated health care agent, or next of kin, depending on state statute. Generally, the next of kin may give consent unless a health care agent has been designated by the patient or a legal guardian has been appointed by the court. Although the following may vary depending on state statute, the generally accepted priority of surrogate consent is health care agent (proxy designated by the patient in advance), legal guardian, spouse, adult child, parent, adult siblings, and aunt or uncle. Regardless of who provides consent, treatment usually can proceed as long as the health care provider believes the surrogate is acting in good faith. In general, if a patient legally designates a health care agent in an advance directive, that agent's decisions supersede the wishes of family members.

*Judicial intervention may be required in the following circumstances:*

- The surrogate or agent appears to be acting in bad faith.
- Members of the same next-of-kin class (for instance, adult children) are in conflict.
- No surrogate or agent is available.
- There is no designated agent, and the surrogate refuses to allow medically indicated treatment.


## CONSENT FOR TREATMENT OF MINORS

In general, a patient under the age of 18 years is considered to be a minor, and consent for treatment must be obtained from a parent or legal guardian. However, there are some restrictions on parental consent. State laws vary and should be consulted.

*The more common exceptions to parental consent include the following:*

- **Emergency situations:** If the delay needed to obtain informed consent from a parent or legal guardian may cause harm, the health care provider may proceed with treatment. The delay need not be life threatening.

- **Emancipated minors:** Emancipated minor status encompasses individuals who are married, parents, financially independent and living away from their parents, and/or members of the armed forces.
- **Mature minors:** These individuals are close to the age of majority and are able to understand and appreciate the nature and consequences of the proposed treatment.

In addition, laws have been enacted in every state to allow competent minors to consent to treatment of venereal diseases without obtaining parental consent.[8] Some states also permit minors to consent to treatment related to pregnancy, contraception, abortion, mental health, and substance abuse. These laws are constantly changing, and it is best to consult legal counsel regarding consent for minors.

## SPECIAL SITUATIONS INVOLVING CONSENT

### Informed Consent for human immunodeficiency virus (HIV) Testing

Many states have enacted legislation that requires specific informed consent for HIV testing. The procedure followed and the forms utilized must adhere to current state and local requirements.

### Consent for Sterilization

Sterilization means any medical procedure, treatment, or operation for the purpose of rendering an individual permanently incapable of reproducing.[9] Many state and local laws specifically address the requirements for obtaining informed consent from a competent adult beforehand. In general, the consent should be in writing, and the patient should have reached the age of majority. The health care provider also should discuss all the risks of the procedure, its irreversibility, and the prescribed waiting period between the discussion and the surgery. Consent must be obtained within a certain number of days prior to the surgery. Alternate methods of birth control should be discussed as well.

Federal regulations include guidelines for the informed consent process when federal funds are involved in reimbursement.[10] The guidelines specify the minimum age of the patient and the minimum waiting period between the informed consent discussion and performing the procedure.

*Federal regulations prohibit obtaining informed consent for sterilization while the patient is:*[11]

- in labor or childbirth
- seeking to obtain or obtaining an abortion
- under the influence of alcohol or other substances that affect the individual's state of awareness

## Medical Research and Experimentation

The informed consent process for medical research and experimentation is designed to protect the rights of the patients involved. Informed consent for research on human subjects, including the use of experimental methods, devices, or drugs, is regulated by federal law. Federal law requires the sponsoring entity to convene an institutional review board (IRB). One of an IRB's major areas of concern is the adequacy of the informed consent. Among the governmental requirements relating to informed consent for experimental procedures are a statement of confidentiality; an explanation of the procedure, including any experimental procedures and their purposes; any reasonably expected discomforts or risks, and the possibility of unforeseeable risks; potential benefits and alternatives; and possible compensation and treatment available should an injury occur.[12] The individual obtaining the consent must answer any questions concerning the procedure and advise the patient that he or she may withdraw participation at any time without prejudicing the quality of further care.[13] Other requirements (not listed here) also may be relevant to a specific case under investigation.

## Refusal of Treatment

In the Cruzan case, the United States Supreme Court established that competent adults have a common-law right to refuse medical treatment or to have unwanted treatment withdrawn.[14] The Cruzan decision was based on the individual's constitutional liberty interest (i.e., the right to life, liberty, etc.). This right, however, is not absolute. The state may intervene when, for example, other individuals in addition to the patient might be harmed by the patient's decision to refuse treatment. Such cases tend to be controversial, and legal counsel should be sought. For instance, one situation is refusing vaccination when such refusal could jeopardize the public health.[15] Another example is a pregnant woman's refusal of treatment, the lack of which could be life threatening to mother and fetus.[16]

## ADVANCE DIRECTIVES

Depending on state statutes, an adult can prepare a document that provides guidance for making health care decisions should he or she become incapable of making decisions at some time in the future. Such documents are called *advance directives*. The most common types are living wills, health care proxies, and durable powers of attorney for health care.

The federal Patient Self-Determination Act (PSDA) (42 U.S.C. 1395cc[a] [1]), enacted in 1990, defines an advance directive as a "written instruction, such as a living will or durable power of attorney for health care, recognized under state law . . . and relating to the provision of . . . care when the individual is incapacitated." The PSDA legislation requires HCOs, skilled nursing facilities, home health agencies, hospices, and HMOs to comply with its provisions.

*Upon admission of a patient to a health care facility or before providing treatment, the health care entity must*

- ask if the patient has an advance directive
- provide written information to the patient on admission about his or her statutory and court-recognized rights regarding advance directives (If the facility or the physician will not honor the advance directive, the patient must be transferred to another physician or facility.)
- document the existence of an advance directive in the patient's medical record

*In addition, health care entities are required to*

- maintain written policies and procedures regarding advance directives
- comply with pertinent state laws
- educate health care providers and the community about advance directives

Health care entities cannot condition the provision of medical care on whether a patient has executed an advance directive.

If a patient lacking capacity has not executed an advance directive, a surrogate generally may consent to treatment, as discussed earlier. If the patient's surrogate refuses to consent to a medically indicated procedure, it may be necessary to consult with the HCO's ethics committee or legal counsel or to submit the matter for judicial review. Protocol depends on institutional policy and applicable state law. Although all advance directives attempt to ensure that the patient's wishes are followed, the documents vary in specific form and contents.

## Health Care Proxy

Various state laws, such as New York State's Health Care Proxy Law, allow individuals to appoint agents to make health care decisions should they become unable to do so for themselves. Subject to any limitations the patient has provided in the proxy, agents can be allowed to make any and all decisions regarding treatment or withdrawal of treatment that competent adults would be allowed to make for themselves. In essence, the agent stands in the shoes of the patient. The exception to this rule in New York State is that the proxy cannot order the removal or withholding of artificial nutrition and hydration unless the patient has stated in the proxy document that the agent knows his or her wishes in this regard.

## Durable Power of Attorney for Health Care

All states have durable power of attorney acts that enable individuals to act on behalf of an incapacitated patient on specified matters. Unless specifically prohibited by case law, attorney generals' opinions or statute, a durable power of attorney can be used for health care purposes by appointing an individual to make health care decisions on behalf of an incapacitated patient. A durable power of attorney for health care may specify the patient's preferences for therapy in specific situations or simply designate an individual to make health care decisions without specific instructions. States vary as to whether they allow such individuals to make decisions about withdrawing or withholding artificial nutrition and hydration.

## Living Wills

A living will is a written statement made by a competent person specifying the types of treatment the person does or does not want under special circumstances. Many states have "natural death" or "living will legislation."[17] The National Hospice and Palliative Care Organization, provides specific guidelines, information, and forms to assist individuals in executing a living will. This organization can be contacted at its New York City office at (800) 989-9455.

## Do Not Resuscitate (DNR) Orders

In keeping with the doctrine of informed consent, which states that every person has a right to determine what shall be done with his or her body, decisions regarding resuscitation in the event of cardiac or respiratory arrest should be discussed with the patient beforehand. Not every patient wants cardiopulmonary resuscitation (CPR) in the event of cardiac or respiratory arrest. This is especially true for patients with incurable, irreversible, or terminal illnesses. In 1974, the American Medical Association issued a recommendation that a patient's wishes regarding CPR be entered into the medical record and communicated to other health care providers. In addition, in response to the perceived legal liability, various health care organizations and associations have developed written guidelines on the DNR issue.

New York State, for example, adopted legislation that regulates DNR policies.[18] The law requires that the patient or surrogate give what could be called an "informed refusal" for CPR. The patient or surrogate should understand the risks and benefits of CPR and the consequences of a DNR order. In addition, the Joint Commission on Accreditation of Healthcare Organizations has developed standards that require each HCO to institute policies on withholding of resuscitative services.

## PRACTICAL IMPLICATIONS FOR CLAIM INVESTIGATION

A lack of informed consent is a common cause of action in medical malpractice claims. A plaintiff generally alleges inadequate informed consent. It also may be alleged that if the informed consent had been properly obtained, the plaintiff would not have consented to the treatment that allegedly caused the harm. These allegations are typically combined with other claims of negligent treatment.

*When investigating an allegation about a lack of informed consent, the following are helpful:*

- Interviewing the physician who performed the procedure and asking for his or her best recollection of the informed consent conversation; including how the patient communicated his or her understanding of the procedure (If the physician has no recollection of the informed consent discussion, his or her usual explanation for the procedure in question should be elicited.)
- Scrutinizing the original informed consent form; asking the physician about any apparent additions or alterations to the form

Any appearance of alterations of the informed consent form may present a problem in the defense of such claims. It is also important to check for a progress note concerning the informed consent discussion and to determine whether any witnesses were present at the time of the informed consent discussion.

## NOTES

1. Schloendorff v. Society of New York Hospital, 211 N.Y. 125, 105 N.E. 92 (1914).
2. Salgo v. Leland Stanford, Jr., University Board of Trustees, 317 P.5 2d 170 (1st) quoted in S. Becker, *Health Care Law: A Practical Guide* (Chicago: Ross & Hardies, 2003), 19-7.
3. F. A. Rozovsky, *Consent to Treatment: A Practical Guide*, 3rd ed. (Gaithersburg, Md.: Aspen Publishing, 2005).
4. Becker, 19-13.
5. Natanson v. Kline, 186 Kan. 393, 409 (1960), quoted in Becker, 19-13.
6. Becker, 19-14.
7. Canterbury v. Spence, 464 F. 2d 772.
8. Becker, 19-60.
9. 42 C.F.R. § 441.251 (2005).
10. 42 C.F.R. § 441.256 (2005).
11. 42 C.F.R. § 441.257 (2005).
12. 45 C.F.R. § 46.116 (2005).
13. Ibid.
14. Cruzan v. Director, Missouri Department of Health, 497 U.S. 261 (1990).
15. Becker, 19-34.
16. Raleigh Fitkin Paul Morgan Memorial Hospital v. Anderson, 42 N.J. 421, *cert. denied,* 377 U.S. 985 (1964), quoted in Becker, 19-34.
17. Becker, 19-50.
18. N.Y. Pub Health Law §§ 2960-2979.

# Chapter 18

# Responding to Adverse Occurrences and Potential Lawsuits

---

> - Responding to Patient Complaint Letters
> - Screening Incident/Occurrence Reports
> - Responding to Serious Adverse Occurrences
> - Preventing Recurrences

This chapter describes how the risk manager handles information concerning potential and actual claims. Depending on the policies of the health care organization (HCO), the risk manager may be able to respond immediately or he or she may work with a response team, particularly if the claim has reached the point of litigation.

## RESPONDING TO PATIENT COMPLAINT LETTERS

Immediately after receiving a letter complaining about treatment rendered, the risk manager may ask an investigator to review the patient's medical records to evaluate the seriousness of the complaint. The first step is a review of the medical record (see Chapter 1). Meanwhile, a prompt, courteous response from the HCO's chief executive officer or president, acknowledging the complaint and, if appropriate, assuring the writer that it will be investigated, is helpful. If necessary, a brief investigation can be conducted so that the HCO staff involved can describe the events in question and clarify any ambiguities. Once the matter has been reviewed, a carefully worded and appropriately sympathetic letter to the writer reiterating the circumstances and any follow-up actions may go a long way in avoiding legal action by the complainant.

## SCREENING INCIDENT/OCCURRENCE REPORTS

HCOs file occurrence reports to track possible patient injuries, watch for recurrent events, detect systems problems, and identify practitioners involved in multiple occurrences. In addition, the risk manager can monitor any persistent pattern of adverse events on an HCO-wide basis.

### Focused Occurrence Reporting

Depending on institutional policies, there may be more than one system of reporting adverse events. Some HCOs supplement the traditional incident reporting system, which primarily captures accidents that are the result of day-to-day patient care (e.g., patient falls, medication errors), with a more defined or formal reporting mechanism. One such method, called "focused reporting,"[1] requires health care providers to report specific untoward events to the risk management department. Clinical departments can streamline the reporting process by developing lists of specific occurrences with defining characteristics. Forms can be designed that allow each health care professional to report the event simply by checking off the applicable boxes (**Exhibit 18-1**).

### Occurrence Screening

Using a defined list of criteria, a quality management professional can screen medical records for adverse occurrence information.[2] HCOs develop screening criteria for high-risk areas or for departments with high numbers of reported incidents. Reviewing the medical record at the time of hospitalization (a concurrent review) or after patient discharge (a retrospective review) can alert the risk manager or individual department head to any deviations from practice, policy, or procedures that could cause patient injury.

**Exhibit 18-1** Occurrence Report Form

THE FOLLOWING IS PREPARED FOR THE HOSPITAL'S QUALITY ASSURANCE PROGRAM.
IT IS CONFIDENTIAL AND PROTECTED FROM DISCLOSURE PURSUANT TO NEW YORK
STATE EDUCATION LAW 6527 (3) AND NEW YORK STATE PUBLIC HEALTH LAW 2805-m.

Form ID:

*ADDRESSOGRAPH*

| PATIENT | MALE | AGE | DAYS | DATE OF OCCURRENCE | TIME | | DEPARTMENT | LOCATION |
|---|---|---|---|---|---|---|---|---|
| VISITOR | FEMALE | | MONTHS | | | A.M. | | |
| | | | YEARS | | | P.M. | | |

ADMITTING DIAGNOSIS                                    PROCEDURE

PERSON PREPARING REPORT    LAST NAME              FIRST NAME

Signature                              Date

**1. FALLS**

| | RELATED TO: | | OCCURRENCE INFORMATION | |
|---|---|---|---|---|
| Assisted to Floor | Ambulating | Assessed at Risk | Yes | No |
| Fall Alleged | Bathroom | Protocol in Place | Yes | No  Unk |
| Fall Witnessed | Bed/Crib | Patient is | Oriented | Confused |
| Found on Floor | Chair | Activity Privileges | Ambulatory | Non-Ambulatory |
| | Other Person | Siderails | Complete | Partial  None |
| | Stretcher/Table | Environmental | Wet | Debris  None |
| | Unknown | Restraints | Yes | No  Unk |

SEDATIVE WITHIN LAST 4 HOURS        Yes  No
IF YES, DRUG

**2. SKIN**
- Break/Tear/Scratch
- Burn
- Decubitus (Community)
- Decubitus (Newly Acquired)

**3. LOST PATIENT PROPERTY**
- Articles/Clothing
- Cash
- Dentures
- Glasses/Lens
- Jewelry

**4. INSTITUTIONAL CONDITIONS**
- External Disaster
- Fire
- HAZMAT Disposal
- Poisoning
- Power Failure
- Service Termination
- Spill/Leak
- Strike

**5. STATUS**
- Ambulatory Sx Admit
- New Onset Condition
- Readmit W/I 30 Days
- Transfer from Dx/Tx Center

**6. OBSTETRICS**
- Apgar <5 @ 5 Minutes
- Brachial Plexus/Erb's
- Circumcision with Repair
- Facial/Bell's Palsy
- Forceps Related
- Hysterectomy - Pregnant Woman
- Infant Abduction
- Infant Discharge/Wrong Family
- Inverted/Rupture Uterus
- Maternal Injury
- Meconium Aspiration
- Neonatal Injury
- Return to OR/OR
- Shoulder Dystocia

**7. PERIOPERATIVE/PERIPROCEDURAL**
W/I 30 DAYS
ASA  I  II  III  IV
Date

- AMI
- Anesthesia Related
- Cardiac Arrest
- Displacement/Break Implant
- Incorrect Instrument Count
- Incorrect Needle Count
- Incorrect Procedure
- Incorrect Sponge Count
- Injury to Liver/Spleen
- Laparoscopic to Open Procedure
- New Onset Neuro Deficit
- Peripheral Neuro Deficit
- Positioning
- Retained Foreign Body
- Return to OR
- Surgical Complication
- Thrombosed Graft
- Unanticipated Organ Removal
- Unanticipated Organ Repair
- Wound Dehiscence
- Wrong Patient
- Wrong Site Surgery

**8. PATIENT ASSOCIATED EVENTS**
- Act of Other Patient
- AMA
- Assault
- Attempted Rape/Rape
- Attempted Suicide/Suicide
- Contraband
- Criminal Activity/Injury
- Elopement
- Employee Actions
- Needlesticks
- Patient Actions
- Self-Injury
- Visitor Actions

**9. INSTRUMENT/EQUIPMENT MANUFACTURER**

SERIAL #

MODEL #

TYPE

| | | | |
|---|---|---|---|
| Battery Malfunction | Mechanical Malfunction | Unavailability |
| Electrical Malfunction | Struck By | Usage |

**10. BLOOD/MEDICATIONS**
TYPE (DRUG, CHEMO, ETC.)

| | | ROUTE | IM | SC |
|---|---|---|---|---|
| Documentation | Physician Orders | | IV | Top |
| Dosage | Rate | | PO | Oth |
| Infiltration | Reaction | | | |
| Non-Prescribed | Route | | | |
| Omission | Self-Medication | | | |
| Patient ID | Technique | | | |
| Pharmacy | Time | | | |

**11. PROCEDURES**

| Angiogram | Dialysis | Pacemaker | Thora/Paracentesis |
|---|---|---|---|
| Biopsy | Intubation | PTCA | Tube/Catheter Placement |
| Cardiac Cath | Invasive Dye | Scan | X-ray |
| Dental | Laser | Scope | Other |

SPECIFY

Implanted Intravascular Device
Central Line Venous Access

**12. UNEXPECTED EVENT**
NON-ILLNESS RELATED

| Aspiration (Related to Conscious Sedation) | Death | Loss of Limb |
|---|---|---|
| | Impairment of Limb | Surgical Intervention |
| CAC/Respiratory Arrest | Loss/Impairment Body Function | |

DESCRIBE OCCURRENCE BRIEFLY

PHYSICIAN/PA/NP FINDINGS

| | | | | | |
|---|---|---|---|---|---|
| No Change in Condition | Cardiac Arrest | Ecchymosis | Hemorrhage | Neurological Impairment | Pneumonia | Seizure |
| Abscess | Contusion | Edema | Infection | Pain | Pneumothorax | Shock |
| Anaphylaxis | Death | Emotional | Inflammation | Perforation | Pulmonary Edema | Sprain/Strain |
| Anastomatic Leak | Deep Vein Thrombosis | Fluid Overload | Laceration | Peripheral Neuro Impairment | Pulmonary Embolism | Tooth Injury |
| Burn | Dehiscence | Fracture | Loss of Consciousness | Peritonitis | Respiratory Arrest | Trauma |
| | | Hematoma | Necrosis | Phlebitis | Rupture | Unknown |

X-RAY:   Pos  Neg

TREATMENT

PHYSICIAN/PA/NP NAME                ID NUMBER            SIGNATURE                              DATE
STATUS:  Attending  House Staff  NP  PA  Other

FOJP © 2004

The risk management department aggregates the data from this occurrence screening process to identify trends that can then be addressed by the relevant departments. The goal is to determine whether the report or screen describes

- an odd occurrence that did not result in patient injury and is not likely to happen again
- a recurrent trend with the potential for patient injury
- an incident with actual patient injury

## RESPONDING TO SERIOUS ADVERSE OCCURRENCES

Once the risk manager receives information about a serious adverse occurrence, he or she takes immediate steps to

- provide guidance to the staff and attending physician in the disclosure of information to the patient and/or family (In most facilities, disclosure is the responsibility of the attending physician.)
- offer guidance to staff members to ensure that the adverse occurrence is documented objectively in the medical record
- initiate an investigation to determine the cause of the occurrence and to evaluate the outcome
- open a claim file, as indicated by the HCO internal procedures or criteria to meet the reporting requirements set forth in the HCO's medical malpractice insurance policy, as well as by any other state and federal regulations regarding incident reporting

Copies of the occurrence report and the investigation report are sent to the HCO's insurer (unless self-insured) as a notification of a potential claim. Generally the original report is kept in a secure place in the risk manager's office, and the information is channeled into the quality management system. The department head needs to be notified if a member of his or her department is involved in a serious occurrence.

It should be noted that the reports of occurrences that are part of the HCO's day-to-day operations (e.g., patient falls, medication errors) are discoverable in most states. This is the case even if these events ultimately become lawsuits.

## PREVENTING RECCURRENCES

### Reporting Sentinel Events

The Joint Commission on Accreditation of Healthcare Organizations (JCAHO) requires that all accredited HCOs establish policies and procedures to identify, report, and respond to any occurrence considered a *sentinel event*. JCAHO uses the term "sentinel" to signify the need for immediate investigation and reaction.

The following events are currently subject to review by JCAHO under the sentinel event policy. Periodically, and when responding to a serious occurrence, the JCAHO website should be checked for updates to the definition:

- "an unexpected occurrence involving death or serious physical or psychological injury, or the risk thereof. Serious injuries specifically include loss of limb or function."[3] Such deaths or serious injuries are those not related to the natural course of the patient's illness or the patient's underlying condition. The term "or risk thereof" is intended to capture "near misses" where recurrence of the event could lead to death or serious physical or psychological injury.
- Suicide of any patient receiving care in a staffed facility 24-hours-a-day or a suicide within 72 hours of discharge
- Unexpected death of a full-term infant
- Abduction of any individual receiving care, treatment or services
- Rape involving a patient and another patient, staff member, or other perpetrator while being treated on the HCO's premises (Specific conditions apply.)
- Hemolytic transfusion reactions
- Surgery on the wrong individual or the wrong body part
- Unintended retention of a foreign object after surgical or other procedure[4]
- Severe neonatal hyperbilirubinemia (bilirubin >30 milligrams/deciliter)
- Prolonged fluoroscopy with cumulative does >1500 rads to a single field, or any delivery of radiotherapy to the wrong body regions or >25% above the planned radiotherapy dose.

Each HCO is encouraged but not required to report any event meeting the above criteria. However, if the JCAHO becomes aware of the occurrence of any sentinel event, the HCO is required to prepare a "root cause analysis" and an action plan within 45 days of the HCO becoming aware of the event.

## Root Cause Analysis

Risk managers are frequently required to facilitate completion of or review root cause analyses. A *root cause analysis* is a study which focuses on systems and processes rather than an individual's performance as the underlying cause of a sentinel event. The goal is to identify changes to a system or process that would reduce the risk of recurrence.

JCAHO has posted on its Web site specific requirements for a root cause analysis to be considered "thorough and credible."[5] In addition, JCAHO has published a tool detailing the areas to be reviewed when conducting a root cause analysis of a specific event.[6]

The following is a typical approach that might be used by a risk manager for this process:

- Identifying the problem related to the sentinel event (e.g., a patient allergic to penicillin was given a penicillin derivative and suffered an anaphylactic reaction)
- Convening a multidisciplinary team, consisting of staff involved in the process being reviewed (in this case medication administration), including front-line staff involved in carrying out the process as well as organizational leaders empowered to implement change, to complete an analysis
  - Reviewing the organization's policy for identifying allergies, and trying to determine why the system failed
  - Describing the steps in the process already in place (A flow diagram of the process is helpful in identifying where the system failed and what opportunities exist to prevent recurrence.)
  - Identifying which step(s) in the process failed or contributed to the event (In this case, although the admitting history docu-

mented the penicillin allergy, there were no allergy labels placed on the record and the allergy was not noted on the physician orders sent to the pharmacy.)
- ○ Identifying underlying causes of the error by outlining the factors that contributed to the event (A cause-and-effect diagram can be helpful in identifying contributing factors.)
  - ▪ competency or credentials of the staff involved
  - ▪ orientation and training related to the process under review
  - ▪ availability of clinical information
  - ▪ physical environment
  - ▪ equipment and supplies
  - ▪ policy and procedure

Root cause analysis involves asking "why" and then asking "why" again to identify the root or underlying causes of the error or failure. Root cause analysis recognizes that human error always has a preceding cause. In this case, in brainstorming for "why" there were no allergy labels on the patient's chart, the team might consider the following questions:

- Is there adequate training on the policy?
- Did inadequate staffing contribute to the failure?
- Was information regarding the allergy communicated to the clinician responsible for placing the labels on the chart? Are labels readily available? Are all staff trained to place labels in the same location on the chart?
- Did failure of any other steps in the process contribute to the event? What redundancies are in place in this high-risk process to prevent failure of one step in the process from reaching the patient
  - ○ Does the pharmacy have a database that checks for allergies prior to dispensing?
  - ○ Was the patient wearing an allergy bracelet?
  - ○ Are medication order sheets required to document allergy history?
  - ○ Is the alert patient queried again regarding allergy history immediately prior to administering an antibiotic for the first time?

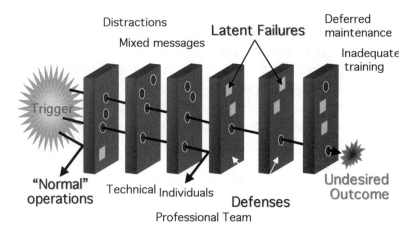

Adapted from: Reason J. Human Error. Cambridge UK; Cambridge University Press; 1990: 208.

**Figure 18-1**    Complex Systems and Latent Failure:
Steps for an In-Depth Review of a Medical Record

Typically, in analyzing sentinel events, the team finds that multiple failures at different steps in the process all contributed to the adverse event. Research in human error indicates that accidents in complex systems occur primarily through a chain of events, with multiple contributing factors.[7] **Figure 18-1** illustrates this concept frequently referred to as the "Swiss Cheese Theory" (i.e., several holes [failures] in the Swiss cheese [process] must line up for multiple defenses to fail, harming the patient)

### Action Plan

Last, the HCO is required to prepare an action plan describing the strategies to be implemented to reduce risk associated with the sentinel event and how the effectiveness of the implemented changes will be measured.

An essential element of this action plan is the identification of potential improvements in the process or system that would reduce the likelihood of a recurrence of the adverse event. In this example, one of the improvements recommended by the team was to review and enhance the orientation and training process for identification and documentation of allergies. In identifying potential improvements to make the process more reliable, the team should consider principles of safe process design, including

- reducing reliance on memory
- using checklists and protocols
- simplifying (reducing the number of steps) and standardizing the process (e.g., making sure that the organizational policies related to labeling records for allergies are consistent throughout the institution and do not vary from unit to unit or service to service)
- building in redundancy, such has having the pharmacy double check with the clinician when allergy history is not documented on the order sheet
- using information technology such as a pharmacy profile that would prompt the pharmacist regarding the allergy prior to dispensing medication

An additional element of this action plan is the development of a plan to implement the changes and of an evaluation tool to review the system or process to measure the effectiveness of the changes. In this case, one example of a measure of effectiveness would be an audit of patient records for documented allergies and the presence of the appropriate label to determine if the enhanced training was effective in improving compliance with the process. This and other monitoring tools can then be used to continue to monitor the effectiveness of the strategies implemented to prevent recurrence of this type of event.

## NOTES

1. McDonough, William J. "Systems for Risk Identification," in *The Risk Management Handbook for Health Care Organizations*, ed. R. Carroll, 4th ed. (Indianapolis: Wiley, 2003), 162.
2. Ibid., 166.
3. Joint Commission on Accreditation of Healthcare Organizations, *2006Hospital Accreditation Standards* (Oakbrook Terrace, Ill.: Joint Commission Resources, 2005), 99.
4. Ibid., 102.
5. Joint Commission on Accreditation of Healthcare Organizations, http://www.jcaho.org/ accredited+organizations/sentinel+event/se_pp.htm#3.

6. Joint Commission on Accreditation of Healthcare Organizations, *Minimum Scope of Root Cause Analysis for Specific Types of Sentinel Events*, http://www.jcaho.org/ accredited+organizations/sentinel+event/se_root_cause_analysis_matrix.pdf
7. J. Reason, *Human Error* (New York: Cambridge University Press, 1990).

# Chapter 19

# Claim Management

- Planning a Defense Strategy
- Handling a Summons
- Setting Loss and Expense Reserves
- Choosing a Medical Expert
- Costs of Defending a Claim
- Reviewing Defense-Related Bills
- Claim Conferences
- Negotiating a Settlement
- Attending the Trial
- Settling Claims Made Prior to Litigation
- Setting Priorities for Investigations

The claim investigator needs to be familiar with the claim management function so that he or she understands the importance of the investigation report and how the information is used to defend the health care organization (HCO).

The risk manager usually is responsible for claim management on a day-to-day basis. Whether or not claim management is the risk manager's primary function, he or she should monitor the HCO's claims. This responsibility may be shared with the insurer's claim manager, who then works with the risk manager and defense counsel to monitor the development of individual cases. This team approach ensures that important issues are evaluated from the HCO's standpoint and prevents any unnecessary lapse in defense activities. It is the risk manager's responsibility to safeguard the HCO's assets as part of the loss prevention program. Active claim monitoring is essential to implement the best possible defense with as little financial loss to the HCO as possible.

The following information outlines the basic claim management principles. (If necessary, please refer to definitions contained in Chapters 11 and 16.)

## PLANNING A DEFENSE STRATEGY

Developing a defense strategy entails evaluating the entire claim and giving consideration to the opinions of the medical experts, HCO administration, and defense counsel.

The risk manager begins to formulate a defense strategy at the outset of each new case. This process involves developing a case management plan toward the ultimate goal of achieving the most advantageous resolution of the claim. As the risk manager learns the facts through the investigation reports and gains more insight into the medical/legal issues of the claim, he or she must revise and refine the management plan accordingly.

*Although much depends on the plaintiff's demands, typical factors to consider in developing a defense strategy and evaluating a claim include*

- the plaintiff's allegations
- severity of the plaintiff's injuries
- facts revealed by the investigator's analysis of the medical records investigation
- results of depositions
- sensitivity of issues involved (e.g., will community relations suffer if the case is pursued to trial?)
- positions, opinion, and philosophy of the HCO administrator/risk manager/in-house counsel
- position of the insurance carriers involved
- position of the individual insured defendants
- anticipated strategy of codefendants whom the HCO does not insure
- venue in which the case is brought
- attitude and reputation of the trial judge assigned to the case
- experience and reputation of the plaintiff's attorney
- willingness of defense witnesses to testify

- any disciplinary actions taken against an insured party
- credibility and appearance of each of the witnesses
- ability and willingness of defense witnesses to testify
- whether motion strategy has been effective and efficiently transacted
- any medical record documentation issues

It is important to remember that a strategy requires continual thought and readjustment as the progress of the case is reevaluated from day one. Some, if not all, claims are discussed in conference before a decision is made.

## HANDLING A SUMMONS

The risk manager generally is involved in handling legal documents—including accepting and handling summonses. State statutes govern the proper service of a summons and the time limit for responding to service. The investigator can interview only those parties who are or were employed by the HCO and were covered by the HCO's professional liability insurance. When interviewing such potential defendants, or HCO employees, the investigator should always emphasize the importance of alerting the risk management department upon receipt of a summons (or any legal paper).

The HCO also should require periodic educational programs for members of the HCO staff so that they know how to respond in the event that they personally are served with a summons.

A typical summons (**Exhibit 19-1**) consists of a caption with the names of the plaintiff(s) and named defendants or codefendants and the name and address of the plaintiff's attorney. The summons is also dated. A summons gives the defendant notice that if he or she does not appear within a certain number of days, judgment will be entered against him or her.

*Once a summons is served, the risk manager or other designated individual should review the following information before accepting service on behalf of the HCO or a named defendant:*

- Is the correct institution named in the caption? Is the institution's address correct?
- If it is possible to determine the eligibility of coverage, was the defendant covered by the institution's insurance policy for the time period in question?

**Exhibit 19-1**    Sample Summons with Notice

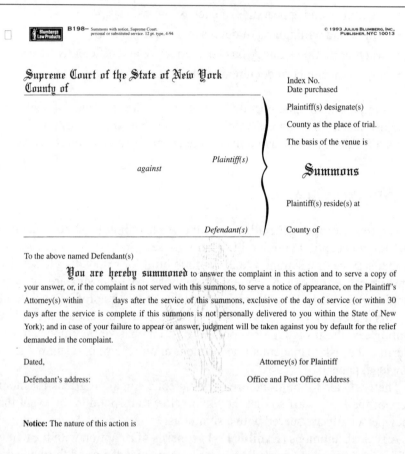

**Supreme Court of the State of New York**
**County of**

Index No.

Date purchased

Plaintiff(s) designate(s)

County as the place of trial.

The basis of the venue is

_Plaintiff(s)_

_against_

**Summons**

Plaintiff(s) reside(s) at

_Defendant(s)_

County of

To the above named Defendant(s)

**You are hereby summoned** to answer the complaint in this action and to serve a copy of your answer, or, if the complaint is not served with this summons, to serve a notice of appearance, on the Plaintiff's Attorney(s) within        days after the service of this summons, exclusive of the day of service (or within 30 days after the service is complete if this summons is not personally delivered to you within the State of New York); and in case of your failure to appear or answer, judgment will be taken against you by default for the relief demanded in the complaint.

Dated,

Defendant's address:

Attorney(s) for Plaintiff

Office and Post Office Address

**Notice:** The nature of this action is

The relief sought is

Upon your failure to appear, judgment will be taken against you by default for the sum of $
with interest from                              and the costs of this action.

**Exhibit 19-1** continued

AFFIDAVIT OF SERVICE

STATE OF NEW YORK, COUNTY OF                 SS:   The undersigned, being duly sworn, deposes and says; deponent is not a
party herein, is over 18 years of age and resides at
That on                                    at          M., at
deponent served the within summons,                        *on*                                                    defendant,

**INDIVIDUAL**
**1.** ☐   by delivering a true copy *of each* to said defendant personally; deponent knew the person so served to be the person described as
said defendant therein.

**CORPORATION**
**2.** ☐   a                          corporation, by delivering thereat a true copy *of each* to
personally, deponent knew said corporation so served to be the corporation described in said summons as said defendant and
knew said individual to be                              thereof.

**SUITABLE AGE PERSON**
**3.** ☐   by delivering thereat a true copy *of each* to                                        a person of suitable age
and discretion. Said premises is defendant's—actual place of business—dwelling place—usual place of abode—within the state.

**AFFIXING TO DOOR, ETC.**
**4.** ☐   by affixing a true copy *of each* to the door of said premises, which is defendant's—actual place of business—dwelling place—
usual place of abode—within the state. Deponent was unable, with due diligence to find defendant or a person of suitable age
and discretion thereat, having called there

**MAILING TO RESIDENCE USE WITH 3 OR 4**
**5A.** ☐   Within 20 days of such delivery or affixing, deponent enclosed a copy of same in a postpaid envelope properly addressed to
defendant at defendant's last known residence, at                                    and deposited
said envelope in an official depository under the exclusive care and custody of the U.S. Postal Service within New York State.

**MAILING TO BUSINESS USE WITH 3 OR 4**
**5B.** ☐   Within 20 days of such delivery or affixing, deponent enclosed a copy of same in a first class postpaid envelope properly
addressed to defendant at defendant's actual place of business, at
in an official depository under the exclusive care and custody of the U.S. Postal Service within New York State.
The envelope bore the legend "Personal and Confidential" and did not indicate on the outside thereof, by return address
or otherwise, that the communication was from an attorney or concerned an action against the defendant.

**DESCRIPTION USE WITH 1, 2, OR 3**
☐

| | | | | | |
|---|---|---|---|---|---|
| ☐ Male | ☐ White Skin | ☐ Black Hair | ☐ White Hair | ☐ 14-20 Yrs. | ☐ Under 5' | ☐ Under 100 Lbs. |
| ☐ Female | ☐ Black Skin | ☐ Brown Hair | ☐ Balding | ☐ 21-35 Yrs. | ☐ 5'0"-5'3" | ☐ 100-130 Lbs. |
| | ☐ Yellow Skin | ☐ Blonde Hair | ☐ Mustache | ☐ 36-50 Yrs. | ☐ 5'4"-5'8" | ☐ 131-160 Lbs. |
| | ☐ Brown Skin | ☐ Gray Hair | ☐ Beard | ☐ 51-65 Yrs. | ☐ 5'9"-6'0" | ☐ 161-200 Lbs. |
| | ☐ Red Skin | ☐ Red Hair | ☐ Glasses | ☐ Over 65 Yrs. | ☐ Over 6' | ☐ Over 200 Lbs. |

Other identifying features:

*Sworn to before me on*                 **Print name beneath signature.** ..........................................................................

LICENSE NO. ..............................................

Index No.
Supreme Court of the State of New York
County of

*Plaintiff(s)*

*against*

*Defendant(s)*

**Summons with Notice**
ACTION NOT BASED UPON A
CONSUMER CREDIT TRANSACTION

*Attorney(s) for Plaintiff(s)*

*Office, Post Office Address and Tel. No.*

- If the employment status can be verified, is/are the defendant(s) currently employed by the HCO?
- If the summons contains a statement as to the nature of the action, is it related to the employee's job?

If the answer to any of these questions is no, service probably should not be accepted. If the process server leaves the summons behind, it should be returned—immediately—to the plaintiff's attorney, along with a brief letter explaining the reason that service was improper.

*After accepting a summons, the risk manager must consider the following:*

- If the institution has applicable insurance, which policy(ies) was/were in effect at the time of the occurrence?
- Are there any restrictions or exclusions of insurance coverage that might be applied to some or all of the allegations? (For example, most insurance programs do not cover undue familiarity and criminal behavior.)
- In cases involving continuous treatment, does the defendant have coverage from another carrier or HCO?
- Was a contractual arrangement in effect between the HCO and another entity that might provide coverage (e.g., residents rotating to another facility, outside food service)?
- Was the defendant's involvement regarding the claimant within the scope of his or her employment?
- Do excess insurance carriers, if any, require notification if potential financial damages seem great?

Once this information has been established, the risk manager should send the original summons, complaint, and relevant information directly to the HCO defense counsel or to the insurance carrier's claim manager (if not self-insured).

## SETTING LOSS AND EXPENSE RESERVES

The loss reserve is the amount of money set aside to pay out to a plaintiff if there is a decision to settle the claim or if a plaintiff verdict is rendered. The expense reserve is the amount of funds set aside to pay legal fees, court fees, clinical expert fees, and so forth, regardless of the outcome of the case. The investigator should keep in mind that the investigation report has great influence on the loss and expense reserves.

The risk manager or insurance carrier claim manager or both generally are responsible for this aspect of claim management. Throughout the life of the claim, the loss and expense reserves will be reevaluated and adjusted continually so that adequate funds are available at the time of settlement or jury verdict. It is also essential to monitor reserves so that the appropriate excess carrier can be notified of possible future indemnities.

It takes a great deal of knowledge and expertise to set reserves. The risk manager can enhance his or her skills by studying a variety of claims and noting their reserving development, reviewing sustainable values, and discussing claims with experienced defense counsel. The risk manager also should be aware of the excess carrier's philosophies on reserving.

To set a basic reserve, the risk manager reviews the facts of the case. The factors involved in establishing a reserve can be categorized into two areas—damages and liability.

Damages consist of injury severity and socioeconomic factors. The severity of the plaintiff's alleged injury is perhaps the most crucial item to be determined. Studies have shown that the more severe the injury, the greater the damages paid out.

*Injury severity is determined according to the following factors:*

- Permanent injuries are more costly than temporary ones, generally because the attendant expenses are higher.
- If the plaintiff can prove past pain and suffering (documentation of a level of awareness), this can enhance the value of the claim.
- Studies have shown that allegations of neurologic impairment (e.g., a brain-damaged infant) are considered the most serious of injuries and thus can be the most costly to the defendant.
- If a plaintiff dies, a wrongful death action may be brought. These cases can be expensive if the plaintiff was a high wage earner and the sole support of a large family. In general, however, if the patient is deceased, the value of the case may be less because costs associated with long-term medical care and years of pain and suffering are eliminated.
- Cases involving loss of reproductive capacity or loss or damage to a sexual organ generally are costly.
- Loss of a parent, in particular a mother, is greater the younger the child.

*Socioeconomic factors include the following:*

- **The claimant's age and professional status:** A young, highly paid wage earner with dependents is more likely to receive a higher award if incapacitated or if death occurs than is an elderly, retired individual.
- **The presence of minor children and/or dependent adults:** The costs of their upkeep or maintenance must be factored in if the case involves the death or disability of the family wage earner.
- **The sympathy factor:** Many cases are lost purely on the basis of the emotional impact of a disabled person on the jury, even though juries are instructed not to consider sympathy during their deliberations.

*The following factors also must be considered in liability claims:*

- **Venue:** Where is the case venued? Could the venue have a negative impact on the outcome of the case? For instance, if a community HCO is being sued in a geographically distant district (where the HCO's reputation is not known), the venue may contribute to an unfavorable outcome because the jurors have no emotional connection to the HCO as a site of community involvement and charitable care.
- **Plaintiff's attorney**
  - Who is the plaintiff's attorney, and what is his or her reputation and experience as a medical malpractice litigator? Does he or she fight for a jury verdict no matter what?
  - Is the attorney considered "cagey" enough to poke holes in a defensible case by taking advantage of even the smallest of gaps in the medical record or testimony?
- **Codefendants' attorneys**
  - Who is the codefendant's attorneys, and what is his or her reputation and experience as a medical malpractice litigator?
  - Will the attorneys seek to blame your HCO and/or individual defendants insured through the HCO?
- **Recent awards:** What was the highest sustained jury award for a similar case in the HCO's locale? When was the award? (If there has been a substantial time lapse since a similar case was reviewed, there is a significant chance that the award will be increased). This information can be obtained from defense counsel or from other firms or publications, such as the local law journal or *Jury Verdict Reporter* (Solon, Ohio).

Such information is of crucial importance when evaluating settlement possibilities, as these figures directly influence the judge's willingness to recommend a reasonable settlement. Media coverage also may affect a jury's estimation of the worth of a case.

- **Parties involved**
  - Are the major tortfeasors (individuals who have committed a civil wrong) covered by the HCO? If so, the bulk of the award most likely will fall on the institution, with very little coverage from any noninsured codefendant to offset the burden.
  - Does the institution insure all the named defendants? If so, that institution must shoulder the entire burden for damages.
  - If the codefendants are the primary tortfeasors, do they have adequate insurance coverage?
- Does the case involve any contracts concerning the providers that might be construed as releasing the HCO from liability or as shifting the liability to another party (e.g., hold harmless and indemnity agreements, defined in Chapter 15)?

Although these factors merit careful consideration individually, they also must be evaluated together to make a reasonable decision regarding reserve and expense allocations.

Clearly, as time passes and more information becomes available about the occurrence and the extent of the plaintiff's injury, the case must be evaluated periodically to assess the need for a possible increase or decrease in reserves. For example, a physical examination by the defendant's medical expert might reveal that the alleged injury has improved or resolved completely. Such a development would call for a possible reduction in the indemnity reserve, but not necessarily in the expense reserve. If the plaintiff continues to allege that he or she has an injury, a private investigator might be brought in to verify the severity of the plaintiff's alleged injury. On the other hand, after reviewing all of the plaintiff's medical records and other pertinent documents, a physician expert might find that there is more negligence than originally believed. Such a finding could necessitate a considerable increase in both indemnity and expense reserves or signal the need to try to settle the case early.

The risk manager's best resources for evaluating reserves are the careful monitoring of correspondence from defense counsel, investigation reports, and his or her ongoing communication with the insurance carrier's claim managers.

## CHOOSING A MEDICAL EXPERT

Retaining a medical expert to review the patient's medical record and other documents is a critical part of a defense strategy. Determinations made by medical experts have a great impact on whether to settle a claim or proceed to trial. Experts are chosen for their knowledge and reputation in a particular clinical area. Compensation for their services should be established at the outset and confirmed, in writing, once they are retained.

*Whether he or she actually chooses the medical expert for a particular claim, it is important that the risk manager or claim investigator be involved in this critical process by ensuring that:*

- all allegations and injuries are known
- the case has been investigated as thoroughly as possible
- all basic information (pathology slides, X-rays, medical records) is available for review
- an "in-house" practitioner with expertise in the particular clinical area has reviewed the case, if necessary, for direction
- a physician from the appropriate specialty is assigned for review
- the expert has good credentials
- the expert is not affiliated with the institution
- the expert was in practice at the time of the allegations and preferably is still in practice
- the expert is willing to testify (at deposition and/or at trial) and is willing to sign any necessary affidavits in support of motion practice

*It is important to assess his or her personality to ascertain whether the expert:*

- is willing to "tell it like it is," rather than "rubber stamp" the defense counsel's position (An expert who is "for the defense at all cost" may not bring the necessary objectivity to the review.)
- is willing to devote the time necessary to review and discuss the case and to testify at the trial
- is cooperative, making himself/herself readily available for meetings with defense counsel
- will make a good witness (The expert should be well groomed and well spoken and not aloof or arrogant.)

An astute risk manager may want to do some "networking" to identify the most qualified expert. One way to start is by asking department chairs for the names of community physicians who have the desired reputation. The local medical society also can be helpful. This is time well spent if the search yields the right expert.

## COSTS OF DEFENDING A CLAIM

Monitoring the cost of defending a claim is another important aspect of claim management. The risk manager and claim investigator both should be aware of the cost involved in defending a claim—defense counsel's fees for reviewing medical records, the cost of filing motions, and the fees involved in expert witness reviews. These costs generally depend on the severity of the case, the amount of time needed for preparing defense strategy, and the number of witnesses deposed. Defense bills should be reviewed by the risk manager or another designated person to make sure the expenses are accurate and appropriate.

## REVIEWING DEFENSE-RELATED BILLS

Legal expenses involved in defending a claim generally are sent directly to the hospital's insurance carrier or, if the HCO is self-insured, to the risk manager. Legal bills may be for professional services rendered, the copying of legal and other documents, telephone calls, and other disbursements made by defense counsel in relation to the case. Bills for court reporters and experts generally arrive separately from defense bills.

*The following guidelines are helpful in reviewing legal expenses:*

- Make sure bills contain an explanation and description of the charges and are reviewed for reasonableness.
- Devise a system that makes it easy to note whether payment already has been made on each bill.
- Review all bills to ascertain that payment is made for services actually rendered and that there are no duplicate bills for the same services.
- Do not pay fees for expert reviews, physical examinations, and surveillance until the reports are in the files.
- Court reporter bills should be itemized and should indicate the total number of pages.

## CLAIM CONFERENCES

A conference is necessary when a claim carries the risk of particularly high exposure or extreme sensitivity. Participants typically include HCO counsel and defense counsel, the risk manager, an appropriate HCO administrator, clinical representatives or the department chair from the specialty involved, the claim investigator, and the chairperson of the medical staff quality management program. The claim conference should be held early in the legal proceedings to begin the development of a strong and unified defense strategy. Additional conferences may be necessary as further investigation is conducted and liability issues are reevaluated. A final conference should be held when the case is placed on the trial calendar, to determine trial and/or settlement strategy.

## NEGOTIATING A SETTLEMENT

Depending on the HCO policy, the risk manager or claim manager may be called upon to negotiate with the plaintiff's attorney during the course of a claim.

There are several ways to define *negotiation*, and certainly there are as many different negotiating styles as there are individuals to negotiate. Essentially, negotiation is the exchange of information necessary to understand opposing positions and ultimately to move those positions to some point of mutual agreement. A negotiation generally is deemed a success when *both sides* come away thinking they have not given up too much and/or received too little in return.

## ATTENDING THE TRIAL

If the decision is made to take a claim to trial, the best way to monitor events, if time allows, is for the risk manager or claim investigator to attend all or part of the proceedings. In addition to having a ringside seat, the risk manager personally can evaluate the plaintiff's impact on the jury, the effectiveness of the defense and plaintiff counsel, witness performance, and the quality of the expert witnesses' testimony. More important, the risk manager can evaluate the proceedings firsthand and thus provide valuable input in the settlement negotiations if the proceedings are not going in the institution's favor.

## SETTLING CLAIMS MADE PRIOR TO LITIGATION

Occasionally patients make claims against an HCO or covered employees without filing a lawsuit. Such a claim usually includes allegations of wrongdoing by the HCO and/or physician that resulted in an injury to the patient. (If the patient is represented by an attorney, contacts should be made only through the attorney.) Negotiations are generally handled by an insurance carrier's claim manager. If the HCO is self-insured, however, the risk manager may be responsible for reviewing the letter of claim and taking the necessary steps to resolve it.

As in all claim investigations, the medical record must be reviewed, parties interviewed, and, possibly, a report prepared. It also may be necessary to have an in-house or outside expert review the case. After all the facts are reviewed, a decision can be made regarding the HCO's position on the claim. If the risk manager's or claim manager's efforts at negotiations are not successful and no agreement can be reached with the patient or with his or her attorney, litigation may ensue.

Early intervention after an adverse occurrence generally is considered the best approach to avoiding litigation.

*Strategies for heading off litigation include*

- waiving any uninsured part of the patient's bill
- having high-ranking administrators and/or the patient ombudsperson visit the patient while in house to discuss the occurrence
- offering counseling services to the patient and family
- offering medical treatment for the injury—free of charge
- offering specific services to the patient and family (i.e., giving them the "VIP" treatment)

## SETTING PRIORITIES FOR INVESTIGATIONS

The HCO's risk management department receives notices of many actual claims (summonses) and potential claims (attorney's request letters, alerts, patient complaint letters). Depending on the department's individual policies, some or all of these cases may be investigated. In a busy department, it is not realistic to expect that all cases will be investigated immediately. However, the risk manager or claim investigator should screen all claims to make a determination regarding the need for an in-depth investigation.

The injury severity code developed by the National Association of Insurance Commissioners (NAIC) is a simple method of evaluating those cases for which a claim file will be opened. The NAIC code ranks injuries from 1 to 9 for increasing severity, with a score of 1 indicating "no physi-cal injury," and a 9 indicating "death" (see **Table 19-1**). Code 10 is for cases not involving an actual injury. Other methods can be substituted.

One can set investigative priorities on newly opened claims by assigning each case an NAIC code according to injury severity (see "Lawsuits" and "Potential Lawsuits").

**Table 19-1**    NAIC Codes

| Temporary/ Permanent | NAIC Code | Description |
|---|---|---|
| | 0) No injury | |
| | 1) Emotional only | Fright, no physical damage |
| Temporary | 2) Insignificant | Lacerations, contusions, minor scars, rash; no delay in recovery |
| Temporary | 3) Minor | Infections, fractures, missed frac-tures; recovery delayed |
| Temporary | 4) Major | Burns, surgical material left, drug side effect; recovery delayed |
| Permanent | 5) Minor | Loss of fingers, loss or damage to organs; includes nondisabling injuries |
| Permanent | 6) Significant | Deafness, loss of limb, loss of eye, loss of one kidney or lung |
| Permanent | 7) Major | Paraplegia, blindness, loss of two limbs, brain damage |
| Permanent | 8) Grave | Quadriplegia, severe brain damage, lifelong care or fatal prognosis |
| | 9) Death | |
| | 10) Legal issue only | Billing disputes, refusal to treat, interprofessional relations |

*Source:* Reprinted with permission from *Malpractice Claims Final Compilation, Medical Malpractice Closed Claims 1975-1978*, p. 8, item 6-13, (c) 1980 by National Association of Insurance Commissioners.

The following guidelines may be helpful in using the NAIC code to set priorities for investigating actual or potential claims.

## Lawsuits

All lawsuits need to be investigated, but not all lawsuits can be investigated immediately.

*An in-depth investigation should be done as soon as possible for*

- high-exposure cases that involve serious injuries (NAIC codes 4–9); cases of high notoriety (e.g., when there is media coverage) fall into this category
- federal court cases that move quickly through the legal process, because of the shorter time frame for discovery
- older cases that may be approaching trial date

*The following types of lawsuits generally can be held for investigation at a later date:*

- Low-exposure cases that involve minor injuries (NAIC codes 0–3)
- Cases in which the allegation and/or occurrence is unknown or unclear—that is, cases in which there has been no apparent occurrence or injury and for which clarifying legal documents (i.e., bill of particulars) have not yet been served
- Any case in which the statute of limitations has expired (such cases should be discussed with legal counsel due to the complex issues involved) (e.g., legal counsel should be consulted on cases awaiting discontinuance for statute of limitations expiration)

## Potential Lawsuits

As discussed in Chapter 1, it is important to investigate all potential lawsuits as quickly as possible. If a prompt response is not feasible, it is important to assess each case and then determine which cases should be given priority. The following guidelines can help in establishing these priorities.

*The cases are grouped into five categories using the NAIC codes:*

1.  **High Priority with an Attorney Involved:** There is serious injury (NAIC codes 4–9), and an attorney has requested the medical record or written a letter asking for compensation for his client.
2.  **High Priority without an Attorney Involved:** There is serious injury, and no attorney is involved. The risk manager can be alerted to this type of situation by a letter of claim or an occurrence via the risk management reporting system or screening obtained during the quality assessment process.
3.  **Low Priority with an Attorney Involved:** There is nonserious injury (NAIC codes 0–3), and an attorney is involved.
4.  **Low Priority without an Attorney Involved:** There is nonserious injury, and no attorney is involved.
5.  **Low Priority:** Billing disputes probably require little or no investigation.[1]

Cases that involve serious injuries (categories 1 and 2 above) get a high priority for claim investigation. The potential for legal action is high, and the need for early evaluation and possible settlement negotiations is obvious. If an investigation is conducted early, important documents can be secured, and the parties involved in the incident can be interviewed while events are still fresh in their minds and while they are still employed by or associated with the HCO.

Additionally, seemingly nonserious injuries in which a well-known medical malpractice plaintiff's attorney is involved should be investigated briefly, and principal parties should be interviewed. The injury may be more serious than it appears in the medical record.

**NOTES**

1.  As noted in Chapter 1, records should be screened for evidence of liability or injury so that the HCO does not institute legal proceedings against an individual who may countersue for malpractice. A system should be devised whereby the HCO's billing department is notified to hold billing in cases of clear liability.

# Chapter 20

# Writing the Report
# Clearly and Concisely

- Audience Analysis
- Concise Writing
- Coherent Writing
- Error-Free Writing
- Resources

The investigation report should be written in clear, concise language. The writing style is especially important because the readers—claim managers, defense attorneys, and the HCO's risk managers—are busy professionals who have many documents competing for their attention. When a piece of writing is simple and clear, readers get the intended message quickly and effectively without having to struggle to understand what the writer meant.

Sometimes people do not realize that writing is a process of revision and editing. Even the most seasoned writer cannot produce a polished text in the first draft. On the other hand, investigators have time constraints that do not allow for endless revising. Therefore, this section has been prepared in order to provide some guidelines for producing readable prose in the most efficient way possible.

## AUDIENCE ANALYSIS

When preparing a report, it is important to think about who its readers will be, what their level of expertise is, and what they do or do not know about the subject of the report. This analysis helps the investigator determine what specific information needs to be included in any given document and what can be left out. The investigator should remember that most malpractice defense lawyers and claim managers have at least a rudimentary understanding of medicine. Thus, for example, it is unlikely that one would need to define *IV infiltrate* in any investigative report. On the other hand, *scotomata*, a visual deficit, should be explained.

*The following questions should be asked as the writing process begins:*

- How much is the reader likely to know about this particular topic?
- What information can be left out because the reader already knows it? (Because readers are busy, they should not be asked to read something with which they are already familiar.)
- What information should be provided so that the reader can understand fully the nature of the occurrence?

One specific point to think about is the use of abbreviations and acronyms. If there is any doubt that readers will not understand an abbreviation or acronym, spell out the entire word or phrase on first reference and put the acronym in parentheses. Then, in subsequent references, one only need use the acronym. (For example, in preparing this text, we spelled out the term *peer review organization* on first reference, followed by the initials, *PRO*, which we then used throughout the rest of the chapter.)

## CONCISE WRITING

Producing dynamic, clear writing is not a matter of accident or even the writer's talent. Following specific guidelines helps turn imprecise, wordy writing into powerful prose. However, we use the word *guideline* very specifically. Writing is a craft; it is not a "science" with a set of rules that can be followed. Although there are some definite, not-to-be broken rules of grammar and punctuation, other principles of writing are better thought of as suggestions that still require the writer to think about when they should and should not be applied. The goal, however, is always the same—to produce writing that is natural and conversational.

*With that said, here are some suggestions for producing uncluttered, readable documents:*

- **Make sure a sentence tells a story about someone doing something:** Sometimes in business, professional writers eliminate "actors" from a sentence so that no one is responsible for the action. This practice tends to make the writing heavy, boring, and unclear. For example, "The decision was made to intubate the patient" is stronger if it is written, "The attending and resident decided to intubate the patient." (Of course, if it is not clear from the review of the record who decided to intubate the patient, the sentence must be written the first way. However, if the actors are known, they should be included in the sentence.)
- **Use simple, short sentences; use more complex sentences selectively when absolutely necessary:** A sure way to lose readers is to write such long sentences that they forget the beginning of the sentence by the time they get to the end. A good way to test if sentence length is too long is to read it aloud. If the reader runs out of breath before reaching the end of the sentence, it probably needs to be shortened.
- **Use simple, specific, concrete words:** Rather than making the writer sound knowledgeable, the use of polysyllabic words, jargon, or highly abstract words often makes it more difficult for the reader to understand the writer's meaning. Instead of "The patient's condition was ameliorated," write, "The patient's condition improved." Rather than "Pursuant to your memorandum dated October 15..." try, "After receiving your October 15 memo...."
- **Use words economically:** Every word on a page needs to justify its existence. That is, each word should further the idea the writer is trying to communicate. If an idea can be expressed in fewer words, those words that do not serve any useful function should be eliminated. Here are some examples of phrases that can be written more economically:

| *Wordy* | *Economical* |
| --- | --- |
| during the time that | while |
| for the purpose of | for, to |
| for the reason that | because |
| at this point in time | now |
| we are in receipt of | we have |
| in the event that | if |

- **Watch out for redundancies and negative constructions:** Both redundancies and negative constructions lead to excess words that may confuse or irritate readers. For example, in the sentence, "The physician had breakfast at 8:00 A.M. in the morning with the incumbent congresswoman from the state of Massachusetts," the words *in the morning, incumbent*, and s*tate of* can all be eliminated without sacrificing meaning. Similarly, the sentence "An outpatient surgery center cannot operate until it has been licensed by the municipality in which it is operated" can be written to read, "Before accepting patients, an outpatient surgery center must be licensed by the municipality in which it operates."
- **Try to avoid nominalizations, the passive voice, and stacked nouns**
  - Nominalizations are verbs that have been turned into nouns (e.g., *discover* into *discovery, move* into *movement*, or *fail* into *failure*). Often, when nominalizations are used in a sentence, the actors disappear. For example, "A review was done of the relevant regulation" can be rewritten with the actor in the sentence as, "I reviewed the relevant regulations."
  - In the passive voice, the subject of the sentence is deemphasized or hidden. An example of a sentence in the passive voice is, "The patient was intubated by the doctor." The sentence is stronger, however, if written in the active voice with the subject first, followed by the verb as, "The doctor intubated the patient."
  - "Stacked nouns" are more than two nouns strung together. An example of a sentence with a stacked noun is, "On the basis of our extensive training needs assessment review, we have concluded that more in-house workshops are needed." This sentence could be rewritten as "We have extensively reviewed our training needs and decided...."

## COHERENT WRITING

A coherent document is logical, consistent, and unified. When a report is coherent, it is easy to follow the writer's train of thought; there are no jarring pieces that force the reader to muddle through the writer's meaning.

*Below are several tips that contribute to coherence:*

- **Make decisions about person, tense, and tone before beginning to write:** These three qualities— the person, the tense, and the tone in which the report is written—should be consistent throughout the entire document.
  - Most investigative reports are written in the third person (*he/she/ him/her/they/them*). Occasionally, the investigator may need to use the first person (*I/me*), especially when reporting on the interview (e.g., "I then asked Dr. Jones her customary practice in this area").
  - Most reports are written in the past tense, because they describe events that already have occurred.
  - Reports should be written in a conversational, objective, and businesslike tone.
- **Use transitions effectively to link one idea to another:** Transitions are those words that tell the reader how one idea relates to another. Simply repeating the same words (e.g., the names of the people involved in the occurrence, the disease involved, the procedures performed) serves as a kind of link, reminding the reader that "this is what this report is about." There are also transitions that "move" ideas. *Here is a list of transitions that show direction:*
  - To move in the same direction: *also, in many cases, as well, too, next, again, in addition, further*
  - To move in the opposite direction: *but, however, on the other hand, on the contrary, nevertheless*
  - To move toward a conclusion: *consequently, so, hence, accordingly, then, thus, therefore, in short, in summary*
  - To go toward words that are more or less abstract: *for example, such as, for instance, as an illustration*
- **Keep related words and ideas together:** Whether combining words into sentences, sentences into paragraphs, or paragraphs into entire reports, similar ideas should be kept together. For example, writing about the patient's postoperative course in one paragraph and then returning to it again four paragraphs later can confuse the reader.

## ERROR-FREE WRITING

It is the investigator's responsibility to guarantee that every report is accurate and error free. To do this, when the report is complete, the investigator should

- check for actual errors
- check for inconsistencies and contradictions
- make sure the reader has all the necessary information
- correct all spelling, grammar, and punctuation errors
- check for consistency in formatting devices (Are all the heading and subheadings formatted consistently? Are bullets used consistently? Are all paragraphs indented an identical number of spaces?)
- check the accuracy of figures
- check the spelling of all names
- beware of ambiguous meanings

## RESOURCES

A good dictionary, a thesaurus, and a grammar handbook should be a part of every writer's library. Below are recommendations for all three kinds of references:

- Recommended dictionaries are *Webster's New Collegiate Dictionary*, the *American Heritage Dictionary*, and *Webster's New World Dictionary*.
- A recommended thesaurus is *Roget's International Thesaurus*.
- Recommended grammar handbooks are
  - Kessler, Lauren, and Duncan McDonald. *When Words Collide*. 5th ed. Belmont, Calif.: Wadsworth Publishing, 2000 (or latest edition).
  - Fowler, H. Ramsey, and Jane E. Aaron. *The Little, Brown Handbook*. 9th ed. Glenview, Ill.: Scott Foresman, 2003 (or latest edition).
- For more information on writing well, read Zinsser, William. *On Writing Well*. New York: HarperCollins, 2001 (or latest edition) and Williams, Joseph M. *Style*. New York: Longman, 2004 (or latest edition).

# Resources

Behrman, R. E., R. M. Kliegman, and H. B. Jenson, eds. *Nelson Textbook of Pediatrics*. 17th ed. Philadelphia: W. B. Saunders Company, 2004.

Braunwald, E., D. P. Zipes, L. Peter, and R. Bonow, eds. *Braunwald's Heart Disease*: *A Textbook of Cardiovascular Medicine*. 7th ed. Philadelphia: W. B. SaundersCompany, 2004.

Brunton, L., J. Lazo, and K. Parker, eds. *Goodman and Gilman's The Pharmacological Basis of Therapeutics*. 11th ed. New York: McGraw-Hill Professional, 2005.

Clemente, C., ed. *Gray's Anatomy*. 30th ed. Baltimore: Lippincott, Williams & Wilkins, 2004.

Cunningham, F. G., K. J. Leveno, S. L. Bloom, J. C. Hauth, L. C. Gilstrap, and K. D. Wenstrom, eds. *Williams Obstetrics*. 22nd ed. New York: McGraw-Hill, 2005.

Kasper, D. L., E. Braunwald, A. Fauci, S. Hauser, D. Longo, and J. L. Jameson, eds. *Harrison's Principles of Internal Medicine*. 16th ed. New York: McGraw-Hill Professional, 2004.

Marx, J. A., R. S. Hockberger, and R. M. Walls, eds. *Rosen's Emergency Medicine: Concepts and Clinical Practice*. 5th ed. St. Louis: C. V. Mosby, 2002.

Townsend, C. M., R. D. Beauchamp, B. M. Evers, and K. L. Mattox, eds. *Sabiston Textbook of Surgery: The Biological Basis of Modern Surgical Practice*. 17th ed. Philadelphia: W. B. Saunders Company, 2004.

# Authors and Contributors

**Nancy Acerbo-Kozuchowski, RN, MS, CPHRM** *Risk Management Consultant & Education Director, FOJP Service Corporation, New York, NY*
Ms. Acerbo-Kozuchowski is the co-author of the first edition of this book. She holds a Masters in Health Systems Management from the Hagan School of Business at Iona College. Starting as a claim investigator at FOJP in 1979, she has held leadership positions and is currently responsible for the development of risk management clinical education courses for FOJP's clients.

**Kathleen Ashton, RN, BSN** *Education Coordinator, FOJP Service Corporation, New York, NY*
Kathleen Ashton received a BSN from Hunter College-Bellevue School of Nursing in 1976. She is licensed as a professional registered nurse in New York State where she worked in staff and management nursing positions for 23 years. Kathleen joined FOJP Service Corporation in 1999 where she is the Education Coordinator in the Claim Services Department.

**Gregory M. Asnis, MD** *Professor of Psychiatry and Behavioral Sciences, Director, The Anxiety & Depression Program, Albert Einstein College of Medicine/Montefiore Medical Center, Bronx, NY*

**Ruth H. Axelrod, RN, JD** *Claims Attorney FOJP Service Corporation, New York, NY*
Ms. Axelrod has be a medical malpractice litigator for 11 years. She has been employed at FOJP for 3 years as a claims attorney. She was graduated from Boston University with BSN 1980 and from Cardozo School of Law 1990 with JD. While on law review she wrote a published Note called, "Whose Womb is it Anyway: Are Paternal Rights Alive and Well Despite Danforth?" 11 Cardozo L. Rev. 685 (1990).

**Allison M. Barth, Esq.** *Counsel, FOJP Service Corporation, New York, NY*

**Peter Bernstein, MD, MPH** *Associate Professor of Obstetrics & Gynecology and Women's Health, Montefiore Medical Center/Albert Einstein College of Medicine, Bronx, NY*

**Lori Breslow, PhD** *Senior Lecturer, Sloan School of Management, MIT, Cambridge, MA*
Lori Breslow, who is a Senior Lecturer in the Communication Program at the MIT Sloan School, has been a communication consultant with FOJP Service Corporation since 1984.

**David Feldman, MD, MBA** *Vice President, Perioperative Services, Vice Chairman, Dept. of Surgery, Maimonides Medical Center, Brooklyn, NY*

**Karen Geller, RN, JD** *Director Risk Management & Regulatory Affairs, The Mount Sinai Medical Center, New York, NY*
Karen Geller is a nurse attorney and risk manager with many years' experience in healthcare. She is active on both the local and national levels in the field of risk management and been a contributor to several risk management publications.

**Jose Guzman, RN, MS** *Director, Risk Management, Hospitals Insurance Company, Inc., White Plains, NY*
A Registered Nurse with over 25 years of extensive clinical and administrative experience; in both acute care, and long-term care settings. He has held various executive leadership positions including Director of Nursing at several long-term care facilities, acute care hospital and in case management industries. Mr. Guzman has held adjunct faculty status at Columbia University in N.Y.C. and has co-authored various publications on acute care and long-term care risk management.

**Vilma A. Joseph, MD, MPH** *Assistant Professor of Anethesiology, Associate Director of Quality Improvement and Research Associate, Director of Anesthesiology /Weiler Division, Montefiore Medical Center/ Albert Einstein College of Medicine, Bronx, NY*

**Irene Kassel BSN, RN** *Operations Project Coordinator, FOJP Service Corporation, New York, NY*
Ms. Kassel practiced nursing in Labor & Delivery and Neonatal Intensive Care at high risk tertiary care centers. Ms. Kassel has authored articles in risk management publications and has been a member of the Risk Management Department at FOJP Service Corporation for the past 17 years.

**Patricia Kischak, RN, CPHRM** *Vice President, Risk Management, Hospitals Insurance Company, Inc., White Plains, NY*
Ms. Kischak entered the field of risk management as a medical malpractice investigator at FOJP and over 19 years she held various management positions at FOJP and was the Director of Risk Management since 2001. She is currently the Vice President, Risk Management for Hospitals Insurance Company, Inc., an an affiliate of FOJP.

Ms. Kischak earned a Bachelor's Degree in Business Management and an Associate's Degree in Paralegal Studies and is currently pursing a Master's degree in Business Administration.

**Steve Macaluso, Esq.** *Associate General Counsel, FOJP Service Corporation, New York, NY*
Steve Macaluso, Associate General Counsel at FOJP, has an A.B. from Harvard College and a J.D. from Harvard Law School. His professional background includes work in the areas of insurance and health and hospital law.[1]

**Monica Santoro, RN, CPHRM, CPHQ** *Vice President, Senior Consultant, New York, NY*
Monica Santoro has worked in healthcare risk management for over 25 years. She has consulted extensively on root cause analysis and contributed to a guide on root cause analysis published by the Greater New York Hospital Association. Ms. Santoro currently serves as the Vice President and Senior Consultant of a major risk and insurance services firm in New York City.

**Joseph Schappert, MD** *Vice Chair, Pathology and Laboratory Medicine, Beth Israel Medical Center, New York, NY*

**Robert Stanyon, MS, RN, CPHRM, FASHRM** *AVP Risk Management & Research, FOJP Service Corporation, New York, NY*
Robert Stanyon is Assistant Vice President, Risk Management and Research at FOJP Service Corporation. He has over 20 years of experience in health care risk management, is a past president of AHRMNY and presently co-chairs the ASHRM taskforce on Online Education. His most recent publications include articles on risk management education using online methods as well as the electronic health record from the perspective of the risk manager.

[1]Special thanks to: Jaime Zaldumbide & Angie Gonzalez

# Index